PRAISE FOR

THE NORDIC THEORY OF EVERYTHING

'Meticulously researched. [Partanen] offers a clear, informative, fact-filled survey of the differences between American and Nordic child care, health care, education, eldercare, and taxation arrangements. It could be a game-changer in national conversations about the roles that governments should play in their citizens' lives.' *Seattle Times*

'Partanen is good at blending the individual stories of her friends in the cold, hard facts of national statistics... Partanen is a careful, judicious writer and she makes a careful, judicious case.' *New York Times Book Review*

'An engaging fusion of reportage and memoir.'
O, The Oprah Magazine

'In this election year, Partanen's sensible book should be required reading for those who wonder why so many Americans feel resentful and alienated.' *Foreign Affairs*

'Partanen's pride in her homeland and genuine concern for the struggles of middle-class Americans infuse her book with candor and charm, and her perceptions about American struggles feel spot-on.' *Booklist*

'A passionate and intelligent argument.' *Publishers Weekly*

'This highly readable and entertaining work is timely, as the conversation about inequality and the role of social services in this country has never been more relevant.' *Library Journal*

'An earnest, well-written work worth heeding, especially in our current toxic political climate.' *Kirkus Reviews*

'If Americans really understood how bad we have it - how unjust and wrongheaded our child care, education, and public health policies are - we'd take to the streets. Anu Partanen rips up the stale stereotypes about Nordic welfare states and shows us all the kinds of human flourishing we're missing out on. This is a dangerous book. Don't let it fall in to the wrong hands.' Judith Shulevitz, author of *The Sabbath World*

'This is a wonderful, hopeful book about what American society could be—not by adopting Nordic 'socialism' but by embracing the values that have allowed Nordic citizens to enjoy more freedom and equality than in present-day America. The American dream was once an inspiration to the world. Anu Partanen shows us how to rediscover it.'

Robert Reich, Chancellor's Professor of Public Policy at University of California, Berkeley

'We are all undeniably obsessed with adopting the idyllic Scandi lifestyle.' *Stylist*

THE NORDIC THEORY
OF EVERYTHING

THE
NORDIC THEORY
OF EVERYTHING

IN SEARCH OF
A BETTER LIFE

Anu Partanen

DUCKWORTH

First published in the United Kingdom by Duckworth in 2018

Duckworth, an imprint of Prelude Books Ltd
13 Carrington Road, Richmond,
TW10 5AA, United Kingdom
www.preludebooks.co.uk
For bulk and special sales please contact
info@preludebooks.co.uk

A catalogue record for this book is available from the British Library

Printed and bound in Great Britain by Clays Ltd, Elcograf S.p.A.

ISBN 978-0-7156-5318-0

4 6 8 10 9 7 5

CONTENTS

THE NORDIC THEORY
OF EVERYTHING

PROLOGUE

Bill Clinton was leaning back, gazing over the rims of his glasses into space. One of his hands held a microphone, the other hand was poised in midair with fingers spread wide. For a brief moment silence descended on the packed ballroom.

When Clinton spoke, he addressed the woman with orange hair sitting next to him on the stage. "There's a huge debate going on in America now," he said. It was September 2010, nearly two years since the financial crisis began. Clinton paused again, his hand now falling and dangling. "About what it takes to be a successful country in the twenty-first century. This debate is also going on in many other countries around the world." Clinton looked out at the audience. "There's a lot of shaken confidence."

Sitting on the other side of the stage from Clinton was a panel of luminaries from the highest ranks of the American elite. There was Eric Schmidt, the chairman of Google. There was Melinda Gates, cochair of the multibillion-dollar Bill and Melinda Gates Foundation. And there was Bob McDonald, at the time CEO of the multinational corporation Procter & Gamble. But Clinton wasn't talking to any of them. He was totally focused on the orange-haired woman next to him.

"How would you advise people everywhere," Clinton asked her, "not to look in the past and blame the past, but just to figure out—wake up tomorrow morning and figure out—what in the living daylights are we going to do now?"

His focus growing more intense, Clinton swiveled his chair away from the audience and pointed himself directly at the woman, his hand jabbing the air like a karate chop as he continued.

"How do we decide what government should do? What the private sector should do? How to design a tax system?" He spun back to face the crowd as he went on. "How to design our relationships with the rest of the world? How to define our obligations to poorer countries? How do you run your business? How would you advise all these people to go back home and start?"

Clinton lowered the microphone, crossed his arms, and peered over his glasses at the woman with orange hair.

"Thanks," she said, giving Clinton a look. "Simple question."

The crowd laughed, and then she began to talk, doing her best to respond to Clinton's daunting interrogation, to the worries and fears that seemed to be on the minds of everyone in the audience.

It was a Tuesday morning at the Times Square Sheraton Hotel in New York City, where the Clinton Global Initiative Conference was under way. More than a thousand people from ninety countries on six continents had traveled there to brainstorm ways to secure a better life for the world's citizens in the twenty-first century. Many of the attendees were current or former heads of state, business leaders, or executives of nongovernmental organizations.

When Clinton had walked onto the stage an hour earlier to welcome the audience and commence the proceedings, he looked well. He'd slimmed down a bit since his years as president of the United States, and though he was visibly aging, he was dressed sharply in a patriotic ensemble of dark blue suit with white shirt and red tie. Relaxed and confident, he had introduced the panelists, including the woman with orange hair. He'd listed her profession—like him, she was a president—as well as some of her other activities, before getting to the part that clearly animated him the most.

"And," Clinton had said, this woman "has a country that consistently finishes in the top five in all global rankings on the quality of education, the way the economy works, the distribution of wealth, and opportunity."

Those were accolades that, not long ago, might have been associated with the world's best-known and most robust countries—perhaps the United States, perhaps Japan, perhaps Germany. But this woman, dressed in a simple beige pantsuit, who'd been invited by the former leader of the free world to share the stage with the globe's most influential titans of technology, industry, and philanthropy, was Tarja Halonen, and she was the president of a much more modest nation, tucked high in the northeast corner of Europe next to the Arctic circle: Finland.

By then Finland had been garnering worldwide admiration for a decade, and now the attention was exploding. It had all started with excitement over the educational achievements of Finland's children. On international surveys Finnish teenagers had ranked at or near the top in reading, math, and science from the year 2000 on. Delegation after delegation from other countries had started making pilgrimages to Finland to visit Finnish schools and talk with Finnish education experts. Soon people around the world were talking about the Finnish education miracle.

Then, just a month before the Clinton conference, *Newsweek* had published the results of a survey it had conducted of nations around the globe. The magazine had set out to answer a question that, in its own words, was "at once simple and incredibly complex—if you were born today, which country would provide you the very best opportunity to live a healthy, safe, reasonably prosperous, and upwardly mobile life?" It defined five categories that measured national well-being—education, health, quality of life, economic competitiveness, and political environment—and compared a hundred nations on these metrics. The result came as something of an unpleasant surprise to the United States and other major powers that might have expected to be at the top. *Newsweek* declared that for a person starting out his or her life at the beginning of the twenty-first century, the best country in the world was Finland. The United States did not even place in the top ten, coming in at number eleven.

The accolades for Finland continued in the months and years to come. The international lifestyle magazine *Monocle* ranked Finland's capital, Helsinki, as the most livable city in the world, while the World Economic Forum's *Global Competitiveness Report* listed Finland as the fourth most competitive country in the world in 2011—a ranking that actually went up to number three the following year. The Organization for Economic Cooperation and Development (OECD) declared Finland the world's fourth-best country for work-life balance. The European Union's *Innovation Scoreboard* named Finland one of EU's top four innovation leaders.

The United Nations even set out to measure the seemingly unmeasurable: happiness. When, in the spring of 2012, the *World Happiness Report* rolled off the presses, Finland had achieved nearly the ultimate ranking, securing a spot as the second-happiest nation on earth. In addition, flanking Finland in the first- and third-happiest spots were two of its close neighbors in the Nordic region: Denmark and Norway.

While gloom and doom rolled across southern Europe as the euro crisis swept the land, the *Financial Times* published a special report on Finland titled "Rich, Happy and Good at

Austerity." Meanwhile, there was one global ranking in which Finland came in dead last: the *Failed States Index*. According to the Fund for Peace, Finland was the least fragile nation in the world. There was icing on the cake, too, when it came to Finland's international reputation: Probably the world's most popular mobile video game, Angry Birds, was the brainchild of programmers in Finland.

Perhaps the biggest shocker, though, came in May 2012, when a politician in Britain, which had long been America's oldest and closest friend in Europe, uttered a comment that would have been unthinkable at any point in the previous hundred years: Ed Miliband, the leader of the British Labour Party, was attending a conference on social mobility, where experts butted heads over the question of whether people around the world were achieving a better life than their parents. For decades, if not centuries, the country that had best secured a person's opportunity for upward mobility had been the United States. No longer, said Miliband. "If you want the American dream," Miliband quipped at the conference, "go to Finland."

At the top of these many different rankings of competitiveness and quality of life, Finland was not alone. As with the *World Happiness Report*, something good seemed to be afoot in the Nordic region as a whole. Near Finland in the rankings were usually some of Finland's neighbors: Denmark, Norway, Sweden, and on some measures Iceland—a group of countries often referred to as "Scandinavia," but that, when including Finland and Iceland, are more accurately known as the Nordic region.

For generations the United States had inspired the world as a model of upward mobility and high quality of life. But now it wasn't just British Labour politicians who were no longer feeling so inspired by America. When Britain's Conservative prime minister, David Cameron, was seeking ways for his nation to support its families, increase the number of women in the workforce, advance childhood development, and generate greater overall well-being, he didn't turn to the United States. Instead he looked elsewhere for inspiration and advice: the Nordic nations. Soon Britain's free-market-friendly magazine *The Economist* was having similar inclinations. It published a special report titled "The Next Supermodel," exploring what the Nordic nations were doing right in order to produce such successful economies and societies.

Nordic culture had been attracting admiration, too, even from within the United States. Sweden had produced the immensely popular musical act Abba, the best-selling crime novels of Stieg Larsson, including *The Girl with the Dragon Tattoo*, the affordable chain store for sophisticated fashion H&M, and the revolutionary furniture retailer Ikea, not to mention the evergreen auto brand Volvo. There had always been LEGOs, the ubiquitous Danish plastic toy bricks; now Denmark was also churning out first-rate crime dramas such as *The Killing*, and Copenhagen's Noma was gaining a reputation as one of the best restaurants in the world. By August 2012 *Vanity Fair* was officially declaring what had gradually become apparent: The world was experiencing a "Scandinavian moment."

For me all this was more than a tad bittersweet. Back in the year 2000, when Tarja Halonen had first become president of Finland, I was a young Finnish newspaper reporter, fresh-faced and twenty-five years old, newly hired by the largest-circulation Nordic daily newspaper, *Helsingin Sanomat*, located in Helsinki. I was a Finn through and through—I'd been born and raised in the small, unassuming country far up north that now, all of a sudden, had become the world's darling.

But as the rest of the world was embracing Finland, I had

done just the opposite. For me it was very much an American moment. Just before *Newsweek* had declared my homeland the best country in the world, I had decided to leave behind everything in Finland to begin a new life as an immigrant to the United States.

From my new perch in America, I gazed back across the sea at the Nordic lands that had been my home. Like a sports fan rooting for her hometown team, I watched Finland's performance in the international surveys and global rankings with pride. At the same time I was distracted by the challenges I faced in my new life in America. Around me, moreover, most Americans didn't seem particularly aware of, or interested in, Finland, or its tiny club of Nordic neighbors near the Arctic circle. Americans were too overwhelmed by the challenges of their life in America. Maybe policy wonks like Bill Clinton and the editors of *The Economist* had the time and energy to get excited about Finland, but really, what could a bunch of tiny, cold, insignificant countries where everybody looks the same, acts the same, and thinks a good time is a plate of pickled herring have to offer the diverse and dynamic United States?

The United States had long been the world's shining beacon of freedom, independence, individualism, and opportunity. Compared with freewheeling and liberty-loving America, the Nordic region could seem not only irrelevant but downright awful. Not a few Americans saw the Nordic countries as a pathetic bunch of "socialist nanny states," coddling their citizens with welfare programs that weren't building happiness but were instead breeding dependency, apathy, and despair. American critics of the so-called Nordic supermodel mostly talked about the high rates of depression, alcoholism, and suicide in my home country and its Nordic neighbors.

In the Nordic countries themselves, too, a lot of people

weren't sure what all the fuss was about. My fellow Finns, in particular, are legendary for their low self-esteem. When *News-week* named Finland the best country in the world, just about the entire population of Finland assumed that the magazine had made some terrible and very embarrassing mistake. And the idea that Finns could be even the second-happiest people on earth struck a lot of people as ludicrous. With its long, dark, freezing winters, Finland makes many of its citizens miserable for sizable chunks of the year, and alcoholism is indeed a real problem there. Sweden, Denmark, and Norway have tended to demonstrate more self-confidence than Finland and Iceland, but none of the Nordic nations could be called a perfect country by any stretch, and Nordic citizens themselves still often feel inspired by the United States, especially by America's pop culture, its entrepreneurial spirit, and its world-class cities such as New York, San Francisco, and LA.

As I settled into my new life in the United States, the American economy began its rebound from the worst of the financial crisis, while back home in Finland, the atmosphere started to feel ever more gloomy. The global recession and the eurozone crisis started to weigh heavily on Finland, slowing the celebrated Finnish economy. Finland's schoolchildren were no longer quite at the top of every education survey anymore, either, even though they still performed impressively well. Overall, if you asked Finns on the street whether their country was a "super-model" for the rest of the world, let alone for the mighty United States, their grumpy retorts, particularly if the weather was cold and cloudy, would most likely be a resounding no.

Yet the longer I lived in America as a Nordic immigrant, something became clear to me. Regardless of whether Finland was the "best" country in the world or not, most people in the United States, as well as many of my Nordic countrymen back home, did not fully realize that to leave Finland or any other Nordic country behind and settle in America at the beginning of the twenty-first century was to experience an extraordinary—and extraordinarily harsh—form of travel backward in time.

As a Nordic immigrant to the United States, I noticed something else, too. Americans, and many others around the world, did not seem fully aware of how much better things could be.

ONE

IN THE LAND
OF THE FREE

BECOMING AMERICAN

OPPORTUNITY

The bride to be was peering through the window. In my memories she is wearing white, but now that I look at pictures from that day, taken some hours before the ceremony, I see that she was in fact at that moment wearing black, and looking anxious. I remember her anxiety because the TV commentators were busy interpreting every expression that crossed her beautiful face. They had little else to go on. All that was known was that bride and groom would soon be getting married in front of more than 150 guests at a castle in Italy. The camera crews and paparazzi hovered outside, reporting as best they could on the arrival of celebrity guests—who was dressed in what, and details of the menu.

I was watching from a hotel room thousands of miles away in Boston, where I'd recently arrived to attend a conference. I flipped through the channels. In addition to Tom Cruise and Katie Holmes's wedding, the news was reporting that the justices of the U.S. Supreme Court had received packages of poisoned cookies in the mail. The sender had helpfully furnished each justice with a letter stating her intentions: "I am going to kill you" and "This is poisoned." That night at dinner, a man from the conference who was standing behind me in the buffet line asked me with a smile if I'd be kind enough to taste the food for him, to see if it was edible. I assumed he was making a joke about the cookies sent to the Supreme Court. I promised to let him know if the food was poisoned. He stared at me, confused. I tried to explain that I was referring to the terrorized justices, and he looked even more bewildered. Soon we were both giggling in confusion. It turned out he hadn't been watching the news and didn't know about the Supreme Court and the cookies. As I sat next to him at dinner, we started to understand each other better. Two hours later, under the branches of a big bush, we kissed. The next day I got on a plane for the ten-hour trip home to Finland.

My friends back in Helsinki were thrilled. You met an American writer! At a conference! So romantic! When they heard that Trevor had called me soon after our meeting to announce his plans to visit Finland to see me, the excitement turned to near ecstasy—now here was a real love story in the making! Trevor did visit, and the visit went well. When our long-distance relationship continued, and each rendezvous was followed by the inevitable separation between continents, my friends started sighing. Do you miss him terribly? You're not too sad, are you?

I did like him. But I wasn't yet convinced that I liked him as much as my friends were convinced that I liked him. Trevor had just moved from Washington, DC, to New York City, and when it became clear that I might start visiting him regularly in Brooklyn, my friends treated the whole thing as if it were a television romance. You'll be just like Derek and Meredith on *Grey's Anatomy*! You'll be like Carrie on *Sex and the City*! (Both shows had been big hits in Finland.)

There was just one problem: I had no intention of moving to America. Trevor felt like Mr. Right, but was I supposed to give up everything I knew just because I was in love? At this point in my life, I had explored the world. I'd spent two years studying abroad, one in Adelaide, Australia, and another in Paris. As a working journalist, I'd managed to visit six of the globe's seven continents, and had even seen the legendary New York City. And what conclusion had I come to? That I wanted to live in Finland.

As I'd worked at my job and traveled and read and lived my life, I'd also decided that a woman is meant to be more than a caretaker for her man and children. She ought to have her own purpose, her own will, her own career, including her own salary—as the British actress Helen Mirren once said, "The greatest gift every girl can have is economic independence." I wanted to be a strong, intelligent, creative woman, not that girl who surrenders everything just for a guy.

The longer Trevor and I were dating, the more heavily this weighed on me. When our long-distance relationship hit the two-year mark we counted fourteen round trips that we'd made between our two countries so we could spend time together. He was becoming my best friend and true love, the one person whose presence made all clouds disappear. How could I throw that away?

It had become clear that if we were going to take the next steps in our relationship, one of us would have to leave a life behind, and there was a list of practical reasons why that someone would have to be me. Technically Trevor could have moved to Finland. But he didn't seem inclined to, and I had to admit it probably didn't make sense. He didn't speak Finnish, whereas I already spoke English. New York is an international city, so I had a better chance of finding work there than he did in Helsinki.

And then there were a few things about Finland itself that, despite its overall high quality of life, I wasn't sure Trevor could handle even if he'd wanted to come.

I had always loved Finland. It's a country of gorgeous summers and quiet natural beauty, not to mention that Finland happened to contain most of my friends and family, whom I adored. Finland's location was convenient to other parts of Europe, making even weekend getaways to places like Paris or Rome doable for the average citizen. All that said, compared with any number of places in the United States, Finland could also feel like the small, cold, dark, and often somewhat monotonous place it was. Finns have long been known for being modest, but extra modesty is not really required when comparing Helsinki to a place like New York.

Finland had its accomplishments to be proud of, to be sure, although the name of Finland's world-famous cell phone company, Nokia, tended to sound Japanese to most people. Perhaps more distinctly Finnish were our designers and architects— Marimekko, Alvar Aalto and his famous chairs, and Eero Saarinen, who designed the St. Louis Arch as well as Dulles Airport in Washington, DC, and the old TWA air terminal at Kennedy Airport in New York. Fans of classical music might know the symphonies of our composer Jean Sibelius. And people who watched *Late Night with Conan O'Brien* might even have heard Conan's frequent jokes about his own eerie resemblance to our orange-haired president. When you're from a small country, you take what fame you can get.

But as Stieg Larsson's *Girl with the Dragon Tattoo* novels made so clear, the Nordic lands have a dark side—and quite literally so. After Trevor's first trip to visit me, he boasted to his American friends that during an entire week in Helsinki in winter he'd seen the sun for just three hours. With so much darkness this far north, many residents throughout the Nordic region, at least those who can afford to travel overseas, consider a midwinter trip to Thailand essential to their mental health. Finns, in particular, also have a tendency to view life as a parade of endless obstacles and disappointments, and to dispense with small talk and niceties; as a result they can seem taciturn and even rude to outsiders. I could imagine Trevor leaving the excitement and sunshine of New York City only to find himself spiraling into a nightmare of dark and lonely depression caused by my introverted homeland.

The more I contemplated the melancholy of the Finnish psyche, it really seemed to me that the citizens of the United States were the ones who deserved to be the best country on earth, with their all-American optimism, gumption, ingenuity, and knack for magically transforming challenging circumstances into profitable advantage. Indeed, I was almost too embarrassed to tell Trevor my own story about the attribute that we Finns seemed most to treasure and inspire in one another, something we called *sisu*—a quality perhaps best translated into English as "grit."

When I was ten years old, my family lived deep in the woods. Like most young kids in Finland, my brother and I were left to our own devices to trek the mile or so to school and back every day. Often we rode our bikes, and sometimes we walked, but during the long winters when the snow piled up too high, there were days when we were supposed to ski to school. I hated skiing, so mostly I insisted on walking anyway. One evening after I'd returned home, my mother asked offhandedly how the walk to school had been that day.

I explained that at first the going had been a bit tricky, since with every step I had sunk into the snow all the way up to my hips. But I'd discovered that if I crawled on all fours I wouldn't fall through. After that the going was easy, I said, so I'd proceeded to crawl on all fours for much of the mile to school.

To my proud parents that was a sign that their daughter had *sisu*. I could imagine the different story that a proud American parent would tell about their child: The kid gets out of the snow immediately, flags down a passing car, and deploys prodigious charm to negotiate not only a ride to school but an entrepreneurial arrangement that leads to the kid becoming the CEO of a million-dollar snow-shoveling business by age sixteen, featured on the cover of *Fortune*. Come to think of it, compared with America, what did Finland have that was so great—anything, really? Was there any reason not to leave?

I made a list of the good and bad aspects of moving to America.

The bad first.

In Finland, in the decade-plus of my working life as a newspaper and magazine writer and editor, I'd lived a comfortable middle-class existence, as had all my friends. I'd always had enough disposable income after taxes to eat out, travel, and enjoy myself, as well as a nice cushion to set aside in savings every year besides. I'd never had to pay extra for things like health insurance, and medical treatment of any kind had only ever cost me small sums, if anything. If I were ever to get seriously ill in Finland, not only would I be treated at no significant cost to me, I would also get up to a year of paid sick leave with job security, and more help after that if I needed it.

What if I were to have a baby or two? In Finland I'd be eligible for a good *ten* months of *paid* parental leave for each child, and without having to worry about losing my job while I was away. My kids would then get inexpensive, high-quality day care. They could attend some of the world's best schools, all completely free, followed by their college educations—also tuition-free.

And like most Finns, every year I took four or even five weeks of paid summer vacation. Though our winters were dark and miserable, our summers were glorious, and when it came to summer vacation, our society, and our employers, considered it important to our health and productivity that we enjoy our time off.

I wasn't exactly sure how all this would work in the United States, but I had certainly gotten the impression that such givens might be more complicated. Moreover, it wasn't as if Trevor was going to become my sugar daddy in America. His books had been successful, and he had some savings, but as a writer and teacher he couldn't do much more with his income stream than support himself.

And as I was contemplating all this in 2008, the collapse of the investment bank Lehman Brothers set off a financial crisis plunging the American economy as a whole into dire uncertainty.

But then there was the good.

Trevor was great. New York was great. The United States had always been the land of opportunity. America was a wellspring of positive energy and creativity, the place that produced so much of the culture that I enjoyed and lived with every day, from the arts to goods and services to technology. I would get to experience the most powerful country in the world firsthand, and start a new chapter of life, away from the safety and complacency of Nordic ways. I would be one of the huddled masses yearning to breathe free, one more participant in the greatest experiment on earth: building a truly diverse nation in which people from all over the world live and work side by side, united by their love of liberty and the chance to excel. The American dream was beckoning. And did I mention those Finnish winters? Or, more important, love?

I asked myself the classic questions: What would I do if I stayed put—same-old, same-old for the next thirty years? Which would I regret more on my deathbed—that I'd stayed or that I'd left? I wasn't a great romantic, but I wasn't a great materialist either. I thought of myself as a realist, and as a realist I believed that on my deathbed I wasn't going to be thinking about safe paths chosen or acquired comforts held onto. I'd be thinking about love lived, courage shown, and risks taken.

In November I quit my job. I gave up my apartment. I got rid of all my possessions. On Christmas Day I said good-bye to my family and friends, and the next morning boarded a plane for America.

ANXIETY

The onset was quick. The panic would seep in from my stomach, with burning waves making their way around my insides while the pressure in my chest grew stronger. A band of dull pain would wrap itself around my skull. I would gulp down air in faster and deeper breaths, but still it felt like no oxygen was getting in. With every breath I would hear humming in my ears.

This was the second time I'd experienced a panic attack like this. The first had been when I was hiking with my mother in the woods of Lapland in northeastern Finland, near the Russian border. My mother had come up with an idea: We should bushwhack through a patch of forest, she suggested, to a cabin she pointed out on the map. She said she'd been there once before, with a group of friends, but I was not reassured when she revealed, cheerfully, that they'd only found it after being lost in the woods for hours. We had no compass with us, but off we went.

Sure enough, within two hours we were lost.

I could feel the anxiety spreading through me, and no amount of reasoning could stop the physical wave of dread. My body grew jittery and my mind rigid; I felt alone and in trouble. Our cell phones had no signal, adding to the sense of isolation—I wondered if we should start building a bonfire to summon help. I told myself to stop being ridiculous—we could not have been far from the marked trails, and we were enjoying a beautiful, cool, clear autumn day—but all I could do was pretend to act calm even though my stomach was churning inside. The possibilities of what could go wrong filled me with dread.

We walked among the pines, passing the occasional reindeer, until eventually we reached a hilltop from which we could see that the sun was already going down, and realized that it would be setting in the west. We aimed ourselves accordingly and soon encountered a fence that was marked on the map. In no time we were back on the trail, right where we'd started. The anxiety dissipated immediately.

I experienced the second attack of anxiety soon after I moved to America. I wasn't doing anything dangerous, yet the physical feeling of dread was exactly the same. At first I thought I was just stressed out by the adjustment to life in a new country. You have to speak a different language all day, and you often don't understand what's going on around you, even in the most mundane of exchanges. But figuring out how to navigate America felt far more stressful than my earlier experiences in other countries—despite the fact that it should have been easier, since I was older, more experienced, and already spoke fluent English.

There were little things, like understanding how much of a tip to leave at a restaurant or hairdresser's, or learning to order at Starbucks, which was more complicated than doing my Finnish taxes. And there were slightly bigger, more mysterious things—things about life in America that Americans themselves didn't seem to realize wouldn't be the norm in many other countries. For example, I tried to open a bank account but I couldn't understand all the different fees, no matter how many times I read the brochures. I was undone by the flood of letters that I received in the United States offering me credit cards, and it was a mystery to me how I was supposed to be able to afford the huge interest rates that were listed in the footnotes of American credit-card agreements. Or why, when I bought a cell phone, I had to buy it from a carrier and commit myself to two years of service, regardless of whether the carrier turned out to be good or bad. In Finland cell-phone companies rarely locked consumers into this sort of straitjacket, and Finnish consumers wouldn't have put up with it if they had tried.

Then there was the matter of trying to get cable TV. After arriving in New York I'd been hoping to subscribe to a couple of channels so I could watch my favorite shows. In Finland that would have been an easy, predictable, and affordable thing to do. To find out how much it would cost me in the United States, I looked online but got dizzy trying to understand the different packages and their pricing. So I called the company, which made me feel like I must not understand English.

"So how much would that be?"

"Ten dollars a month. For the first three months."

"Okay, and how much after that?"

"I can't tell you. It depends on the price at the time."

"I don't understand. Does the price change every day like the stock market?"

"You'll have to call us after the first three months to get the price."

"But you can't just start charging me some random price on my credit card that I haven't agreed to, right?"

"You have to call us. Otherwise the subscription will continue automatically with the new price."

The unknowable "new price," of course, would be much, much higher. It was all part of a way of doing things in the United States that, as I would gradually realize, forced you to be constantly on guard, constantly worried that whatever amount of money you had or earned would never be enough, and constantly anxious about navigating the complex and mysterious fine print thrown at you from every direction by corporations that had somehow managed to evade even the bare minimum of sensible protections for consumers. Things didn't improve when it came time to file my first tax return for Uncle Sam. I tried to research my tax situation on the Internal Revenue Service Web site, and was soon tearing my hair trying to comprehend the pages and pages of fine print and the endless exceptions and loopholes. In Finland filing my taxes had always been quick and simple. But here in America, buried under IRS instruction booklets and terrified I might make some crucial and costly mistake, I gave up and hired an accountant, something I'd never had to do back home.

My spirits would fall even further whenever I read one of the many magazine or newspaper features profiling superachieving, high-earning Americans who rose at four in the morning to answer e-mail before heading to the gym at five and then hitting the office by six to get started on their ninety-hour workweeks. Mothers in America seemed capable of miracles—returning to work just a few weeks after giving birth, pumping milk between meetings, and working at home on the weekends by managing children with one hand and their BlackBerrys with the other. I was certain I could never function at that level. The logical conclusion that began to settle on me was that I could never make it in America.

Instead I became transfixed by the news stories I read about another kind of American. These were citizens who'd perhaps made one bad decision, or who'd had a bit of bad luck. They'd fallen ill, lost their jobs, gotten divorced, gotten pregnant at the wrong time, or been hit by a hurricane. They found themselves unable to pay their medical bills, or their house was being foreclosed on, or they were working three low-paying jobs and still not making ends meet, or sending their children to a horrible school, or leaving their babies with random neighbors because they couldn't afford day care, or all the above.

I also became obsessed with news stories about epidemics in the United States of food-borne illness, toxic plastic bottles and toys, and antibiotics pumped with such abandon into farm animals that we were all going to die from diseases that in the recent past could easily have been controlled by those same drugs. Sometimes as I sat on the couch staring at my laptop, Trevor would pause whatever he was doing and gaze at me. "You have that face again," he'd say softly, lifting a finger to stroke my brow. Without realizing it I'd begun squeezing my forehead into a permanent frown.

After a while it was no longer a mystery to me why I was endlessly panicked. Just as in the forests of Lapland, my brain was processing my interactions with my environment, and the message it brought back was clear: I was lost in a wilderness. And in the American wilderness, you're on your own.

I blamed myself. Obviously I just wasn't tough enough and smart enough—American enough—for this exciting and dynamic country. My troubles were not that serious. Getting all anxious about them, or about the possibility of what might happen, was embarrassing. My mother would certainly say that I had lost my *sisu*. Where was the girl who'd crawled uncomplainingly for a mile through the snow? More self-reliance, less whining, I told myself. More can-do, less I'm-scared.

With my confidence and self-esteem under assault, and feeling the pressure to perform, I found it easy to start questioning things about myself, and about the part of the world that I'd come from. I started to think the American criticisms I was hearing of Nordic societies must be right. Nordic crime novels and design trends might be popular in America, but many politicians in the United States pointed to the way the Nordic states coddled their citizens with indulgences that hadn't been earned, and in the process crushed anyone with even a shred of entrepreneurial spirit. The result was nations of helpless, naive, childlike people who lived in a state of unhealthy dependency on their governments. Of course such a society would produce a sissy like me.

For hours I would sit—my forehead furrowed into that frown—pondering my people's inadequacies and my own weaknesses. Americans were often quick to point out that Nordic nations had produced no Steve Jobs, no Google, no Boeing, no General Electric, and no Hollywood. We were perceived as having little diversity and our GDPs were dwarfed by America's—with the exception of Norway, which had oil—

and we possessed none of the most respected universities in the world, none of the greatest innovations, and none of the wealthiest self-made men and women. We weren't risking our lives and treasuries fighting wars that might need to be fought for the benefit of all. We might be well intentioned, but we were not exceptional. That is what America was. Exceptional.

I still thought Americans might be failing to appreciate some of the good sides of Nordic life, but mainly I came to accept the view that we Nordics just weren't as competitive, creative, self-sufficient, or strong. Just a few months after leaving Finland, I'd gone from being a successful and happy career woman to an anxious, wary, and self-doubting mess.

As I got to know my new acquaintances in the United States better, however, I was surprised to discover that many of them suffered from anxiety just as severe as mine—or worse. It seemed that nearly everyone was struggling to cope with the logistical challenges of daily life in America. Many were in therapy, and some were on medication. The National Institute of Mental Health (NIMH) estimated that almost one in five adult Americans suffered from an anxiety disorder, and the most commonly prescribed psychiatric drug in the country—alprazolam, known to many Americans as Xanax—was for treating anxiety.

Soon I didn't feel so alone, or so crazy. This may sound strange, but imagine my relief when I heard about a study conducted in 2006 by a life insurance company in which 90 percent of the American women surveyed said that they felt financially insecure, while 46 percent said that they actually, seriously, feared ending up on the street, homeless. And this last group included almost half of women with an annual income of more than one hundred thousand dollars a year. If American women making more than one hundred thousand dollars were afraid of ending up in the gutter—and this study had been conducted even before the financial crisis—then perhaps I was channeling the same unease that Americans themselves were feeling in droves. The difference was that for me, the fear was brand-new and strange, while for them it was just life. So maybe I had it backward. Maybe I wasn't racked by anxiety because I came from a foreign country. Maybe I was racked by anxiety because I was becoming an American.

As the months passed and I did my best to settle in and learn to live with this uncertain new existence, it seemed that all around me Americans were becoming more unsettled, more unhappy, and increasingly prone to asking what was wrong with their lives and their society.

Since I'd arrived in the United States a couple of months after the Wall Street collapse, people were talking more and more about the huge gap between the very rich in America and the rest of us, and about stagnation in the incomes of the middle class. Politicians were also fighting, of course, over what to do—if anything—about the tens of millions of Americans who lacked health insurance. In the meantime the nation was buckling under the astronomical costs of medical care, burdening everyone else. At parties or get-togethers, a frequent topic of conversation was the fights that people were having with their health-insurance companies.

Lots of people were also discussing how America could improve its failing schools. I read about poor families trying to get their children out of terrible schools and into experimental ones that might be better. Well-to-do families were competing ever more fiercely, and paying ever-larger sums, for coveted spots at good schools, and at the same time competing ferociously in the workplace for the salaries they needed to pay the out-of-control expenses of not only private schools but also of college down the road.

The American dream seemed to be in trouble.

Unprepared for all this, I struggled to reconcile myself to it all—to my new home, to the excitement of this country's possibility, but also to the intense anxiety and uncertainty that America wrought, on me and seemingly most everyone I met.

Which was about the time that Trevor asked me to marry him.

Officially we were wed on a crisp December day at City Hall in Lower Manhattan, with Trevor's best friend and his wife as our witnesses, followed by champagne on the Brooklyn Bridge. The following summer we staged a modest wedding party back in Finland to celebrate with our families and friends. On a beautiful August afternoon filled with bright sunshine we said our vows in a birch grove by the sea in Helsinki.

Just as we were leaving Finland and returning to our anxiety-filled lives in America, the late-August 2010 issue of *Newsweek* hit the stands. The cover was a swirl of flags of different countries around the world. In the center of the vortex was a teaser reading, "The Best Country in the World Is . . ." The winner, I quickly learned, was the country I had just given up.

I sat on my couch back in the United States and read about the advantages of Finland I'd chosen to forsake. While my fellow-American inhabitants and I were increasingly stressed out, overworked, unhealthy, underpaid, insecure, and uncertain whether our children's lives would be any better, back home in Finland the middle-class friends I'd left behind were enjoying a healthy work-life balance, enough free time and disposable income for truly rejuvenating vacations, and a universal and affordable health-care system good enough not only for Finns, but apparently also for the global soccer star David Beckham. When Beckham had torn his Achilles' tendon a few months earlier, of all the best doctors around the world—including the United States—that he could have gone to see, he'd chosen to fly to Finland for his surgery.

Many of my friends in Finland were having kids, and while bringing up children is never easy, their family lives sounded to me surprisingly sane, helped along by the sorts of things *Newsweek* noted: long parental leaves, easily affordable day care, and an excellent public education system. According to *Newsweek*, a young person's chances of enjoying a good quality of life were better in Finland than anywhere else on the planet.

Nothing about the *Newsweek* survey inspired me to ditch my newfound admiration for the United States. But it did give me back something very important that I'd lost: self-confidence. It also pushed me to compare other aspects of my life in America with life back home. And as I did, I began to wonder if *Newsweek* had simply scratched the surface of a much more important story.

DEPENDENCY

Since the dawn of the modern era, people have been lamenting the way modern life uproots the traditional support structures of society, most especially family and community, leaving insecurity and anxiety in their place. Back in the days when several generations lived together under one roof, sharing chores and domestic duties, surrounded by a tight-knit village where everyone knew one another and pitched in, a person could feel secure—at least when it came to the sorts of problems that family and neighbors could help you solve. Day-to-day life was likely to be relatively predictable, and you might well die in the town where you were born, surrounded by the same people you'd known all your life. For the most part in modern societies, those days are considered long gone.

On the other hand, modernity had brought some tremendous improvements to human existence, and I certainly felt that many of them were on especially splendid display in America. Indeed, perhaps the biggest benefits of modernity were also some of the most cherished and fundamental principles of the United States: freedom, independence, and opportunity. People around the world had long looked to the United States as the champion of these core modern principles. Most people, including myself, assumed that part of what made the United States a great country, and such an exceptional one, was that you could live your life relatively unencumbered by the downside of a traditional, old-fashioned society: dependency on the people you happened to be stuck with. In America you had the liberty to express your individuality and choose your own community. This would allow you to interact with family, neighbors, and fellow citizens on the basis of who you were, rather than on what you were obligated to do or expected to be according to old-fashioned thinking.

The longer I lived in America, therefore, and the more places I visited and the more people I met—and the more American I myself became—the more puzzled I grew. For it was exactly those key benefits of modernity—freedom, personal independence, and opportunity—that seemed, from my outsider's perspective, in a thousand small ways to be surprisingly missing from American life today. Amid the anxiety and stress of people's daily lives, those grand ideals were looking more theoretical than actual.

This wasn't just in New York City, nor was it limited to

certain social classes. As I ventured beyond New York to rural Maine, to Washington, DC, to small-town Ohio, to southern Virginia, to the West Coast, what struck me was not that people felt they had a great deal of freedom, or could fully be individuals, or enjoyed a fair shake at success. Rather, in order to compete and to survive, the Americans I encountered and read about were being forced to depend more and more on one another, in a throwback to the traditional relationships of old. And in the process, individuals were becoming beholden to their spouses, parents, children, colleagues, and bosses in ways that constrained their own liberty. The demands and tensions caused by this state of affairs seemed to be making everyone's stress and anxiety even worse—even in the areas of life that they cherished the most, such as right at home, in the family.

One of the things I most came to admire after moving to the United States was the way American families did things together, stuck up for one another, enjoyed one another's company, and entertained a certain amount of discussion and democracy among its members. I loved the way young and old were not separated into rigid, distinct, and mutually incomprehensible worlds that overlapped only when parents issued orders. American families in the twenty-first century, it seemed to me, managed to be admirably wholesome and progressive at the same time.

American parents clearly spent a lot of time with their children and gave them plenty of love, attention, and encouragement, and this seemed identical to what my friends and acquaintances back in Finland were doing. Both my American and Finnish friends with children shuttled their kids to music lessons and soccer practice, bought them toys, read books with them, and posted pictures of them on Facebook.

And yet the differences nagged at me. When I visited some-one's home in the United States, I couldn't shake a strange sen-sation that I had never quite had back in Finland: that somehow the children were taking over their parents' lives. As usual I blamed myself for being a stodgy, closed-minded Nordic, inad-equate to the cutting-edge innovations of American life.

As I struggled to understand my vague sense of confusion about this, I also met many American parents who felt they needed to direct all of their young children's playtime toward activities that were productive, educational, and goal-oriented. This, I realized, was related to the race to steer even toddlers toward a good school, as early as possible. At what cost, I won-dered, to a child's creativity? And later in a child's young career, I heard about schoolteachers who discovered that a mom or dad was the one doing much of a student's homework. Again, this was in order to secure the good grades that would become criti-cal when trying to find a better school or apply to college. What kind of dependency, I asked myself, did that instill in a child?

When the college race rolled around, anxious American par-ents were forced to micromanage the ever more cutthroat appli-cation process, too. Then, because college was so expensive, once their child was accepted, many parents still spent large sums on tuition, room and board, and health insurance, and maybe even furnishings and a car. It was only natural that in return for all this, some parents expected frequent reports from their children about their activities, even as their children were leaving home and trying to forge their own adult identities. I read about uni-versity students who remained tethered to their parents through texting exchanges and phone chats several times a day.

At the lower end of the income spectrum, teenagers were losing out on college opportunities because their parents didn't know how to manage the application process. Among the few underprivileged students who had, against the odds, been accepted to a good college far from home, many dropped out, feeling they needed to be closer to their families.

I was surprised by how frequently I heard even grown adults in the United States say that their parents were their best friends. This level of dependency among older children on their parents was almost unheard of back in Nordic countries.

And then came the kicker. In America, after children grew into adults with their own children and responsibilities, the codependent child-parent relationship seemed to flip 180 degrees. I met middle-aged adults overwhelmed by the enormously time-consuming and expensive burden of micromanaging the lives of their elderly parents. They were strung out by the tasks of coordinating medical care and treatment, and handling the logistics, and often the costs, of bills and insurance, on top of trying to juggle their own careers and parenting their own kids. In Finland this kind of dependency was unheard of. Of course my Finnish acquaintances back home visited their aging or ailing parents regularly and helped them with small tasks, but being saddled with the kind of caretaker duties Americans were involved with was, in most cases, unimaginable.

My own parents in Finland, both well-educated urban professionals, had always been supportive of me, but they had also made a point of letting me manage my own affairs from an early age. When I was nine and came up with the idea of learning to ride horses, I looked up local stables in the yellow pages and called to book a lesson myself. Then I phoned my mother at work and asked if she would pay for it, and she agreed— and that was how things usually went. Once I'd begun regular riding lessons, my parents occasionally drove me to the stables, but mainly I rode my bike or took the bus. When I turned seventeen, I traveled alone with a friend to Amsterdam. At the age of eighteen I became, as all Finnish eighteen-year-olds do, very much an adult in the eyes of society and the law. When I selected my university major—journalism—I barely discussed it with my parents. After all, I had left home, and my parents weren't paying my college tuition.

The Finnish approach to parenting that I'd grown up with was by no means perfect. In some families it could erect a wall of stoicism between children and adults, where asking for help was considered a sign of weakness. Perhaps as a result, Finnish parents today have gotten more involved in their children's everyday activities compared with when I was a kid. Personally, I'd always had a warm relationship with my mother and father, and I'd always been able to count on their help if I needed it. But very much on purpose, they had also not been intimately involved in managing many of the important decisions in my life. For the most part my Finnish acquaintances had also grown up with a similar degree of affection for their parents, while developing a considerable degree of independence from them early on as well.

I soon discovered that my apprehension about certain aspects of American family life was entering the zeitgeist. Experts on childhood development were pointing to the dangers of "helicopter parenting," noting the difficulties that young adults often encountered establishing themselves as individuals after their parents had cushioned them from failures and made decisions for them for two decades or more. Television shows such as HBO's *Girls* were making comedic hay from such problems—the series begins when Hannah, a twenty-something writer, hears that her parents are finally going to cut her off, after having supported her all the way through college and for two additional years after graduation. More seriously, Americans were increasingly worried about the potentially deleterious long-term effects that dependence on overinvolved parents might cause a person later in life—"How to Land Your Kid in Therapy" warned one widely read cover story in the *Atlantic*. The pharmaceutical industry was doing its part, raking in profits from sales of antianxiety and antidepressant drugs.

As I compared my friends in Finland and America, I realized that a simpler style of parenting—one that would let kids make mistakes and develop independence, that would let them find and pursue opportunity themselves—was a luxury that many American families simply felt they could not afford. In America the primary factor in achieving the possibility of a stable middle-class existence seemed to boil down to one thing: having proactive, tireless, micromanager parents. It was a recipe not for raising independent children well equipped to handle the challenges of modern life for themselves, but rather for raising children handicapped by an almost premodern form of dependency. Yet the root of the trouble did not seem to be emotional or psychological at all, but rather structural—the result of such problems as failing public schools and soaring college costs.

Ditto when it came to grown children having to take care of their aging parents. In the United States, it was nearly impossible to get good-quality, inexpensive senior care. So adults were overburdened with the task of caring for their own parents.

I didn't have kids of my own yet, and my aging parents were back in Finland, so for the moment I was free simply to contemplate the remarkable differences in these relationships between the two countries. But there was a second kind of relationship that I was personally participating in by now that also made life in America radically different from life in Nordic countries: the relationship between women and men.

I'd grown up inspired by the example of strong American women—politicians, artists, authors—who were true to themselves rather than just devoted to finding and pleasing a man. When I'd needed a boost to pursue a goal at the office, or to stick up for myself in a relationship or social situation, I'd found encouragement reading the work of American women writers. After moving to New York I hadn't always felt comfortable among the perfectly manicured, high-heeled, well-toned, and fashionably dressed power ladies of Manhattan—I'd been accustomed to more understated appearances back in oversensible Finland. But during a stint working in the Manhattan offices of a major finance magazine, I did find myself in awe of the can-do attitude and bold resolve of the American women around me.

There was a flip side, however. Once I'd settled in the United States myself, I began to experience some confusion about my new life as a woman in America, especially when it came to the question of getting married, and the nature of the relationship between spouses.

I'd been watching American TV shows and movies for a long time, and I'd gotten used to seeing women obsessed with locking in the perfect marriage. The first American soap opera was finally beamed into Finnish living rooms in the early 1990s—*The Bold and the Beautiful*. It was an immediate sensation, so much so that Finns started naming their newborns Ridge and Brooke. The show's impact for me was learning two new English words. The first was "commitment," the thing that women on the show demanded endlessly from their men. The second word I learned was "libido," the thing that other characters on the show used to explain why for the dreamy men, "commitment" would always be impossible.

Nevertheless the women's persistence was sometimes rewarded when one of the men offered up a sparkling diamond ring, usually immersed in a flute of champagne. (This always struck me as risky. Since Nordic winters are so long, dark, and cold, even the daintier ladies among us are not above snatching up the nearest alcoholic beverage and chugging it without a second thought.) Among my friends and me, the English word "commitment" became a kind of oversize caricature of what we should hope for from a man. We'd say it with soap-opera gravitas in our best imitation of an American accent, then collapse into laughter. Later I watched the women on *Ally McBeal* and *Sex and the City* do their best to reel in a man, too, though the tone of those shows was a tad more sophisticated. After that their place was taken by the bridezillas of American reality TV.

These women depicted on screen were an exaggeration, of course, but after I moved to the United States, it gradually dawned on me that the quest for the ideal man hadn't been exaggerated as much as I'd thought. In real-life America, commitment was important, and the perfect husband would, needless to say, also be handsome, kind, romantic, trustworthy, hardworking, and good with kids. But after living in America for a while, I realized there was an undercurrent to the quest for commitment that I hadn't noticed before—even though, I now realized, there had been plenty of evidence for it on *Sex and the City*. In the United States, when a woman sought commitment from a man, there was often an implicit or explicit understanding that what she was looking for was someone who, perhaps even over other qualities, was well paid.

The first visible hint of this was the diamond engagement rings worn by American women. Even Trevor, my low-paid writer-teacher American boyfriend, had proffered a diamond engagement ring when he popped the question. He'd been lucky—he'd inherited the ring from his grandmother. With a small diamond flanked by two opals, it was the most beautiful thing I'd ever owned. Truly a token of his love, it made my heart swell. But my feelings for the ring were mixed. Where I came from, engagement rings were usually nothing more than simple gold bands worn by both the man and the woman, like American wedding rings. Only later, at the wedding itself, might the man give the woman a second ring, perhaps with some stones, though rarely would it contain anything as pricey as a diamond. When I wore my diamond engagement ring from my American fiancé, sometimes I felt embarrassed to be wearing something so expensive in plain sight. But more to the point, I wondered why the symbol of our future matrimony had to be a display of money. And why should it display not my financial power, but his? Rubbing my fingers on the smooth opals and sparkling diamond, I felt like Gollum in *The Lord of the Rings*, both loving and hating this precious thing.

Not all American marriages were stories of grateful women marrying rich men, of course. Yet the American reality was that getting married was still understood as an act of financial commingling. For proof of this one needed to look no further than the first few lines of a typical U.S. tax return. The IRS rewards married couples for pooling their incomes and filing their taxes as a joint unit. This is a startling practice to anyone from Finland, where each individual is always taxed independently— marital status has nothing to do with paying your taxes. The Finnish approach is deliberate; each spouse can easily track exactly what he or she has individually earned and paid, and contributed to the family, and everyone is taxed similarly without regard to their relationship status. Indeed, in Finland, a policy like America's would be considered government meddling in matters of private morality. By mixing American spousal finances even more tightly together into a muddled knot, the effect of this IRS-inspired commingling is to promote further financial interdependence between spouses.

Just as in the relationships I'd observed between parents

and children in the United States, the unspoken dependencies built into these financial bonds between married men and women struck me as peculiar remnants of a bygone era. It was as if America, land of the Hollywood romance, was in practice mired in a premodern time when marriage was, first and foremost, not an expression of love, but rather a logistical and financial pact to help families survive by joining resources. That, of course, begged the question of why such an old-fashioned pact might be necessary in what was supposed to be one of the most modern countries on earth.

I gradually discovered that again I wasn't the only one wondering what was wrong with marriage in America. Among well-educated women, for example, there was more and more talk—some of it in the form of several widely read magazine articles—about the increasing difficulty of finding a man worth marrying: a man of equal or preferably higher stature in education, social status, and salary. Successful career women who'd labored hard to secure a degree from a brand-name college or graduate school, and who themselves might already have landed a high-profile job, wondered whether they'd now have to settle for a spouse with lesser qualifications, status, and income.

Among the less privileged, meanwhile, American marriage appeared to be in a state of full-blown crisis. A much-discussed study had found that among white people in their thirties and forties, less than half of those with only a high-school education were tying the knot. Critics debated the causes of this reality, but what was remarkable to me was that this discussion, too, ultimately circled around the financial axis—whether the men were suffering from a lack of paychecks, or the women from an abundance of welfare checks. In all these cases the problems, and the possible solutions, seemed peculiarly linked to a couple's, or a family's, income—traditionally the husband's, but now sometimes the wife's—which then became the glue that held marriages together, or alternatively, the wedge that drove them apart.

From a Nordic point of view all this was extremely peculiar. I'd always thought of a romantic relationship between two people as a union of equal partners, lovers, and friends—and never as a financial arrangement. This wasn't just naïveté. When I was growing up in Finland, my father advised me to choose a profession that would pay well, but never once did he suggest that I find a husband who would be well paid. My mother, for her part, had set a clear example ever since I can remember—she was a dentist who had her own clinic, and she'd made good money throughout my childhood. As for my Finnish friends and I, we never sat around discussing what sort of salaries we hoped for in a spouse. Finances seldom came up as a factor in the marriage equation. People generally assumed that both partners would have jobs, but that was about it.

However, now that I was a woman in America—a woman who didn't make a lot of money herself, and who had just married a man whose income was also relatively modest—I realized that all this consideration of marriage as a financial arrangement did indeed have a certain compelling, if sad, logic. In America, if you were contemplating getting married and starting a family, you first needed to think very carefully about your finances. How much debt did you have in student loans? Could you afford health insurance? For that matter, how much would it cost just to give birth? The maternity benefits of different health-insurance plans varied dramatically. I was stunned when I learned of a young couple who had health insurance, and nevertheless had ended up owing the hospital twenty thousand dollars for the birth of their baby.

Then there was trying to care for a baby once it was born.

Under American law, companies with fewer than fifty employees weren't required to grant any parental leave at all; if you were a woman who wanted to care for a newborn, you might actually have to quit your job. Then who would pay the bills? Larger companies had to grant only three months of maternity leave, and likewise, that was unpaid. Some employers might offer more generous benefits, but generally speaking prospective parents in the United States faced enormous challenges simply in arranging and paying for their lives if they wanted to have kids. Often the livelihood of one of the spouses was at stake, and needless to say it would usually be the mother's. Which meant the husband needed to earn all that much more. Suddenly the obsession for commitment from a well-paid man started to make a whole lot more sense.

If you managed to calculate your way through those first few months, you would immediately face another financial crisis when your baby got a little bigger. If both parents went back to work, could they afford a nanny or private day care, either one of which was a huge expense? When the child grew even older, American parents would then have to tally up the enormous costs of trying to afford a house near a good public school, or paying tuition for a private school, assuming their child could even get in—not to mention the costs of saving for college.

I admired the ingenuity and stamina that American couples brought to the task of teaming up to build a family, but I was not surprised that marriage was in retreat. Maybe this was because life in America was transforming the whole institution of wedlock between spouses into an unappealing morass of squandered careers, insane schedules, and lost personal liberty. When money and access to money predetermined every major decision affecting a family and a child's future, it was no wonder that an American woman might pay attention to a potential husband's paycheck and benefits package, no matter how modern-minded she was.

Simmering resentment between spouses was, of course, another key driver of the therapy industry in the United States, as psychologists and psychiatrists profited from lucrative couples counseling, at least among people who could afford it. But to me, having come from Finland, once again the root of the problem didn't seem emotional or psychological. It seemed simple and structural. American society, despite all its high-tech innovation and mobility, just doesn't provide the basic support structures for families—support structures that all Nordic countries provide absolutely as a matter of course to everyone, as does nearly every other modern wealthy country on the planet.

There was no doubt that for Trevor and me, our lives and any plans we might have for a family were subject to debilitating economic uncertainty, tied to the nature of our careers and incomes. Like not a few other Americans, I imagine, I found myself in the evenings nursing a bowl of ice cream in front of the British TV sensation *Downton Abbey*, fantasizing that I had married a wealthy aristocrat who commanded a vast estate, humming with helpful staff.

An estate that, better yet, would also include a well-equipped private medical wing, and a staff of doctors and nurses so that we wouldn't have to rely on the fickle whims of our employers for health care. Which brings me to the third kind of relationship that confused me in America: the relationship between people and their employers.

One of the most heartbreaking episodes I witnessed after moving to the United States involved an American acquaintance who was battling cancer. To make matters even worse, it was clear that the person's domestic relationship was fraying at the same time. The peculiarly American twist on the story was this: If the couple split up, the young cancer patient, with many months of expensive treatment ahead, would be left without health insurance, since it was being provided through the domestic partner's employer. The unhappy relationship seemed to last much longer than it should have, hurting everyone involved far more than necessary. The trauma of the situation had been vastly multiplied simply because of the total dependency of everyone in the equation on the employer.

Far less tragic than the story of my friend with cancer, yet still stifling to acquaintances I'd gotten to know in a variety of circumstances, were the cases of people taking a job they didn't really want, simply because they needed the health insurance. Others hesitated to change jobs, or decided not to make an otherwise positive career move, because they'd have to give up their health coverage. Less obvious than the matter of health care, but also insidious, was the hesitancy of practically every American I met to take their full allotment of vacation time, as allowed by their employer, no matter how paltry. Never mind actually leaving work every day at five.

Gradually it dawned on me how much people in America depended on their employers for all sorts of things that were unimaginable to me: medical care, health savings accounts, and pension contributions, to name the most obvious. The result was that employers ended up having far more power in the relationship than the employee. In America jeopardizing your relationship with your employer carried personal risks that extend far beyond the workplace, to a degree unthinkable where I came from.

Americans have a reputation for changing jobs often, but as a result of their dependence on employer-provided benefits, my American acquaintances all seem far more beholden to their

bosses than the Nordics I know. Americans hardly take any parental leave, and clearly feel obligated to work extremely long
hours, with little say over how these hours are arranged.

By contrast, I had worked a number of high-pressure jobs
as a journalist in Finland, and while I'd often put in extra hours
or worked on weekends before a big deadline, overall I'd never
had to worry whether or not I could later take time off to make
up the difference, or take my full four or five weeks' vacation
every year. Moreover, it wasn't even in the realm of possibility
that all my health care could be compromised by anything to
do with my job. My Nordic friends, too, never thought twice
about taking their genuinely restorative vacation time; in fact
they were often encouraged to do so by their bosses. They enjoyed the full parental leaves they were entitled to in order to
raise a healthy baby, and they freely asked their employers for
part-time hours for periods of time when their children were
young.

People throughout the Nordic countries are far less concerned that such requests will reflect badly with their employers or have negative repercussions for their careers. The reason
is quite simple: In the Nordic countries the basics of health
care and other social benefits and essential services simply do
not depend on one's employment to the degree they do in the
United States.

By now I was used to hearing the Nordic countries dismissed
as "socialist nanny states." But ironically it was here in America
that businesses trying to manufacture products and make a buck
had somehow gotten saddled with the nanny's job of taking care
of their employees' health. Surely, I thought, Milton Friedman,
the great free-market economist, must be turning in his grave!
From a Nordic perspective, it seemed ludicrous to burden for-
profit companies with the responsibility of providing employees

with such a fundamental, complicated, and expensive social service.

People in the United States were aware of this contradiction, of course, and in discussions of the American business landscape, experts often pointed to the burdens that health-care obligations placed on companies, especially on small businesses. But no one seemed to be talking about the other side of the coin: the unhealthy dependence on employers that this creates among employees receiving, or hoping to receive, these benefits. It was an old-fashioned and oppressive sort of dependence, it seemed to me, completely at odds with the modern era of individual liberty and opportunity. I could see the consequences in the lives of everyone I knew.

In Europe, and especially in the Nordic countries, it had become a bit of a cliché to criticize Americans as superficial and obsessed with money, work, and status, rather than the more important things in life, like family, time off, and love. After living in America myself, however, I'd come to feel that this criticism was unfair. The Americans I'd gotten to know were thoughtful, loving, and kind people, and family was of particular importance to them. But after seeing for myself how American society forced people into situations that warped some of their most fundamental relationships—the relationships between parents and children, between spouses, and between workers and employers, especially—I could understand where the cliché was coming from.

I also wondered if this situation might not be intimately tied to a fourth fundamental relationship in America: the one between government and citizen. So much of the political debate in the United States revolved, at its core, around the idea that having too much government created a culture of dependency among its citizens, and that the result of this dependency was to ruin families and businesses. But while America might indeed have too much government and be suffocating under an unhealthy culture of dependency, it seemed to me that the size of the government wasn't so much the issue. Rather, it was how government was being used, and to what end. From a Nordic perspective, America's problem wasn't too much modernity. It was too little.

At the beginning of the twenty-first century the Nordic countries were being admired for being the most successful and well-adjusted region of the globe, but what exactly had they done? Were they really a group of small, isolated, homogeneous populations stuck in their welfare-sucking ways? Or was the reality exactly the opposite?

The fast-paced, stressful nature of modern life in a globalized world might be inevitable, but leaving people to muddle through it by falling back on old-fashioned family- and village-based support structures that no longer functioned the way they once did—that was by no means inevitable. The more I experienced life in the United States, the more I began to think that what Nordic societies had figured out was how to take modernity even further—further than America had. One might even say that Nordic societies had succeeded in pushing past outdated forms of social dependency, and that they had taken modernity to its logical conclusion. The Nordic nations had found an approach to government that deployed policies in a smarter way to create in individual citizens not a culture of dependency, but rather, a new culture of personal self-sufficiency that matched modern life. The result had been to put into daily practice the very ideals that many Americans could only fantasize about achieving in their personal lives: real freedom, real independence, and real opportunity.

One of the beautiful things about the Nordic approach also turned out to be that when you pushed modernity all the way, and freed people up so they had true personal independence, they didn't lose their connections to family, community, and one another after all. On the contrary, the Nordic experience suggested that when you took old-fashioned familial dependency out of the equation, children became more empowered, spouses more satisfied, and families more resilient—and even happy.

With some smart policy choices, the United States could surely achieve similar results. But first America might need its own version of what I had started referring to as the Nordic theory of love.

TWO

THE NORDIC THEORY OF LOVE

PIPPI LONGSTOCKING'S MAGIC

IS THE SWEDE A HUMAN BEING?

Pippi Longstocking is a rebellious girl of superhuman strength with two perky red braids and a face full of freckles. Her mother is dead, and her father is always away traveling, so she lives by herself in a big house along with a monkey and a spotted white horse that she can lift above her head. Pippi is sometimes abrupt with people, and her manners aren't the best, but her heart is in the right place.

Pippi is the star of a Swedish children's book series by Astrid Lindgren, first published in the 1940s. The Pippi Longstocking books have since been translated into seventy languages and adapted numerous times for film and television—including several American screen adaptations, the first hosted by Shirley Temple in 1961. In neighboring Finland, I grew up reading and loving Lindgren's books, loving Pippi, and especially loving her horse, which she brought indoors and rode bareback.

But Pippi is also a legend among children and families all over the world, not just in the Nordic countries—my American husband, Trevor, remembers having the Pippi Longstocking books read to him as a kid, too. But what is it, exactly, that captivates so many people about Pippi?

Pippi's best friends in the stories are the two children next door, Annika and Tommy. Unlike Pippi, they belong to an intact and idyllic nuclear family. The significance of Pippi's character and her relationship with Annika and Tommy was never explicitly clear to me as a child, or even as an adult, until a man named Lars Trägårdh pointed it out to me.

Lars Trägårdh is a Swedish scholar and historian who lived in the United States for decades and knows the country intimately. As a boy Trägårdh had dreamed of coming to America, and after high school in Sweden he was accepted by Pomona, a small liberal arts college in California. As he set out to do what millions of Americans do every year—apply for financial aid to help cover the cost of his college tuition—he got his first taste of how things worked in the United States. The financial aid office at Pomona gave him two sets of forms to fill out. One asked about his income and savings. The other asked about his parents' income and savings.

Trägårdh was confused. He was already eighteen, legally an adult. In Sweden his parents no longer had any responsibility for him or any legal right to be involved in his affairs. He supported himself, and he didn't understand what his parents' money had to do with his college expenses. Trägårdh remembers that when he explained all this to a financial aid officer at Pomona, he was told that in America, parents love their children so much that they happily spend tens of thousands of dollars—today it could easily be hundreds of thousands—on college.

The exchange led Trägårdh to a lifetime of thinking and

writing about the American dream, and how it compares to the Nordic dream. The son of a single mother, he did receive the financial aid he needed, and once he finished his studies at Pomona in the 1970s, he ran a café in San Francisco, became an entrepreneur and started his own computer business, and then eventually returned to academia and earned his PhD from UC Berkeley in the early 1990s. He taught European history for a decade at Barnard College in New York City until he moved back to Sweden with his American wife. His current work at a Swedish university focuses on children's rights and social trust—the moral glue that helps hold societies together.

Some years ago Trägårdh and a coauthor came out with a book called *Är svensken människa?* (Is the Swede a human being?) This somewhat startling question refers to the title of a past work that many Swedes would probably recognize, but that requires a little explanation for the rest of us, and that, in a roundabout way, gets us back to the subject of Pippi Longstocking.

In the 1940s, around the same time that Astrid Lindgren was writing the first of her stories about the vivacious and likable Pippi, another Swedish writer was analyzing the Swedish character and writing a very different sort of book, with that provocative question as his title. His name was Sanfrid Neander-Nilsson, and as far as he was concerned, the Swedish national character was ice cold, inward-turned, sad, depressed, and almost animal-like. It was a portrait of Swedes who yearned for solitude and feared other people—nothing like Pippi Longstocking.

A characterization of Swedes as the ultimate loners may seem surprising, especially considering Pippi Longstocking's global popularity. But there is some truth to it—we Nordics aren't known to be especially outgoing, and we probably deserve our reputation as stoic, silent types who can be a bit dour.

That said, the stereotypical Nordic person would probably also be thought of as someone who, although perhaps not particularly talkative, is sensitive to the needs of his or her fellow human beings, especially since we're sometimes believed to have socialist tendencies. It follows that we ought to have a collective mind-set and some solidarity, not be extreme individualists.

In fact, however, a powerful strain of individualism *is* part of the bedrock of Nordic societies—so much so that Lars Trägårdh felt it was worth dusting off the old question "Is the Swede a human being?" and taking a fresh and more positive look at Nordic individualism. After years of observing the differences between Sweden and the United States, Trägårdh identifies in his book some fundamental qualities at the heart of Swedish society—qualities that also exist in all Nordic societies—that help explain Nordic success. Indeed, Trägårdh's findings tell us a lot about why the Nordic countries are doing so well in surveys of global competitiveness and quality of life. And for me Trägårdh helped explain why I'd been feeling so confused by American relationships, especially those between parents and children, between spouses, and between employees and their employers. It all came down to the Nordic way of thinking about love—perfectly exemplified by Pippi Longstocking.

Trägårdh and his collaborator—a well-known Swedish historian and journalist named Henrik Berggren—put together their observations on individualism and formulated something they called "the Swedish theory of love." The core idea is that authentic love and friendship are possible only between individuals who are independent and equal. This notion represents exactly the values that I grew up with and that I feel are most dear to Finns as well as people from the other Nordic nations, not just Swedes, so I like to call it "the Nordic theory of love."

For the citizens of the Nordic countries, the most important values in life are individual self-sufficiency and independence in relation to other members of the community. If you're a fan of American individualism and personal freedom, this might strike you as downright all-American thinking.

A person who must depend on his or her fellow citizens is, like it or not, put in a position of being subservient and unequal. Even worse, as Trägårdh and Berggren explain in their discussion of the moral logic of the Pippi Longstocking stories, "He who is in debt, who is beholden to others, or who requires the charity and kindness not only from strangers but also from his most intimate companions to get by, also becomes untrustworthy. . . . He becomes dishonest and inauthentic."

In the realm of Pippi—who, let's remember, is a strong superhuman girl living alone in a big house—this means that exactly because she is totally self-sufficient, her friendship with the children next door, Tommy and Annika, is a great gift to them. That's because they are absolutely assured that Pippi's friendship is being given freely, no strings attached. It's precisely because Pippi is an exaggeration of self-sufficiency that she draws our awareness to the purity and unbridled enthusiasm of her love, and elicits our admiring affection. In real life, of course, a child Pippi's age would still have a healthy dependency on her parents, the way her neighbors Tommy and Annika do. But Pippi illustrates an ideal of unencumbered love, whose logic, in Nordic thinking, extends to most real-life adult relationships.

What Lars Trägårdh came to understand during his years in the United States was that the overarching ambition of Nordic societies during the course of the twentieth century, and into the twenty-first, has not been to socialize the economy at all, as is often mistakenly assumed. Rather the goal has been to free the individual from *all* forms of dependency within the family *and* in civil society: the poor from charity, wives from husbands, adult children from parents, and elderly parents from their children. The express purpose of this freedom is to allow all those human relationships to be unencumbered by ulterior motives and needs, and thus to be entirely free, completely authentic, and driven purely by love.

I wanted to talk with Trägårdh myself about all this, so I contacted him in Sweden from my new home in New York. As we chatted on Skype, he explained that these were precisely the reasons why he'd felt so at odds with his American college's financial aid policy. "In the United States there is both a moral, and to some extent legal, expectation that parents provide for their children even after the children have come of age," Trägårdh said. "But this expectation also means that parents have power over their children."

Freed from such expectations, people in Nordic societies can raise their children primarily with the goal of helping them become independent and capable of handling life on their own. The prevailing expectation is that every person should be able to craft his or her own life, without an excessive financial debt to one's parents, for example, that might skew one's decisions. There is a corresponding expectation that no one should be penalized in advance by the unlucky accident of having parents who might, for whatever reason, have less than robust finances. Similarly a wife should not be put in a position of being financially overdependent on her husband. Or vice versa, for that matter. And people should be able to make choices related to their employment without worrying whether they will still be able to receive, say, treatment for cancer.

All this creates relationships that are much freer of resentments, guilt, and baggage. In this sense, then, the Nordic theory of love is an intimate philosophy for how empowered individuals can engage in personal relationships in the modern age. Liberated from many of the more onerous financial and logistical obligations of the old days, we can base our relationships with family, friends, and loved ones more on pure human connection. We are also freer to express our true feelings in our relationships with others.

At the same time the Nordic theory of love has become an overarching philosophy about how to structure a society. As such, it has inspired the broad variety of policy choices in the Nordic nations that together ensure a single, predominant goal: independence, freedom, and opportunity for every member of society. Most of the major decisions the Nordic nations have made, whether related to family policies, education, or health care, have followed from, and are direct manifestations of, the Nordic theory of love. While the inspiration for these decisions may originally have been rooted in Nordic cultural values, the policy choices themselves are not questions of culture—they are exactly that: policy choices. How all this has worked, however, is widely misunderstood in America.

THE MARCH OF MODERNITY

In the United States the biggest perceived enemy to individual freedom is the state, and Americans do have a point. History has proved beyond a doubt that the state can be used to oppress and even completely destroy individual liberties. After all, for decades America's worst enemy was the Soviet Union, where the state often controlled even the most intimate details of people's lives. When American critics of Nordic success condemn countries like my own as "socialist nanny states," they are voicing a real fear that citizens could become docile lambs, subject to increasing government influence and control.

Every time I hear an American refer to Finland as a socialist country, however, I feel like I've been suddenly transported back to the 1950s. Finns of my generation and older have a pretty good idea of what socialism is, not to mention communism, having grown up with the Soviet Union right on our doorstep. Our nation fought three brutal wars against socialism in the twentieth century to protect our freedom, independence, and free-market system.

A little history: Until the early twentieth century, Finland was ruled alternately by Sweden and Russia, but gained its independence in 1917 when the Communist revolution in Russia overthrew the czars, creating the soon-to-be Soviet juggernaut. Finland was immediately plunged into a bitter struggle that pitted Finland's own working class—sympathetic to the Russian Communist cause—against our own conservative capitalists. In a short but vicious civil war, the free-market forces in Finland won, crushing the socialist uprising.

Then, when the Soviet Union threatened Finland's independence two decades later, Finns beat back socialism both times, preserving Finnish freedom and independence—at great sacrifice. Nearly a fifth of Finland's entire population fought against the Soviets, and many more participated as nurses and in other supporting roles. Some 93,000 Finns perished out of a population of 3.7 million.

Here's how we in Finland understand socialism: The government controls production and bans ownership of property—no private factories, companies, or stores, and no free markets. No one is allowed to accumulate any personal riches. There is only one political party, few personal freedoms, and little or no freedom of speech. Socialism is one step away from communism, which Karl Marx defined as a situation in which the government, or indeed, the state itself, has become expendable.

The idea that a contemporary Nordic society is anything like this sort of socialism is absurd. The notion that even a liberal American leader such as Barack Obama could be considered a socialist, as some of his conservative critics like to claim, seems to us downright comic. In fact such stereotypes quickly wear thin for us Finns. The number of Finns who sacrificed their lives fighting socialism and communism in the twentieth century is roughly the same as the number of Americans who died in America's two hot wars against communism—Korea and Vietnam—and that's out of a population about one-sixtieth the size of America's. Over the past seventy years what the experience of the Nordic nations actually suggests is that even the United States, with its already very impressive commitments to freedom, might actually be able to learn a few things from us about freedom and free-market capitalism.

Indeed, what if the entire purpose of the state in the twenty-first century, as agreed upon and expressly stated by its citizens, was not to take more power away from the people, but just the opposite: to push the modern values of freedom and independence even further, to provide the people with the logistical foundation for the most comprehensive form of individual liberty possible? It is exactly this exceptional commitment to individualism that defines the Nordic social contract today. And the results of this approach are plain to see from the Nordic region's rankings in global surveys, not only in quality of life but in economic dynamism as well.

All the advantages I gave up when I left Finland and moved to America—universal public health care, universal affordable day care, real maternity benefits, high-quality free education, taxpayer-funded residences for the elderly, even the separate taxation of spouses—were not gifts from the government to make me a servile dependent on the state's largesse. Rather the Nordic system is intentionally designed to take into account the specific challenges of modern life and give citizens as much logistical and financial independence as possible. This is actually the opposite of a community-centered system, or socialism, or whatever you want to call it. This is also why the supposed social solidarity of people in the Nordic nations is not really as noble an undertaking as it is often made out to be.

Here's how Trägårdh puts it: "The Swedes like to flatter themselves into thinking that they are just very altruistic people, always doing good things," he told me. The same could be said of Finns, or other Nordics. However, what really motivates Swedes and other Nordic citizens to support their system isn't altruism—no one is that selfless—but self-interest. Nordic societies provide their citizens—all their citizens, and especially the middle class—with maximum autonomy from old-fashioned, traditional ties of dependency, which among other things ends up saving people a lot of money and heartache along with securing personal freedom. According to Trägårdh and Berggren, Nordic countries are, in fact, the most individualized societies on the face of the earth.

I know just how horrible this might sound to some Americans. Surely it brings to mind a totalitarian state—one that has cleverly severed all emotional ties between people in order to make citizens into slaves of the system. You could also be forgiven for harboring a dim view of Nordic society simply from living in Finland. Finns themselves love nothing more than to grumble and complain constantly about how everything in their country is terrible—how the social services are terrible, how burdensome family relations are, how children are growing up miserable, how the government is a terrible bureaucratic overlord. Part of this is simply human nature: People always find fault with their situation no matter how good they have it. But the reality is that many Finns really have no idea how good they *do* have it, because they've never been on their own as a citizen of a place like the United States. Even many of my cosmopolitan and well-educated Finnish acquaintances still don't understand, for example, even after I've explained it to them for the hundredth time, that despite the passage of ObamaCare (the Affordable Care Act), the United States still does not have a universal public health-care system. It's simply unimaginable to them that an advanced rich country could be so backward.

Despite the genuine grumbling you hear in Nordic societies, if you compare statistics on family life in Nordic countries during recent decades with those in other countries, it becomes clear that loving families, well-adjusted children, and caring communities are by far the Nordic norm. When UNICEF looked at children's well-being throughout the different rich nations of the world—considering such metrics as childhood poverty, children's health and safety, family relationships, education, and behavior, including diet, teenage pregnancy, and bullying—the Netherlands, Norway, Iceland, Finland, and Sweden ranked best. Sad to say, the United States came in near the bottom. A study by Save the Children deemed Nordic nations the world's best countries for mothers, while the United States came in thirty-third. How is that possible? It's possible because freeing people from the shackles of financial and other sorts of dependency on one another enables them to be more caring toward each other, not less. This is precisely the Nordic theory of love in action.

But surely all this Nordic talk of extreme individualism and independence means that even if Nordic people love their families, the bonds of family ultimately are weak. Indeed, by dispensing with many of the financial interdependencies that require a husband and wife to stay together, doesn't the Nordic arrangement encourage families to break apart?

Actually, by empowering individuals for the modern age, the Nordic theory of love has given the family a reboot, making it, in a sense, more up-to-date and relevant—and better prepared for the challenges of the twenty-first century. In a report prepared for the World Economic Forum in Davos, Switzerland, titled *The Nordic Way*, Trägårdh and Berggren write: "The family remains a central social institution in the Nordic countries, but it too is infused with the same moral logic stressing autonomy and equality. The ideal family is made up of adults who work and are not financially dependent on the other, and children who are encouraged to be as independent as early as possible. Rather than undermining 'family values' this could be interpreted as a modernization of the family as a social institution."

An example that Trägårdh uses to illustrate the Nordic theory of love, and to show how Nordic societies value family, is elder care. In the United States, if your parents develop a long-term health condition in their old age, taking care of them and paying their medical bills can steal away years of your life. In the Nordic countries, if one or both of your parents are chronically ill, you can rely on your country's universal health-care system to handle the logistics and medical treatment. The result? You are freed up to do the more rewarding, loving things in the precious time you have left with your ailing parent, which the social workers can't do: go for a walk, talk, read, just spend time together.

"When surveys ask elderly Swedes whether they prefer to be dependent on their own adult children or the state," Trägårdh told me, "they say the state. If you rephrase the question and ask if they'd like their children to visit them, they all say yes. So it is not that the elderly in Sweden don't want to have relationships with their children. It's that they don't want to see them on terms and conditions where they are being reduced to a state of dependency in relation to their own children."

Despite the doubts that some Americans still seem to have about the Nordic countries' commitment to free markets, Sweden, Finland, the United States, and other wealthy industrialized nations are all societies immersed in modern capitalism. It is precisely life in this modern free-market world that is breaking down the old-fashioned, traditional relationships of family and community, gradually equalizing gender roles, and encouraging individuality and independence. Critics sometimes argue that the Nordic countries have little to teach the rest of the world, because their success is specific to an isolated group of small, culturally uniform, ethnically homogeneous countries. But this misses the larger point. While the Nordic theory of love may have emerged as a set of cultural ideas specific to the region, the smart social policies that have resulted happen to dovetail perfectly with the universal challenges that all nations are facing as modernity inevitably advances.

Today the United States is at once a hypermodern society in its embrace of the contemporary free-market system, but an antiquarian society in leaving it to families and other community institutions to address the problems the system creates. Seen from a Nordic perspective, the United States is stuck in a conflict, but it's not the conflict between liberals and conservatives, or between Democrats and Republicans, and it's not the old debate about bigger government versus smaller government. It's the conflict between the past and the future. Much of America's government does look ridiculously bloated and intrusive in all the wrong ways for modernity. The way the United States government micromanages society with case-by-case policies, and hands out uniquely tailored gifts left and right to special interests, strikes a Nordic as a clearly outdated way to govern. And whether the United States wants to admit this to itself or not, staying stuck in the past is putting itself at an ever-increasing disadvantage in the world.

As the world continues to evolve and change, all nations need new ideas. One of America's best-known commentators, the columnist David Brooks, expressed this need particularly well in relation to the United States in an article he titled "The Talent Society." "We're living in the middle of an amazing era of individualism," Brooks wrote, expressing a view that's actually almost identical to Trägårdh's. The evidence that Brooks cites makes it clear that the changes caused by the relentless advance of modernity are happening whether we like it or not. Whereas a few generations ago it was considered shameful for people to have children unless they were married, for example, now more than 50 percent of births to American women under thirty occur outside of marriage. More than 50 percent of American adults are single, and 28 percent of households consist of just one person. There are more single-person American households than there are married-with-children households. More Americans consider themselves politically independent than either Republican or Democrat. Lifetime employment is down, and union membership has plummeted.

"The trend is pretty clear," Brooks concluded, articulating his own version of how old-fashioned, traditional relationships have given way to personal independence: "Fifty years ago, America was groupy. People were more likely to be enmeshed in stable, dense and obligatory relationships. They were more defined by permanent social roles: mother, father, deacon. Today, individuals have more freedom. They move between more diverse, loosely structured and flexible networks of relationships."

Brooks paints a picture of an America that allows "the ambitious and the gifted to surf through amazing possibilities," but where the people who lack these skills fall further behind. Though this captures America's dilemma to a degree, it's not the complete picture. When it comes to "the ambitious and the gifted," we need to add that for the most part, it's only the ambitious and gifted lucky enough to have access to substantial private resources who find opportunity in America today.

Brooks says it is time to build new versions of the settled, stable, and thick arrangements of the past that Americans have left behind. This is exactly what the Nordic region has set out to do, and the Nordic theory of love has turned out to be a solid foundation for what Brooks calls the "diverse, loosely structured, and flexible networks of relationships" that characterize our current cultural and economic life. In an age when people are experiencing more freedom than ever, Finland and its Nordic neighbors have found a way to expand personal liberty while also ensuring that the vast majority of individuals—not just the elite—have new ways to be stable and be able to prosper.

As the twenty-first century progresses, countries that can figure out their own version of the Nordic theory of love will have a long-term advantage. Good quality of life, worker satisfaction and health, economic dynamism, and political freedom and stability are all interconnected. Given all that, if the United States were able to borrow anything from the successes of Nordic societies to reinvigorate its own success—just supposing—where would it begin?

Well, from a Nordic point of view, a pretty good place to start would be at the beginning, with babies.

THREE

FAMILY VALUES FOR REAL

STRONG INDIVIDUALS FORM
A BEAUTIFUL TEAM

IT STARTS WITH CHILDREN

When my American acquaintance Jennifer realized she was pregnant, she asked her friends for recommendations for good obstetricians. She called the doctors to see whether they accepted her insurance, and which hospital they were affiliated with. When Jennifer found a doctor she liked and could see without additional costs, she started going for regular appointments. Most of the visits focused on medical care, and she remembers getting general advice about becoming a new mother only in regard to the possibility of post-partum depression. On matters such as breast-feeding, she consulted the Internet and her friends.

At the time she was working for a large media company in New York City. Her workdays would often stretch until seven or eight at night. Now that she was pregnant, she asked her boss if she could transfer to a position with shorter days and

more predictable hours. Although he wasn't required to accommodate her request, her boss was generous and agreed. A few
months before her due date Jennifer suffered early labor pains,
and her doctor assigned her to bed rest. Again her employer was
generous, allowing her to work from home until the baby was
born, for which she was grateful.

After giving birth she stayed in a semiprivate room in the
hospital for three days with her insurance covering the costs
while she recovered from her cesarean. Then she started her
three months of unpaid maternity leave. The short-term
disability insurance offered by her employer paid her salary for
ten weeks, and when she returned to work, her husband used
accrued vacation time to stay home with the baby for another
month.

Jennifer had started looking for day care early, since she
knew it would be an ordeal. She researched a variety of day-
care centers to determine their quality and reputation, checked
waiting lists, compared prices, and asked for recommendations.
Eventually she settled on one that would cost her and her husband $1,200 a month for one child, or $14,400 a year, a typical
price in the New York City area. Her baby started there at the
age of four months.

By the time Jennifer got pregnant again, she was working
for a much smaller company. The hours were more manageable, but her health insurance had changed, and she couldn't
see the doctor from her first pregnancy anymore. Since the new
company employed less than fifty people, she was no longer
entitled to any leave, nor did the new company offer short-
term disability insurance. So even though she suffered severe
back pain throughout her second and third trimesters, she had
no choice but to go to the office every day, where she spent six
months in agony. After she gave birth via C-section, her doctors

encouraged her to get up and start moving. She went home after a few days. Soon after returning she was on the couch, holding the baby, when she felt the sickening sensation of something leaking all over her. The surgical wound had opened, and she had to visit her doctor's office to have it stitched closed again. Her new employer was more generous than it needed to be, and offered her six weeks of paid maternity leave. Since her husband had not accrued enough new vacation days to take time off, after that her son joined his sister in day care—at the age of six weeks. "I had a C-section, and that's a major abdominal surgery," Jennifer said later. "So you're going back to work after six weeks, not having slept the whole time, after a major surgery, and with an infant. If you ask me, it's barbaric."

In the system she was in, Jennifer could actually count herself lucky. Her first employer allowed her to work from home, and for both pregnancies, her health insurance covered all the costs. This is not always the case. On average, women with insurance pay several thousands of dollars out of pocket for giving birth in the United States. Women without insurance face costs that can quickly climb into the tens of thousands of dollars.

As for time off, Americans who have worked for a company with more than fifty employees for more than a year have the right to a total of twelve weeks of family or medical leave annually—*un*paid, of course—but that leave can be used up by any of the following events: the birth of a child; an adoption; caring for an ailing child, spouse, or parent; or an illness. In 2012 this law covered only slightly more than half of American workers. For everyone else there is no universal guarantee of any leave for any reason—not for having children, not for getting sick. The small businesses that Americans applaud as the backbone of the U.S. economy have a darker side: the utter lack of any security for their employees. Technically companies are not allowed to fire someone for getting pregnant. The truth, however, is that it happens all the time.

When it comes to family and medical leave for workers, the United States is utterly out of line with the contemporary norms of modern nations. While Nordic citizens often don't realize how good they have it, Americans seem not to realize how terribly they are being treated. According to a UN report from 2014 surveying 185 countries and territories, only two did not guarantee any paid maternity leave; Papua New Guinea and the United States. The United States is also one of only a handful of countries that don't guarantee their workers any paid time off for illness—others include Angola, India, and Liberia.

As a result, when Americans have children, their options vary widely depending on where they live, for whom they work, and how high up the job-skills and corporate ladders they've managed to climb. Some states and cities require companies to give their employees some paid time off for illness. California is one of the few states that offer paid family leave for workers who have contributed to the state's disability insurance program—but only for six weeks, and only at about half their normal pay. Advocates for family leave in the United States celebrate California's example as progressive, and it is certainly a start. But by the standards of any Nordic country, a paltry six weeks at half pay is still way behind the times.

It's true that some of the better American companies offer their employees paid sick days as a benefit, and some even offer paid family leave. Google's five months of paid maternity leave have often been hailed as outstanding. Some companies also subsidize short-term disability insurance for their workers, which then might cover part of an employee's salary during unpaid parental leave, as it did during Jennifer's first pregnancy. Many new moms use a combination of sick days and vacation time to create some paid parental leave, but that robs them of a much-needed chance to rest later in the year.

Overall the reality in the United States is grim: In 2015 only one in ten Americans working for private companies had access to paid family leave—although 87 percent did get at least some unpaid leave. Fully a third of private-sector workers had no access to any paid sick days. A quarter had no paid vacation. Even for those who did have paid vacation, the average length of the allotted vacation for a full-time worker in private industry was, after one year of employment, just ten days. That increased, after four more years, to an infinitesimally more generous total of fifteen days. Between 2006 and 2010, nearly a third of American working mothers reported taking no maternity leave whatsoever. For those who did, the average length of the leave was ten weeks.

Jennifer wrapped all this up for me succinctly: "In this country you are at the mercy of your employer. You really don't have any rights. Because of that you live in a constant state of worry."

In countries informed by the Nordic theory of love, the American response to the birth of a baby makes no sense. As wealthy, modern, industrialized nations, the Nordic countries have realized that the productivity of their workers and businesses, as well as the long-term health of their societies and economies, depends first and foremost on healthy relationships between children and their parents, between spouses, and between parents and their employers. Thus the Nordic response to the birth of a baby is rather different.

In Finland, when a woman I got to know named Hanna realized she was pregnant, she phoned the local maternity clinic operated by her town close to Helsinki and made an appointment to see a nurse. When she arrived for that first appointment, she and her baby were immediately gathered into the embrace of the comprehensive system of care that Finland has set up to nurture all families—which is to say every Finnish family in the entire country, regardless of income, municipality, or employment.

Throughout the pregnancy the nurse, and less frequently the doctor, monitored Hanna's health while they counseled her on breast-feeding, foods to avoid, and feelings that might arise during such a significant life event. The nurse ran tests on Hanna to check for any early signs of trouble, and discussed her health history with her, the risks of alcohol and drug use, and the dangers of smoking. Whenever Hanna had a question, she could go see the nurse for advice, or simply call a help line set up for expecting and new parents.

Hanna's pregnancy proceeded smoothly, and she ended up only needing to see the doctor a few times. The nurse signed her up for the usual two ultrasounds, and neither revealed any problems. Hanna decided to pay for two additional sonograms at a private doctor, just for her own satisfaction and peace of mind. If any problems had arisen, however, the public health-care system would have sprung into action. When my Finnish sister-in-law Veera's belly appeared unusually small during her first pregnancy, she was immediately sent to the hospital for additional checkups. In her case, happily, everything turned out to be fine. The same applied to another friend who experienced mild heart arrhythmia during her pregnancy.

For Hanna and her husband, Olli, the total cost of all this attentive prenatal care—apart from the two private sonograms—was, well, zero. Hearing this, an American might have one of two reactions. Hanna and Olli must be paying exorbitantly high taxes to subsidize all this public welfare, leaving them pathetically poor compared with an equivalent American family, who could at least choose what kind of health insurance they wanted to pay for. Or the American listener might feel sorry for Hanna and Olli, concluding that they must be very poor to begin with, or an at-risk family, to have qualified for so much free monitoring, counseling, and help.

Setting aside for the moment the question of taxes—a very interesting question indeed, which I'll return to later—Hanna and Olli are neither poor nor at-risk. They met when they were both students in one of Finland's most prestigious university programs in industrial engineering and management, at what is today Aalto University. By the time Hanna got pregnant, both she and Olli were working in high-powered jobs at successful management-consulting firms in Helsinki. The care they received during Hanna's pregnancy was pretty much the standard care anyone in Finland would receive. Some of my friends in Finland find all the questions from the nurses about their private lives slightly intrusive, but mostly they take it all in stride, because they know that the clinics are working to ensure the well-being of their child. Many are very happy to receive so much help, especially since the free visits continue after the baby is born, when new parents are most likely to have questions and feel overwhelmed.

As Hanna's due date approached, she and Olli were offered a choice of hospitals nearby. They got to tour the facilities in advance, where they learned about the birthing stools, bathtubs, and pain relief methods the mother could use while in labor. Then, when Hanna finally went into labor, both she and Olli stayed in a private room in the public hospital for four days, with their newborn in a crib next to them. The specially trained nurse-midwives running the maternity ward checked on the family several times a day, while Olli took charge of changing diapers and picking up meals and medications.

This, too, is all standard care for all Finnish parents. My sister-in-law, Veera, still reminisces warmly about all the helpful advice she got from the public hospital staff after the birth of her first child, including lessons on how to bathe the baby, change diapers, and breast-feed. The hospital's nurse-midwives were a godsend, Veera told me, and the private room she and my brother Mikko stayed in for three days was a blessing for a young family trying to get its bearings. "And it wasn't just some oatmeal for us," Veera said happily a few years later, as we looked at photos of the births of their two children. "All the best yogurt, muesli, dried fruit—the works."

Hanna and Olli needed less guidance in caring for their new baby because they already had one small child at home—a baby they'd recently adopted. However, since the birth had left Hanna with some physical trauma, she was provided with a physical therapist right away, so she could begin her healing process while still at the hospital. Hanna related all this to me a couple of months after the experience, as we sat in the kitchen of her home on the outskirts of Helsinki. "I really think it all worked extremely well," she said, as her new baby, Oliver, slept in his crib beside us. "I had a fairly difficult birth, but I have gotten all the care I've needed, and nobody rushed us to leave the hospital before I was ready."

For all this, however, Hanna and Olli did have to pay. I'm sorry to say that the bill came to a staggering $375.

Not everyone's experiences of giving birth in Finland are always rosy. If there is a rush, mothers might have to share rooms or give birth in a hospital that wasn't their first choice. Municipalities do have different routines and facilities. Giving birth can be a harrowing experience under any conditions. Yet most of my Finnish friends tell me glowing stories of the care they received during their pregnancy and delivery. One couple

I know stayed in a private room in the hospital for a week because the mother was having trouble getting started with her breast-feeding. Until the medical staff was sure the baby was properly receiving nourishment, the hospital never once suggested that they should pack up and leave. This extended private stay, admittedly, did bring their hospital bill up a bit—to about five hundred dollars.

This is what the Nordic theory of love looks like in Finland when a baby is born. As much as possible, the theory is that parents should be able to focus on welcoming new life into the world and loving their newborn, rather than being overwhelmed by the logistical challenges involved. The other Nordic countries all have similar practices, too, though with some local variations. The Danish attitude toward childbirth tends to be a bit less doting than the Finnish, with more emphasis on natural birth, without epidurals or long hospital stays; that said, treatments like acupuncture to ease labor pains are routine. My Danish friend Brandur was promptly sent home in the wee hours of the morning after the birth of his and his wife Hannah's first baby, while Hannah and the baby stayed behind. "The hospital is not a hotel," a nurse informed him brusquely, sending the giddy man off to find a cab and, as Brandur remembers, "talk way too much to the taxi driver." When another Danish acquaintance, Sigrid, had her first child by cesarean, she was grateful that the nurses let her stay in the hospital for a week to help ensure she was breast-feeding without trouble; by contrast, after her next two vaginal deliveries they let her go home a few hours after giving birth. She and her husband thought this was perfectly fine, as did the other Danes I know who had had similar experiences. A Swedish friend of mine, meanwhile, gushed about how much time the nurses always had for her during her pregnancy, while two other Swedes felt that the same service was even a bit too much, with all that sitting and chatting about feelings. Some Swedes I know got private rooms for their deliveries, some didn't. On average, all they had to pay was the grand fee of about fifty dollars for their hospital stays.

Once a new baby has been brought safely into the world, the Nordic theory of love has some things to say about its first year of life. Nordic nations have realized that it is in the best long-term interests of everyone, including businesses, to support families in raising children. After all, in the long run, happy family members are more productive, and businesses will have a wider pool of healthy, productive, well-adjusted workers to draw on in the future. So when it comes to granting parental leave after a baby is born, the Nordic approach is also quite different from the American.

Throughout the entire Nordic region, the universal *minimum* amount of parental leave that new parents receive, regardless of where they work, is nine months. While on leave the parent who stays home also receives at least 70 percent of his or her pay for the entire duration of the leave. Some countries do put a cap on these payments, but only for people who have particularly high salaries. Some Nordic countries offer a variety of options, too; in Norway families can choose eleven months at full pay or thirteen months at 80 percent. But the basic duration and pay of parental leaves are universally guaranteed. Parental leave policy is not dependent on the whims of different employers of different sizes, or on the vagaries of different local arrangements. Nordic parental leaves are a function of a simple, straightforward, uniform national policy, and pay is furnished through taxes managed by each country's social security system. To make things fair, Nordic parental leaves are funded by all employees and employers, not just the firms that happen to have hired pregnant women or women with small children.

That said, Nordic parental leaves are also flexible. Parents can tailor the allotted time off to their individual needs, portioning it between the mother and the father, and adjusting the timing. Moreover, all Nordic countries have earmarked some leave specifically for fathers, to encourage their active participation in child rearing, and to lessen the stigma that men might experience in the workplace when they become active, involved parents.

In Finland the first four months of parental leave go specifically to the mother, and the leave begins at least five weeks before her due date. After she gives birth she then has three months to recover and breast-feed the baby, which most Finnish mothers choose to do. Nevertheless all new fathers can also take three paid weeks off at the same time to help around the house and bond with the baby. As for the subsequent six months, parents can divide that allotment between them as they like. Finally, the father has another six weeks of paternity leave to use on his own, which is not available to the mother. Again, this is not dependent on the particular policies at the workplace, but rather is a universal right of any new parent, man or woman.

The system functions smoothly and is widely accepted as the norm, by employers as well as families. What's more, after the ten months of parental leave are used up in Finland, one parent can *still* stay home, without losing his or her job, until the child turns three. The parent doesn't continue to receive a portion of his or her salary during this period, but does receive a small home-care allowance. At the end of the parent's period of home leave, up to three years, he or she is welcomed back and reintegrated into the original workplace.

When Hanna and Olli had adopted their first child, a baby from Kenya, the Kenyan adoption agency required the new parents to stay in Kenya for more than a half year as part of the process. Hanna took a year of paid maternity leave, while Olli also took a leave of seven months, though for both parents to take such long leaves at the same time was unusual, and Olli's had to be unpaid. Then, with the birth of their second child, Hanna began her maternity leave a month before her due date and planned to stay home for a year and a half. After the baby was born Olli took off two weeks, and was eligible for more leave later.

When both parents return to work, the Nordic theory of love comes into play in a new way. At this stage of a young child's life, Nordic societies want to ensure that both parents are able to focus again on being fully engaged and productive employees, while at the same time also remaining good parents. In America day care is often one of the most vexing logistical challenges that parents face, and one of their most exorbitant expenses. By contrast, Nordic societies have decided to free parents from this burden as it is good for all the individuals and institutions involved: employers, parents, and—not least, of course—the children themselves. Thanks to the Nordic theory of love, every parent in Finland, Sweden, Norway, and Denmark has easy access to inexpensive, convenient day care, publicly subsidized and generally paid for on a sliding scale according to a family's income. Access to day care begins as soon as parents complete their initial parental leaves, and day-care centers are regulated to ensure high quality. Privately run day care is certainly also available in many places, if parents prefer that option.

In Finland, because parents are guaranteed the right to return to their jobs for up to three years after the birth of a child, most families opt to have one or the other parent care for their children themselves at home for the first two years, after which the vast majority chooses one of the excellent public day-care centers. Low-income families get the service for free, and high-income families pay up to a cap, which for 2016 was about $350 per month or $4,200 per year for a first child, with the incremental costs reduced for each additional child.

Hanna and Olli wanted to give their adopted child the chance to attend an English-language day care because of his international background, so Hanna went online to check out the list of local day-care centers, picked two private facilities close to their home, and sent each an e-mail. One accepted their son immediately, and the matter was settled. Because even private day-care centers are subsidized, Hanna and Olli paid only a little more than the monthly fee they would have for public day care: about $370.

I asked Hanna if she was worried that taking such long parental leaves might hurt her career, and whether Olli had also worried about the same thing, since he'd taken seven months off himself—after all, management consulting is an infamously cutthroat business. What's more, Hanna's company operated all over the world and its roots were in the United States—Hanna had even spent a year in the company's American offices.

"I think Olli wondered about that," Hanna told me, "and I did somewhat, too." But she felt the local branch of her employer in Finland had been nothing but supportive of her two maternity leaves, and that she and Olli had been able to reintegrate quickly. "Once we got back to work after the first kid, we both discovered that it was pretty easy to get back on track at work. I don't feel I have to worry about that now with the second baby."

Some other Nordic countries have even more helpful arrangements to facilitate the experience of working parents, first in providing parental leaves, and subsequently in providing day care. In Sweden families receive 480 days of paid parental leave—approximately sixteen months—to use at any time they like before a child turns four, and part of these days can be saved and used anytime before the child turns twelve. The day care in Sweden costs even less than in Finland. While Finns often opt to care for their small children at home for longer periods, other Nordics tend to return to work when a child reaches the age of one. In addition to parental leave and universal day care, in most Nordic countries parents are also entitled to work shorter days until a child enters its first years of school. And if a young child is sick, one parent may stay home for several days.

Nordic societies recognize that for individuals to give fully to their jobs as employees and as parents, they need time to rest, recuperate, and just enjoy each other's company. This means giving workers—all workers, at the top and the bottom—substantial paid vacations every year. In Finland employees earn two days of paid vacation for each month worked during the first year of employment, and after that the guaranteed length of annual paid vacation for full-time workers is thirty days—the equivalent of five weeks. The other Nordic nations have similar arrangements. Even Hanna and her husband, Olli, in Helsinki, with their intense jobs, are encouraged by their companies to take full advantage of their substantial paid vacations, because the time off makes them not only better human beings but better workers. Olli takes at least five weeks off a year, Hanna takes six.

It is worth emphasizing that no employer of any size in Nordic countries can deny parents access to any of these policies. They are enshrined at the national level. Inspired by the Nordic theory of love, this is the commitment that Nordic societies have made to families—and, more specifically, to children.

Although all these social policies might seem geared primarily toward parents, there is another way of looking at them:

as primarily ensuring a good life for children. In this sense the modern Nordic goal of supporting every individual's personal liberty to the greatest extent possible actually begins at the very beginning of every individual's life, when they are newborn. From a Nordic perspective a failure to ensure sufficient parental leave is nothing short of a violation of fundamental human rights—specifically, of a child's basic human right to be cared for, to be nurtured, and to have parents who are able and present to do the job and do it well.

This attitude is anything but altruistic. In the Nordic view ensuring a child's fundamental rights to be properly cared for is an investment in the future of the society. Supporting the psychological, physiological, and financial well-being of families through paid parental leaves, sick days, and genuinely recuperative vacations helps ensure that children grow into healthy and productive members of society rather than into prisoners, patients, or the unemployed. Subsidized day care, meanwhile, lets able-bodied mothers and fathers get back to economically productive work, and gives all children the benefit of early-childhood education. Parents retain the primary responsibility for raising their children, of course, but society supports them in the task, because doing so is good for individual children and beneficial to society as a whole.

An American friend of mine in New York once fumed to me about a female colleague of his who was asking to work part-time from home after having children. In the man's opinion this would make life harder for her colleagues. "She chose to have children," he said angrily. "Now she wants everyone else to accommodate her choices. It's not our problem." In a Nordic country you'd be hard-pressed to hear such an unforgiving view, even among the childless. Still, I could certainly see his point. As a person without children myself, I too had worked longer hours than my colleagues with small children, and had paid taxes that were higher than my taxes might otherwise have been in order to support the cost of their parental leaves and day-care services. However, I still thought of children's well-being as everyone's benefit, and their poverty or unhappiness as everyone's problem. In addition, a child's right to a good childhood seemed to me inalienable, and certainly not subordinate to the comforts of adults. Perhaps most important, though, I was just being selfish: I knew that if I did ever have children of my own, exactly those same support structures would be there for me.

In addition, if I ever had my own kids in Finland, I could look forward to one of my country's most beloved traditions, something that Americans would find extremely strange: receiving my very own baby box.

OF BABY BOXES AND BOOMERANG KIDS

One of the most illuminating collisions of cultures I came across during my first years in the United States was an article published on the Web site of the *Atlantic*: "Finland's 'Baby Box': Gift from Santa Claus or Socialist Hell?" The American author, a political scientist named Dominic Tierney, described for American readers one of Finland's most uncontroversial and beloved traditions: a box filled with brand-new baby equipment, including clothes, bedding, moisturizing cream, a baby toothbrush, a reusable diaper set, a chew toy, and a picture book, that is sent to families of all newborns. The box itself is also specially designed to be used as a crib, and has a little built-in mattress. Finns think this special delivery helps new families who are tight on money, and it's certainly convenient for families who are busy. New parents can opt out of the box, and receive instead a payment of $150, but most families take the box. The box also encourages everyone to visit the maternity clinic before giving birth, since the box is only delivered after your first appointment. My friends in Finland praise the baby box: What first-time parents would ever think of buying baby nail clippers or a bath thermometer in advance? Many of them use the sturdy box as the baby's first bed. Finland's baby box is perhaps one of the first tangible expressions of the Nordic theory of love. Your parents will certainly do their best to love you, but you're not left entirely dependent on their resources at the start of your life.

Tierney, however, anticipated a probable reaction to all this in the United States: "The baby box might strike some Americans as the epitome of the nanny state. Can't people get their own crib?" Finnish parents who aren't destitute can certainly buy their own crib—in fact I'm pretty sure all of them eventually do. But for parents with less means or just fewer friends and family, the baby box is vital, and because it's sent to everyone, there's no stigma attached. It's also a great deal, since the government, as the nation's largest purveyor, can negotiate a terrific price on the contents of the box. The clothes come in cheerful colors with designs that change every so often. One year, the graphic design students at Aalto University in Helsinki competed to create a stylish look for the box itself. And just in case an American might assume that Finnish playgrounds each winter become a sea of identical, government-issued snowsuits that call to mind a communist children's brigade, I can assure you that Finnish parents swap, inherit, and buy most of their children's clothing beyond what comes in the box. On the whole Finns tend to see the baby box as a delightful rite of passage, and a symbolic welcome from society at large. It says: We honor your choice to have children, and we support you in the adventure; you're not alone.

America has its own version of the baby box, the baby shower. It's hard to imagine many occasions that are more full of promise and love than a party where family and friends gather to give the parents-to-be baby-related gifts. At the same time the American baby shower is also symbolic of what's to come. A family's resources and connections will affect not only what a child receives at a baby shower but whether a child goes on to get good medical care, good day care, enough parenting, and a good education. The poorest families in America can get some assistance from social programs or scholarships, but for the increasingly beleaguered middle class as well as the well-to-do, the accident of birth confers advantage, or disadvantage, as the case may be.

Policies based on the Nordic theory of love don't disappear because a child starts to grow up and is no longer a helpless toddler. On the contrary, Nordic societies believe that helping children develop a healthy independence from the random lottery of their parents' resources, connections, and skills is arguably even more important when children begin to transition toward adulthood. In a variety of ways Nordic societies continue to help children attain a degree of logistical independence from their parents as the children mature.

But first let's return to Tierney, because it is precisely this possibility that occurs to him. In his article on the Finnish baby box, he echoes the sentiments many Americans might have about the potential perils of the encroaching nanny state: "Isn't there a slippery slope here? When the baby has outgrown its first set of clothes, why doesn't the state provide a second baby box, followed by a child box, and then an adult box?"

It's a fair question. And the answer to this question lies in a recent phenomenon that I had never heard of until I moved to America: "boomerang kids."

Some years ago an American sociologist named Katherine S. Newman noticed that since the 1970s, the number of Americans between the ages of thirty and thirty-four who were living with their parents had risen by half. The number of young adults in their late twenties and thirties who had never left the nest at all was also rising. The phenomenon was particularly pronounced in the United States, but it was visible in other places such as Japan, Italy, and Spain as well. "Why," wondered Newman, "in the world's most affluent societies, are young (and not so young) adults unable to stand on their own two feet?"

Newman's team discovered a variety of stresses that were prolonging the dependency of children on their parents, causing these grown children to "boomerang" back home. Globalization was dragging down young people's wages. Helicopter parenting and consumerism were creating children who preferred expensive shoes and vacations to paying for their own rent and groceries, and parents were continuing to indulge them. In families where old-fashioned ideas persisted, young women were avoiding leaving home to get married because if they did, they would be expected to become the chief caretaker not just of their own children but of their in-laws and grandparents, too. The pressures of modern life, in combination with the persistence of social structures from the past, were changing young people's experience of adulthood, essentially preventing them from growing up.

Then Newman turned her attention to another part of the world: the Nordic region. "Citizens of Norway, Denmark, Finland, and Sweden could be forgiven for wondering what the ruckus is about. . . . Young people typically leave home at age eighteen in Stockholm or Oslo. Living with one's parents in Copenhagen or Helsinki past the age of eighteen will set tongues wagging; it's a social curiosity."

Newman was seeing the results of the Nordic theory of love in action. As children mature toward adulthood, Nordic social policies help them depend less and less on their parents for logistical and financial support. Just a few major examples: Nordic college students are not dependent on their parents for college tuition, as university studies are mostly free of charge, nor must they later try to make their way into the world saddled with huge student loans. College students are also not dependent on their parents for living expenses; instead they receive student stipends until they graduate. Nordic young adults are not forced to move back in with their parents, because they can qualify for decent affordable housing or rent subsidies. If economic times are tough and they have trouble finding a job at first, unemployment benefits are also substantial enough for them to live on. Since young people usually lack work history, the payments are low, and even benefits aligned with previous earnings drop significantly after a year or two, but some form of cash assistance continues to be available. In return unemployed people are required to visit councilors at employment offices and show proof of serious efforts to find work or education. All told, thanks to these various forms of freedom from the old-fashioned logistical dependence on one's parents, children in Nordic countries have an easier time successfully managing the transition to adulthood.

What a disaster, an American might think, that young people could end up on welfare straight out of school. And the American-style family-support model has its upside. Relationships between parents and their grown children seem to be tighter in the United States than in the Nordic countries, whether out of free will or by necessity. But the increasing number of boomerang kids shows that the need to be dependent on one's parents as an adult can be just as debilitating, corrosive, and downright damaging to a person's sense of independence, maturity, and self-reliance as other forms of assistance. In fact a good argument can be made that dependence on family can be even more damaging. Rather than being able at least to live on one's own, boomerang kids end up regressing to the arrangements of childhood. The Nordic theory of love would hold that the relationship between parents and grown children ought to become one of equals, so that they can express love, affection, and support for one another as self-sufficient adults. Instead boomerang kids and their parents must revert to a complex and prolonged negotiation of financial and psychological dependency, which easily becomes laced with embarrassment, anxiety, resentment, and guilt.

In addition, when family is all that is left to cushion individuals against the ever-harsher realities of life, a deeper, more insidious corrosion can start to eat away at the fundamental relationships of the family. The challenges of our economically uncertain times are taking a greater and greater toll on those families who have fewer resources available to support either their young or their adult children, and in the United States that increasingly includes not just the poor but ever larger swaths of the middle class. For Americans who love family, the irony of this sad state of affairs couldn't be more poignant. One of the main casualties of America's excessive dependence on family support is turning out to be marriage itself.

MARRIAGE MISSES THE POINT

In January 2014, Senator Marco Rubio of Florida gave a speech on the fiftieth anniversary of Lyndon B. Johnson's famous War on Poverty. "For most Americans, their primary aspiration is to achieve a better life," Rubio, the son of Cuban immigrants, said. "For some, that means becoming wealthy, and there is nothing wrong with that. But for most, they just want to be able to live a happy and fulfilling life. To earn a livable wage in a good job. To have the time to spend with family and do the things they enjoy. To be able to retire with security. And to give their own kids a chance to do as well or better than themselves."

I could imagine any Nordic politician saying exactly the same thing. These are universal dreams for people in all countries. Rubio then went on to mention the growth of income inequality in America, which he found startling, and talked about the forces that he felt were keeping poor Americans down: the loss of low-skill jobs, an expensive tax code, burdensome regulations, and an unsustainable national debt. He lamented the lack of social mobility, and mentioned possible solutions, such as requiring that the long-term unemployed take training courses in order to continue receiving unemployment benefits—a policy that Finland has had in place for years. But he also said something that you'd be unlikely to hear in any Nordic country: "The truth is, the greatest tool to lift children and families from poverty is one that decreases the probability of child poverty by 82 percent. But it isn't a government-spending program. It's called marriage."

This sounds romantic and uplifting. Who'd oppose marriage? What this statement is actually saying, though, is that the solution to the financial and logistical struggles of American families in the twenty-first century is decidedly not to do what every other modern industrialized nation has done—that is, providing sensible support for children, such as paid parental leave, or other universal policies that protect the basic rights of children. No. According to this American line of thinking, the number-one best solution to the problem of people not having enough money is marriage.

To a Nordic ear, the idea of promoting marriage, one of the most precious of human experiences, as a policy solution to poverty sounds like something from the distant past. Marriage today shouldn't be used to force people into a pact of financial dependency as it was in the old days, back when every decent person—especially every decent woman—sacrificed his or her true desires and set aside any qualms about the union for the sake of familial legacy and property. This is exactly the sort of old-fashioned arrangement that modernity is supposed to have freed us from.

Protecting that freedom and opportunity is what the Nordic theory of love is all about. Marriage today should be a commitment by two individuals who want to give their love and care freely, as unencumbered and self-sufficient equals. That they choose to enter the relationship purely out of love is exactly what creates such a profound bond. The stoic, taciturn Nordics turn out to be some of the most genuine romantics on earth.

Nevertheless Rubio's proposal admittedly has a certain un-fortunate and inevitable logic. In the United States, surprising as it may sound, couples who live together with their kids are usually married; unmarried mothers are, for all practical pur-poses, single parents. Worried about this fact, commentators point to studies showing that children born outside marriage are more likely to live in poverty, to fail in school, and to suffer physiological, social, and emotional problems.

To someone from a Nordic country, it is perfectly logical that American single-parent families are poorer than families with two parents. Obviously it's harder to raise children on one income, and the American government doesn't provide sufficient support for single parents. Curiously many Americans see the same situation and manage to come to the opposite conclusion. They conclude that the decline of marriage and the rise of child poverty are, indeed, the government's fault—but not because the government has left single-parent families to their own devices, as a Nordic person might suggest. Rather many Americans say it is because excessive government programs have made single parenting more attractive than getting married.

The benefits that American single parents receive are actually downright pathetic compared with the benefits they receive in most advanced nations, including the Nordic countries. When Legal Momentum, a women's advocacy group, looked at single mothers in seventeen high-income nations, American single mothers came out the worst off. They had the highest poverty rate, were most likely to lack health-care coverage, got the least income support, and could only dream of the parental leaves, sick days, and public day-care services that single parents in other countries can rely on.

By this strange American logic, which blames the troubles of single parents on too much government help, if anyone in the world should be motivated to churn out babies outside of wedlock and mooch off the state, it should be Nordic parents, with all those generous policies to support children, including a variety of helpful cash benefits alongside affordable day care.

So has the Nordic theory of love, and all the supportive

family policies it has spawned, indeed caused Nordic families to fall apart?

If you look at the statistics on Nordic children born outside marriage, you might well conclude that the Nordic family has been decimated. Nordics have some of the highest rates of children born outside marriage of all wealthy countries. Sweden, Norway, and Iceland actually have more births outside marriage than within it. The trend is a bit less pronounced in Denmark and Finland, but it's still clear, with more out-of-wedlock births than in the United States.

Is that the most useful measurement, though? It's worth stopping to ask whether in this day and age, marriage per se is still the relevant indicator it might once have been. When you look at statistics about family structure instead, the picture changes dramatically. It turns out that Nordic children actually are more likely to have two parents in their home than American children are, even if their parents are not married.

The sociologist Katherine S. Newman has written about this phenomenon as well: "The patterns of family formation Americans associate with the poor—single-parent households, cohabitation, and out-of-wedlock childbearing—are very common across the classes in the Nordic countries." Inspired by the Nordic theory of love, Nordic societies have simply chosen to embrace the sorts of flexible arrangements that go with modernity, and to recognize people's fundamental humanity nonetheless. In Finland this acceptance extends even to the highest office in the land. Finland's president, Tarja Halonen, had been a single mother, and at the time of her election, she was in a long-term relationship with a man who wasn't her child's father and didn't live with her. (After the election, he did move with her to the presidential residence, and eventually the couple did get married.) Outsiders to the region often imagine that Nordic culture binds Nordic people to some sort of Lutheran morality code. However, in reality Nordic societies have already accepted that today's adult relationships come in many shapes and forms, and that the focus of all family policies should be on supporting individuals within families, regardless of how those families want to arrange their private affairs.

Married and cohabiting couples in Nordic countries, as well as single parents, all get more or less the same benefits for their children, and if a child has only one parent, society steps in to support that parent with his or her emotional, financial, and logistical hardships—not for the benefit of the parent, mind you, but in order to secure the best possible childhood for that child. The Nordic way is not to push single parents to find a new spouse; not being married itself isn't the problem.

Still, to be fair to Rubio, aren't the Nordic countries at least in danger of creating their own "welfare queens," who keep having children and milking the government for cash, without ever working themselves? After all, in Finland a woman could easily spend six years at home without losing her job, if she were to have two or three children in a row and take care of each of them at home for two or three years. The answer is that the key to keeping welfare queens—or, for that matter, welfare kings—at bay is linking a person's benefits to his or her previous salary. If a woman has not worked at all before having a child, her maternity benefits are going to be very small. In Finland the monthly maternity benefit for someone who has not worked before giving birth is about six hundred dollars before taxes. The allowance for taking care of a one- or a two-year-old at home is even less than that. It's not the kind of money that entices parents to forget about jobs, even if they might qualify for additional assistance. Extended time on minimum benefits is not what most people want from life.

Parental leaves are meant to be breaks in a steady career, not a way of life, and Nordic policies ensure that for the vast majority of people, that is exactly what they are. As a result Nordic single parents are just as or even more likely to be working than American single parents—in large part because they can. While in the United States single parents can face tremendous obstacles in trying to keep their jobs while caring for a newborn, and additional difficulties affording day care and transportation to work, in Nordic countries single parents are actively helped and pushed to continue their careers.

The American fear that government assistance automatically weakens families, encourages single parenthood, and creates welfare queens is not borne out by the experience of the Nordic countries. Although the reason for this may seem counterintuitive, it's exactly because Nordic societies do *not* subsidize marriage and the joint enterprise of a family that the family becomes stronger. From the perspective of implementing the Nordic theory of love, focusing on the family is a mistake. A family will not function well as a team unless it is first composed of strong, self-sufficient individuals. So instead Nordic societies work to ensure independence for the individual members involved. For fathers and mothers the result is to make the prospect of remaining engaged in the life of the family less difficult. This approach creates fewer strains between family members, because those individuals don't have to make the sort of extreme sacrifices that can cause them to lose their independence, which so often forces families in America to fall apart—or stops them from forming in the first place.

The most plausible explanation for why Americans—and particularly working-class Americans—are not getting married anymore has nothing to do with lack of morals, and nothing to do with government welfare programs. It comes from Jennifer M. Silva, a sociologist and author of *Coming Up Short: Working-Class Adulthood in an Age of Uncertainty*. Silva spent several years interviewing young working-class Americans about their lives.

"These are people bouncing from one temporary job to the next; dropping out of college because they can't figure out financial aid forms or fulfill their major requirements; relying on credit cards for medical emergencies; and avoiding romantic commitments because they can take care of only themselves," Silva has written. "Increasingly disconnected from institutions of work, family and community, they grow up by learning that counting on others will only hurt them in the end. Adulthood is not simply being delayed but dramatically reimagined along lines of trust, dignity and connection and obligation to others."

These young adults are finding that even their own families can't shield them from the effects of globalization and the challenges of American life today. Worse, they're learning to view another person's company as a potential burden instead of a source of support. If you can barely take care of yourself, joining forces with someone else who is also struggling could just make matters worse. As Silva puts it, "The insecurities and uncertainties of their daily lives have rendered commitment a luxury they can't afford." Yet, true to their American upbringing, they are quick to blame themselves for not managing to build a more stable life. They have nothing to compare their American existence with, and they don't realize how out-of-date their own society's structures are for the challenges they face. Tragically, America appears to be raising a new generation of young people afraid to form bonds at all.

It's impossible not to be shocked by how old-fashioned these problems and debates sound if you're from a Nordic country, where these issues are hardly debated anymore. Declining marriage rates and changing family structures are irrelevant, if they're considered problems at all, and workplace flexibility has long ago been guaranteed by rules enforcing healthy amounts of paid leave. Nordic societies have already transitioned toward the primary and more contemporary goal of supporting the independence of the individual, so that the individual can then afford to make supportive and loving commitments to other people, like pairing up and starting a family. In this sense the Nordic approach has truly become more laissez-faire than America's. The result has been—no surprise to any Nordic citizen—stronger families.

Another result has been something that makes those families even more resilient: stronger women.

STRONGER MOTHERS, HAPPIER FATHERS

The Nordic countries as a whole are particularly proud of their achievements in securing equal rights for women. In Finland it has become common for women to hold close to half the seats in parliament; the offices of prime minister and president have both been held by women; and about half the cabinet ministers are typically women. The equalization of gender roles is by no means complete, but compared with the United States, the difference in Nordic countries is apparent everywhere.

So I admit I was surprised by how much parenting in America is still the woman's responsibility. In most cases it is the woman who has battled her employers for parental leave, researched day-care options, and arranged work around her children's schedules. She takes them to the doctor, she prepares school lunches, she stays home from work when they're sick.

American mothers spend about twice as much time caring for their children as do fathers, and when it comes to housework in general, American women spend about triple the amount of time on it that men do. American women spend far more time than men doing such unpaid work—substantially more than Nordic women do in relation to Nordic men. Of course there are exceptions. It is more common now for American men to become stay-at-home dads while the mother works, but they are still a small minority.

In Finland fathers routinely change diapers, cook meals, pick the kids up from day care, and sit by the playground. For my male friends in Finland, posting updates and photos on Facebook that depict them caring for their infants or toddlers is something to "humblebrag" about, to the extent that it's become a point of pride and a kind of competition. "It's almost like you're not a real man anymore if you haven't done your share of diaper duty," a Finnish father told me.

Mothers usually stay home for at least a year or even two, and fathers might stay home for another six months or so while the mother returns to work. Partly women take more time off because maternity clinics in Finland promote the World Health Organization's recommendation that children be exclusively breast-fed until the age of six months, and continue to be breast-fed, while also receiving complementary foods, until the age of one or even later. The more educated the mother, it turns out, the longer she breast-feeds.

Americans often view maternity leave as a time for a mother to recover from giving birth, and anything longer as an entitlement that unfairly gives women benefits that men and their childless colleagues don't get. Nordic societies see this question differently. For starters, in the Nordic view long leaves for both parents are seen as crucial to allow the child to form strong bonds with both the mother and the father. The other rationale is that long leaves not just for mothers but for fathers allow both parents to get into the groove of sharing responsibilities at home and work equally, from the beginning. This, in turn, supports gender equality.

Gender equality in Nordic societies is thus not an abstract goal, pursued for its own sake. Instead it serves the larger goals of the Nordic theory of love: that all individuals be self-sufficient, so that they can give more purely and generously of their affection and care. Parental leave policies that give time to both parents promote exactly this result. Between spouses, a more equal division of housework on the one hand, and a more equal division of paid work on the other, increases both spouses' autonomy. Both parents earn their own money, and both parents have their own fully developed relationships with their children. By ensuring independence for each parent this way, the family as a whole grows stronger. Spouses avoid the dependencies and resentments that arise when one person pursues a career and controls the money, and the other person manages all the housework and the children. And in the sad event of a divorce, since both parents already have their own careers and their own intimate knowledge of how to care for their children, they can remain stronger both financially and emotionally even on their own, which is good for the kids. To put it bluntly, fathers stick around and women can support themselves, reducing the risk of the kind of poor single parenthood that worries American policy makers.

To encourage men to take advantage of their parental leaves, the Nordic countries have launched special paid leave that is "daddy-only" time off. If, after a mother returns to work, the father doesn't take advantage of this special chunk of leave, the family loses it. Iceland has become famous for its so-called 3+3+3 model, in which a total of nine months of parental leave are divided into three equal blocks of three months each. One of these blocks can be used by either parent, but of the two remaining blocks, one belongs to the mother and one to the father. If the father doesn't take his personal allotment, the mother is not eligible to take it instead.

In Norway the father similarly has a special share of ten weeks that are daddy-only, and in Sweden daddies get an exclusive three months. In Finland the father's personal share is nine weeks, of which three can be taken at the same time as the mother. Of course fathers can stay home even longer, if they choose to use part or all of the leave available to either parent.

Daddy-only leaves have made a huge difference. Their introduction has encouraged Nordic fathers to take a much greater share of parental leaves than before, and the impact on families is profound. Studies in several countries show that when fathers as well as mothers take parental leaves, the family dynamic changes for the better, with men taking a more active role in raising children. Men also participate more in household tasks such as cooking or shopping, and women end up spending a fairer share of their time in paid work.

To a more old-fashioned way of thinking, where the man is seen as the sole breadwinner for the family, this sort of change might not be considered progress. But there's another way of looking at it. Even in the United States more and more men are realizing that they've been denied the satisfactions of bonding with their own children, and denied the right to help raise them. Surveys show that increasing numbers of American men want to take paternity leave. Unfortunately they're often stymied in this by employers who don't offer such leaves.

Even when employers do offer paternity leave, American

fathers still have a hard time taking advantage of it, for fear of being marked as less committed to the company, and thus hurting their chances for promotion, or worse. Not just in the United States but in many other countries, men regularly face harassment in the workplace if they cut back work hours to help care for their children. Part of the whole point of Nordic daddy-only leaves is that these policies are implemented at the national level, making fathering an equally legitimate pursuit for all men. The Nordic example has shown that employers and coworkers much more willingly accept a man's decision to stay home when they know that otherwise, his family would lose their right to that time and money.

The results in Nordic societies are obvious—in the workplace, yes, but also at the playground. A Finnish friend of mine, Saska, had two children in the early 1990s, and then, after getting remarried, had another two children twenty years later. "When I became a father for the first time, I was the odd one out, sitting by the sandbox with all the mothers," he told me. "Now I'm just one of many fathers sitting there by the sandbox." But, he added with a laugh, "They're all twenty years younger than me." While two decades ago a father might have been embarrassed to stay home, now Finnish fathers are more likely to be ashamed if they don't take time off, and many feel a responsibility to be involved in most aspects of their children's lives, whether doctor's appointments, day care, or school field trips. The daily grind with young kids can numb the mind of any adult, of course. However, many Finnish men are discovering an unexpected bonus of more-involved fathering, which has nothing to do with the kids. Participating in one's share of toilet training actually seems to forge closer bonds not just with one's children but also with one's fellow parent, leading to a happier and deeper relationship. For many of my own male friends in Finland, it's no longer a question of whether or not to take paternity leave; taking time off for fathering has become the normal way of life. And as far as I can tell, they're all glad they've done so.

Their spouses—the mothers—have been glad too, of course, but also surprised at how well it's worked out. "I can still remember how great it felt when my husband was home on parental leave, and my son cried for him instead of me when he fell," said Kaarina, a Finnish freelance writer. She and her husband, a craftsman specializing in building custom stone walls, split their parental leaves evenly, taking turns every six months. "It felt wonderful, because it reduced my guilt," she explained. "As a mother you always wonder whether in the end it really should be you who stays at home—if it's wrong for a mother to be out there working. Basically you're just overestimating your own importance. And when my son's first reaction was to cry for his dad, I knew that our choice was right, and that the child was perfectly cared for. That it really doesn't have to be always me. I had always known it rationally, but at that moment I believed it emotionally. It was a huge relief."

THE TROUBLE WITH SUPERMOMS

The admiration I've long felt for American women couldn't have been greater when Marissa Mayer, an executive at Google, was named CEO of Yahoo, even though she was pregnant at the time. She promptly announced that her maternity leave would last just a few weeks, and went on to build a nursery next to her office so she could see her baby all day. I doubted whether a Finnish woman could be hard core enough to do the same, no matter how high up the corporate ladder. The Facebook executive Sheryl Sandberg, in her book *Lean In,* encourages women to strive for more responsibility at work despite the demands of motherhood. Her stories of pumping milk during conference calls, and combing through her children's hair searching for lice while flying on a private jet to a conference, were tales from the world of American supermoms, and that world has always struck me as no place for merely mortal Nordic mothers.

Nordic mothers work, but rarely at the same relentless pace as many American mothers. While the slower pace and time off can certainly be healthier for mothers and their children, it would be disingenuous not to admit that long maternity leaves can also be a double-edged sword. Taking too much time off can deny women crucial work experience, as well as promotions and raises, not to mention some of their income, along with pension contributions. In addition employers may discriminate against young women in hiring, if it seems likely that a new female employee will soon drop out for a few years to have kids. Sadly for Nordic women, statistics substantiate some of these fears. For example, for all the gender equality in Nordic societies, Nordic women are still less likely to work as managers than are American women. So, is the answer for Nordic women to become American-style supermoms, "leaning in" more at the office while also doing full duty as parents?

When we compare the plight of Nordic and American mothers, a paradox emerges. In the Nordic countries, one parent is expected to stay home for the first year or so of a child's life, and yes, the mother often ends up taking more of that time off from her career than does the father. In the United States, on the other hand, it is perfectly acceptable, and often compulsory, for both parents to return to work very soon, even when the child is still only a few months or even weeks old. The mother then becomes a supermom, heroically juggling her job and her kids. While this is also not ideal for American women, at least the American mother doesn't miss out on six or nine or even twelve months of her career with every new child, the way a Nordic mother would.

But that is not the whole story. In the United States it's also perfectly acceptable, and quite common, for one parent to drop out of the workforce entirely and never return—or not for many, many years. In the vast majority of cases, the parent who drops out of the workforce in the United States is the mother. And it seems that this trend has actually been increasing. Among American mothers with children under the age of eighteen, nearly a third of them have become stay-at-home mothers, the highest level in two decades, according to 2012 statistics from the Pew Research Center. In the Nordic countries, by contrast, for either parent to abandon work entirely for parenting is seldom seen as necessary, or even desirable. After the first year or so of parental leave in a Nordic country, or after the first couple of years in Finland, where mothers tend to stay home a bit longer than their Nordic neighbors, both parents are expected to go right back to work. As a result, in all the Nordic countries, women over the age of twenty-five participate in the workforce at higher rates than do women in the United States. So while America may have more supermoms, it turns out that asking women to become supermoms is not a solution. Instead women are just dropping out.

One of the reasons that American women so often seem stuck between two restrictive options—supermom or stay-at-home mom—is that day care in the United States is so absurdly expensive. While close to a third of American mothers may be giving up their careers and staying home, that still leaves more than a half of American two-parent families in a situation where both parents are working, and thus in desperate need of child care. For these families the astronomical fees for day care are a disaster. In the United States the average annual cost of full-time child care for an infant in a day-care center ranged from $4,800 per year in Mississippi to $22,600 in the District of Columbia in 2014, with the cost exceeding $10,000 per year in twenty states, according to the nonprofit group Child Care Aware. Care for a four-year-old costs only slightly less. If a family has more than one child, as most do, these costs naturally double or triple. The federal government and certain states might subsidize costs for low-income families, and tax credits also help, but even so, paying for child care takes up a huge chunk of the American family budget, especially for those with less-than-stellar salaries.

Among my own friends and acquaintances in the United States, most are caught in the middle: not wealthy enough to have one parent stay home while maintaining a middle-class lifestyle, but also not wealthy enough to pay for nannies or day care without difficulties. Many of them, ever the heroic super-parents, demonstrate tremendous creativity in solving their day-care dilemmas. They work part-time and swap child-care duties with friends midweek; they share nannies, enlist relatives, and work from home. They cajole employers for flexible schedules, and some have even gone into debt to pay for a good preschool. Many testify to living constantly on the brink of financial insecurity. For the fortunate ones their parents help shoulder the costs.

Much as I admire all this resourcefulness among my American friends, I also can't help wondering: Is this a smart way for a society in the twenty-first century to allocate its precious human resources? All this creativity in figuring out child care uses up vast amounts of everyone's energy and brainpower, and steals away many hours and days that could be better spent. It always seems to me a surprising waste of time and potential.

For citizens of Nordic societies, for the most part, these problems simply don't exist. A simple and universal commitment at the national level to paid parental leaves of a realistic length alleviates much of the financial stress and workplace demands on families with babies. Then, when children are a little older, a straightforward commitment to making high-quality child care affordable and universal makes life for working parents far more manageable; statistics show that between the ages of three and five, the vast majority of Nordic children are being cared for in high-quality professional day-care facilities. The result is that Nordic women can simultaneously have careers and be moms at substantially higher rates than American women, and all without having to be supermoms.

It's true that Nordic women have room for improvement in one area compared to their counterparts in the United States: American women who do work may reach higher positions in their companies. However, as a whole, American women are falling behind. Various studies show that the ideal arrangement for women's careers seems to be paid parental leaves that are generous, but not too generous—less than two years, or maybe even less than a year—and, crucially, the sharing of parental leaves, as well as any reductions in working hours required for parenting, evenly with men.

When the World Economic Forum measures the gap between men and women in different countries around the globe in four fundamental categories—(1) economic participation and opportunity, (2) educational attainment, (3) health and survival, and (4) political empowerment—Nordic nations consistently rank as the most equal societies on earth. By comparison, how does the United States fare? In 2015 the United States ranked twenty-eighth. The annual report has specifically noted that in the Nordic countries, women's participation in the labor force is among the highest in the world; salary gaps between women and men are among the lowest in the world; and overall, despite a slight disadvantage for Nordic women in corporate management, women in Nordic societies nevertheless still have abundant opportunities to rise to positions of leadership.

The Nordic theory of love has provided a vision: how independent individuals can actually create stronger and more resilient familial teams than spouses who are tied to each other in relationships that are unequal, or that involve financial and logistical dependencies. In turn, the Nordic countries have provided the policies to make this vision come true: straightforward social policies, at the national level, that make sense for families in the twenty-first century—and that could be adopted by any country that wants to achieve similar results.

Continuing to live in the past is costing Americans dearly. American families pay in lost income, in stress, and in hardship—all of which spawn an enormous burden of anxiety that I could observe all around me, and that I started to suffer from myself soon after I settled on American shores. American women in particular are paying a terrible price, in lost opportunities. American children are paying a price, too, in ways we might not even understand yet, because society is not protecting their right to high-quality day care. And the American economy is paying as well. A 2014 report by the White House Council of Economic Advisers noted that policies such as paid family leave, flexible work schedules, and affordable child care that help women work can make a significant contribution to economic growth.

But at the most basic level, it can all be said simply: The American family deserves better.

FAMILIES FOR TOMORROW

How could the United States as a nation begin to address these challenges? For starters Americans could look at reforms that are already under way. In addition to California, New Jersey and Rhode Island have instituted statewide paid parental leave policies for mothers and fathers alike, funded entirely by employee contributions, with no direct costs to employers. Many companies have started to offer their own paid parental leaves, with Silicon Valley giants like Google, Facebook, and Yahoo leading the way. If some of America's most forward-thinking businesses and states are doing it voluntarily, why not level the playing field, embrace the future, and institute more realistic paid parental leaves as a national policy? Would that be too costly for American businesses across the board, and for the American economy as a whole?

So far California's paid family leave policies have demonstrated that when more generous parental leaves are offered, American employees gratefully take them, and families clearly benefit. The California program allows eligible workers just six weeks of paid family leave, which certainly isn't much by Nordic standards. However, according to the 2013 *Economic Report of the President*, this alone more than doubled the overall use of maternity leave, increasing it from around three to six or seven weeks for the typical new mother, which is a great start to a better life for babies, not just for moms. A 2010 survey by the economist Eileen Appelbaum and the sociologist Ruth Milkman, studying the results of the California initiative, demonstrated that thanks to the new policy, mothers were breast-feeding longer, and fathers were taking more paternity leaves. Such developments could certainly be considered small but promising first steps toward something akin to an American version of the Nordic theory of love.

Implementing better family policies has been difficult, however, because businesses worry about the cost. Indeed, before the California plan was enacted, the business lobby opposed it as a "job killer." To what extent are these fears justified? Six years into the new California leave program, the same survey by Appelbaum and Milkman found that none of the fears that businesses had harbored about the costs of granting leaves had materialized. In fact, the vast majority of businesses reported that the program had a positive effect, or no noticeable effect, on productivity, profitability, turnover, and employee morale.

Considering such positive results at the state level, it seems reasonable to hope that America could move toward better family policies nationwide. At the end of 2013, New York senator Kirsten Gillibrand and Connecticut representative Rosa DeLauro did introduce a law in Congress called the Family Act, which built directly on the examples of California and New Jersey. The law proposed a system of small employer and employee payroll contributions, which in turn would provide all workers with up to twelve weeks of partial income during leaves for having a child, recovering from a serious health condition, and caring for a sick family member. The system would be run through the Social Security Administration.

The White House, too, has been pursuing improved leave policies for workers in both small and more significant ways. President Obama pushed for more paid sick days for workers across the country, and better parental leave policies for federal employees. More significantly, several budgets from the Obama White House proposed money for a "State Paid Leave Fund" to help states launch their own paid leave programs.

However, at the national level and in many states, resistance to such federal initiatives remains powerful. Surely, opponents say, it would be too expensive to grant American workers more generous parental leaves—let alone help them out with universal, high-quality subsidized day care—and the American economy would suffer, losing ground in the global race to compete. But when it comes to family policies and international competitiveness, it increasingly looks as if American politicians may just not be very well informed.

Increasing paid leave for workers is part of a worldwide trend, heading in the direction that the Nordic countries have taken. There is a branch of the United Nations that determines decent work standards for all workers around the globe; it's called the ILO (International Labour Organization), and it has won a Nobel Peace Prize for its work. The ILO has concluded that today a reasonable and humane *minimum* for paid maternity leave is fourteen weeks, at a pay rate of at least two-thirds of previous earnings. To make this work, and work fairly, some form of public funding is essential for paid family leaves, the ILO points out. Sticking private companies with the cost of parental benefits would be unfair for two reasons: the burden on corporate balance sheets, but also the risk that companies might start discriminating against women in hiring because of the higher costs of maternity leaves. More and more countries are both extending the length of these leaves and increasing the amount of the benefits.

Americans seem to think that granting such leaves requires altruism, but that misses the point. Other international organizations—the Organization for Economic Co-operation and Development (OECD), the European Union (EU), the World Economic Forum—now encourage their member nations to guarantee their workers paid parental leaves and subsidized day care. They do so because it's clear that these things are good for economic growth. Studies demonstrate the ways that family-friendly policies tailored to today's realities benefit a country's economy. Family leave policies and affordable day care increase women's participation in the labor force, help employers retain workers, and improve the health of women and children.

Nations that have enacted such policies have not experienced harm to their businesses or their economies. In addition their long-term prospects for economic growth have improved, because fertility rates have risen. The OECD, the EU, and the World Economic Forum now pitch these policies to politicians and businesspeople alike in terms not of doing good but of making money. And what these organizations are saying is true. Any American corporate leader who wants to create healthier, happier, and more productive employees—and, crucially, retain them—should be lobbying for mandatory universal policies enacted at the highest levels of government, because that will prevent competing companies from undercutting their efforts. When every company must offer the same benefits across the entire nation, and the burden of paying for parental leaves is shared through some form of public funding, a fair and level playing field is created for all businesses, allowing all to benefit.

My friends back in Finland can plan their families knowing that they have ample parental leave, that the day care is good and cheap, and that the public health-care system will take care of them. Of course arranging family life is never easy, and most of my friends also rely on grandparents and other relatives for help. But if you want to have a family in a Nordic country, you just go ahead and do so. And once you do, the time and energy that you spend on your kids can be focused mostly on loving them, being with them, and raising them, not working so hard to afford them that you never get to see them.

Everyone complains no matter how good they have it, even in Finland. But most of this is a matter of tweaking life, not of trying to secure the fundamentals. It's almost funny how frequently the same friends who cheered on my romance with Trevor and my move to New York now tell me that I shouldn't think about money if we want to have kids. Yeah, right, I say to myself. *You* try coming to America and having kids, and not thinking about money!

The Nordic countries have managed not just to bring more women into the labor force, but in the process to make the Nordic theory of love a reality. Their overall goal is to support the individual, regardless of gender, and in the process produce healthier workers, better work-life balance, and more well-being for children and their parents. In strengthening individuals, Nordic societies have empowered them to form even stronger family teams. There is no reason why the United States couldn't do the same.

But there is also another way to strengthen individuals that involves every society's most precious resource—its children.

FOUR

HOW CHILDREN ACHIEVE

SECRETS FOR ATTAINING EDUCATIONAL SUCCESS

THE RISE OF THE EDUCATION SUPERPOWER

When I married Trevor and moved to America, I gained a wonderful extended family in the United States. Among the first Americans I got to know well were Trevor's cousin Holly and her husband, John. They live in a medium-size town in the southeastern United States, and they quickly became two of my favorite people in the world. Holly is thoughtful, smart, and always interested in sharing her experiences and learning about those of others. John is quick-witted, funny, and incredibly gracious at welcoming new people into a group, including a foreigner like myself. Holly works in academia, John in the private sector. They are both highly educated and hardworking, and they have two school-age children.

After marrying, Trevor and I began to think seriously about starting a family. I'd accepted by then that it would be a logistical and financial struggle in the United States to care for an infant. But what about later, when a child was ready for school? In an effort to understand what I could expect, I turned to a mother whose judgment I had come to trust: Holly. What was it like for her and John to arrange their children's education?

As Holly described the process, it sounded like the work of a private investigator. She'd asked countless people for their impressions and advice, trying to ascertain the word on the street, and spent long hours researching different options trying to narrow down their choices. She visited as many of the pre-schools in their area in person as she could. All of which, she added, was exactly what she'd gone through when she'd tried to find day care a few years earlier.

After identifying a good preschool, Holly continued her re-search and in-person visits in order to secure her children the next rung up the ladder: spots at a good kindergarten and ele-mentary school. "I visited several schools," Holly told me. "You could say I was consumed by the question."

There were pros and cons to consider. The public school in their neighborhood had performed poorly in recent statewide tests. On the other hand, while visiting to observe a few classes there, Holly found the principal impressive and dynamic. She spoke with families whose children had attended the school and were happy with it, but she was still bothered by what she called "the whole public school approach." From what Holly could tell, the classes were too large, too many of the assignments involved rote memorization and problem sheets, and the opportunities for children to go outside for recess or physical education were too few. From her research, she was aware of what lay behind these problems. American public school students were required to take a barrage of standardized tests, and the results of those tests could determine a school's future, for better or worse. With so much pressure on teachers to improve test results, Holly worried that constant test prep would be taking the place of education that could truly engage students in creative learning.

Holly and John couldn't afford to send two kids to private school, so there weren't any private schools on their list. That changed when friends told them about a private school nearby that granted financial aid even to middle-class families. As she walked around the school and learned about their programs, she started, as she put it to me, to "salivate." The school had a thoughtful and creative curriculum with no standardized testing. It regularly sent students out for recess and PE regardless of the weather. All students took music, arts, drama, science, and foreign languages, unlike in the public elementary schools she visited. When the school came through with the financial aid, the family decided to go for it, even though paying for the remainder of the tuition was going to be tough. Holly maintained a resigned sense of irony about the decision. "My goal in sending them there is not that they get ahead and can go to Harvard," she said. "I'm basically sending them to private school so they can have recess and art."

I had known that trying to secure a good-quality and well-rounded education for one's children in America could be a fraught business, but my conversation with Holly nevertheless left me in something of a state of shock. The complexity of the variables and potential costs involved was daunting.

Soon after, I was chatting with a friend of mine back in Finland named Noora, a very attentive, thoughtful, and engaged mother of two children. She and her husband lived in a little town in southern Finland, and her daughter was about to start school. I asked Noora if she had looked into different schools for her daughter. She had not. They had received a letter from the municipality assigning their daughter to a school, and even though a close friend of the family was the principal of another school nearby and suggested their daughter go there instead, Noora and her husband saw no reason to complicate things. After all, she said without a second thought, both of the public schools nearby were terrific.

Still thinking back to Holly's experience, I asked Noora if she was concerned whether her daughter would do well in school or not. Noora looked a little surprised by the question. "I'm sure she'll do fine," she said. "I hadn't even thought about it." She paused. "Why do you ask?"

It's hard for a Finn today to grasp the degree to which education is a critical and life-altering topic of discussion in the lives of people in other countries. It may also be hard for them to understand why Finland's education system has been the subject of such intense interest and scrutiny around the world. When my new American acquaintances started asking me questions about Finnish schools, I thought they were simply being polite, seeking a way to demonstrate interest in my home country. Yet I soon learned that for my American friends, family, and colleagues, education is a forbidding maze that must constantly be probed and navigated, full of dangers lurking around every corner that threaten to thwart the best efforts of a family to help its children get ahead. American parents are constantly talking about education because it is a constant and conspicuous source of anxiety.

A great many Americans now seem to agree that their education system needs serious reform. Many public schools are failing, private schools are increasingly competitive and exorbitantly expensive, and charter schools—funded by the government but run by private operators—have scored some successes yet have also created new problems and uncertainties, and they remain limited in their availability. The children of the rich in America are now outperforming children from middle-class and poor families by the widest margins in decades. Families scramble to secure their children a spot in a good school, and struggle to afford either the cost of a house in a decent public school district or ever-increasing tuition for private school. And of course paying for college gets more and more difficult as tuition skyrockets. Overall the United States fares poorly in international comparisons of student achievement. The beneficiaries of the current system mainly seem to be the for-profit companies that sell tutoring services, testing services, and, increasingly, education itself to worried parents. The question on everyone's mind is, How do we go about improving schools?

From what I remember of my own education in public schools in Finland—and tellingly, I don't remember much—it was nothing special. My teachers were kind but mostly boring. Not unlike many of today's American public school students, my Finnish classmates and I learned by rote memorization. I recall that many students in my middle school were terribly rude to the teachers. Gym was a traumatizing experience that my generation still talks about like a stint in the army. In our academic classes we got plenty of homework, and took our share of standardized tests. On international surveys in those days, Finland's education ranking was not noteworthy. But since then things have changed—dramatically. In the span of a few decades Finland has managed to turn its schools completely around and create one of the highest-achieving public education systems the world has ever seen.

Outside Finland this education miracle has gained fame

primarily through a particular study: the Programme for International Student Assessment (PISA), conducted every three years by the OECD, a Paris-based group whose members include the world's major industrial powers. The survey compares fifteen-year-olds in different countries in reading, math, and science. Finnish students have ranked at or near the top in all three subjects on every survey since 2000, neck and neck with such superachievers as South Korea and Singapore. In the 2012 survey, which focused on mathematics, Finland slipped slightly. Shanghai took the highest score, with its fellow Asian cities and countries like Singapore, Hong Kong, and Taiwan close behind. In Europe, Finland also lost some ground in math, to the likes of Liechtenstein, Switzerland, the Netherlands, and Estonia. While the competition with other countries is likely to get only tougher, for all practical purposes Finns have, so far, remained near the top. As of the 2012 results, in all three subjects combined Finland ranked third after Korea and Japan among the thirty-four OECD countries, and sixth in mathematics.

How does this compare with the United States? Throughout the same period the performance of American students in the PISA survey has been middling at best. In 2012 the United States came in twenty-first in combined performance in reading, mathematics, and science among the thirty-four OECD countries, and in mathematics it performed below average at twenty-seventh.

Finland's success has been especially notable for another reason. It's not just that some of its schools have performed well; almost all of them have. No other country has so consistently had so little variation in outcomes among schools. Moreover, within individual schools, the gap between the top- and bottom-achieving students has been also extraordinarily small, meaning that just about all Finnish students have done really well. And finally, Finland has achieved these results with remarkable tranquility. Finnish children get very little homework, their school days are short, and most children attend their neighborhood schools. My Finnish friend Noora is not the only parent in Finland who'd be surprised to learn how much effort American parents put into ensuring their children's education.

Finland's unorthodox success has led to a steady stream of foreign delegations visiting Finnish schools, and to global media coverage, with report after report marveling at the Finnish education miracle. That has included lots of enthusiastic attention from people in the United States, but also attention from some Americans who dismiss Finland's experience as irrelevant. I was curious whether Finland really had anything to offer the United States. As I started looking into the history of Finnish education, I discovered that the mess America is stuck in today is more or less exactly the same situation that Finland found itself in decades ago. And in line with the goals of the Nordic theory of love, the approach Finland took at the time to solve its own education mess has some profound—and profoundly surprising—implications for America's choices today.

When Finland emerged from its years of war against the Soviet Union in the late 1940s, it embarked on a new journey. Finland was poor, with little in the way of natural resources besides forests, and lacking the legacy of overseas colonization that had enriched some of its European neighbors. This predicament forced Finland's leaders to conclude that Finns could be only as successful as their brainpower could make them. Individual Finns also came to see educating the minds of their children as the best way for the next generation to get ahead. Education became Finland's best hope for preparing its population for a new economy based not on agriculture or manufacturing, but on knowledge. Although the future high-tech knowledge economy was still decades away, Finland's inherent disadvantages gave it a head start in building an education system for the twenty-first century.

At the time, however, there were huge problems to overcome. Finnish society was riven by stark inequalities, including inequalities in education even more severe than those found in America today. All Finnish children were forced into two possible tracks of middle school—the common "folk schools" or one of the more academically oriented private "grammar schools." The grammar schools functioned more or less in the way high schools do now. They were also a prerequisite for a university education. However, the grammar schools charged tuition, and often didn't exist in small towns. The upshot was that only children of well-off families living in larger towns or more urban districts could even hope to go to college.

My own grandmother was one of the casualties of this system. She'd grown up in a small farming community, and possessed an exceptional intellect. Her teachers at the public elementary school had recommended she continue her studies at an academic grammar school. That, in turn, could have led her all the way to a university education. But her mother, a single parent, couldn't afford the grammar-school tuition. Despite my grandmother's talents, she was entirely dependent on her family to fund her education, which came to an abrupt end. She quit school after six years. Although she did receive some vocational training after that, she soon became a homemaker, caring for my father and his brother, and later for us, her grandchildren.

By the time my parents went to school, the system had improved somewhat. There were more schools, and the government had started to provide subsidies to the private grammar schools, requiring in return that they enroll some poor but bright children tuition-free. Even so, most young Finns still left school after just six years of basic education. Only about a quarter made it to a grammar school.

That was not enough to provide educated workers for the growing ranks of Finland's knowledge-based businesses. Finnish companies wanted better-educated employees to help them compete internationally, and to foster innovation—a situation not unlike that of America today. However, Finns back then were sharply divided on the best way to reform the education system—as Americans are today. Finns debated angrily for two decades over whether or not Finland should create a unified public school system. Critics asked whether it was reasonable to try to educate all students to the high levels that the elite pupils in grammar schools were achieving. Did society really need all young people to be so well educated, or was that a waste of scarce resources, particularly when there were other problems to solve? And was it fair, or even necessary, to expect all young people to learn not just Finnish and Finland's other official language, Swedish, but also a foreign language, as the grammar schools required?

Finally a special committee published its recommendation: Finland should create a unified public school system. Reactions were all over the map. Primary school teachers believed that every student could learn equally well, while university professors tended to be skeptical. Politicians were divided. One Finnish education expert describes the dire prophesies that were made at the time: "Some predicted a gloomy future for Finland if the new ideas related to common unified public school for all were approved: declining level of knowledge, waste of existing national talent, and Finland, as a nation, being left behind in the international economic race."

What these pessimists failed to see, however, were the benefits in terms of the Nordic theory of love. High-quality public education for all would empower each individual, freeing him or her to receive a good education regardless of accidents of birth, family background, and family finances. Children would no longer be dependent on the vagaries of their parents' skills or incomes. Everyone would benefit—individuals and society as a whole—if educational opportunity was universal, and if achievement was solely a reflection of the merits of each individual's own work and talents. Ensuring a high-quality education not just for a few, but for all, would be crucial to building a society composed of independent, self-sufficient human beings, and a society of independent, self-sufficient human beings would be one in which people were less likely to develop unhealthy dependencies on one another—and, it should be noted, on the state. Finland would reap the benefits in dynamism, economic growth, and human capital, while people's lives would improve and become more satisfying, as every individual reached his or her full potential.

The advocates for universal high-quality education won the day, and the first and most basic phase of Finnish school reform was finally implemented in the early 1970s. The initial goal was slowly and carefully to combine the two parallel tracks of folk schools and grammar schools into a single comprehensive system. This approach, it was hoped, would bring the more academically rigorous program to all students. By the end of the 1970s, every municipality in the country had implemented the new system.

But once the new framework was in place, Finland had to make an even more critical commitment to its children. And that's when things got really interesting.

WHERE EXCELLENCE COMES FROM

Pasi Sahlberg is a lean, sandy-haired fifty-something who wears stylish, snugly tailored suits. He looks like he could be an engineer in the high-tech corporate sector. Sahlberg is actually one of the leading Finnish authorities on education reform. He is a teacher, scholar, and former director of the Center for International Mobility in Finland's Ministry of Education. In recent years he's been a visiting professor at the Harvard Graduate School of Education. Before he moved to Cambridge, part of Sahlberg's job back in Helsinki was to host the delegations of educators coming from all corners of the globe to learn from the Finnish education miracle. In addition, Sahlberg himself has traveled around the world giving presentations on Finland's approach to education.

Back in December 2011, Sahlberg made just such a trip to a private prep school in New York City. As he sat in an Upper West Side classroom at the Dwight School, directly across from Central Park, surrounded by students, teachers, and visitors, America's fascination with Finnish education was on full display. Sahlberg chatted with the students about differences in the American and Finnish education systems. How prestigious was teaching as a profession? What were schooldays like in the two countries? How did the SAT compare with the Finnish national matriculation exam? Yet one of the most remarkable things that Sahlberg said passed practically unnoticed. "And," he mentioned at one point, "there are no private schools in Finland."

It is hard to exaggerate the significance of what Sahlberg had just said. Technically, a small number of independent schools do exist in Finland. Some are Waldorf schools, which follow a free-spirited educational philosophy emphasizing creativity and the arts, first developed in Germany. Some teach in a language other than Finnish or Swedish, and others are religious. However, all of them must be licensed, and just about all of them are required to follow Finland's national core curriculum. Most important, though, just about all these independent schools must also still be publicly financed through taxes. Only a few are allowed to charge a small tuition of a few hundred dollars. As a consequence these independent schools cannot be compared to American private schools, which create their own curriculum and fund their operations through tuition. There are some private vocational schools in Finland and there are a few international colleges offering foreign degrees, but there are no private universities offering Finnish degrees. The implications of all this are profound. Even though other choices are available, practically every person in Finland still attends public school, whether for pre-K or a PhD.

How is this possible? In a way the answer is simple: Finland has enshrined the right to a high-quality, free education for all citizens in the Finnish constitution, and has held itself to that commitment as a society. Just as with good parental leaves and affordable day care, the Nordic theory of love has led Finland as a nation to decide that universal access to good schools is also essential to guaranteeing the fundamental human rights of a child growing up in the modern age. The lottery of whether or not a child is born into the sort of family wealth necessary to fund a private education should have nothing to do with it. As a result Finnish parents don't spend their time looking into private options or figuring out how to pay for them, nor is there a need for families to spend extra money on a house in a particularly good public school district.

The son of two teachers, Sahlberg literally grew up in a Finnish school. He taught mathematics and physics in a junior high school in Helsinki, worked his way through a variety of positions in the Finnish Ministry of Education, and spent years as an education expert at the OECD, the World Bank, and other international organizations. Partly in an attempt to answer the questions he always gets asked, in 2011 he published a book called *Finnish Lessons: What Can the World Learn from Educational Change in Finland?*

From Sahlberg's point of view, American school reformers have been consistently obsessed with certain questions: How can you keep track of students' performance if you don't test them constantly? How can you improve teaching if you have no accountability for bad teachers or merit pay for good ones? How do you foster competition and engage the private sector? How do you provide school choice?

Most of this misses the point, Sahlberg believes. After his visit to the Dwight School, during a lecture at Columbia Teachers College later that day, he acknowledged that in the United States parental choice in education means offering charter schools and private schools as an option for parents. "People believe that a school has to be like a shop, where parents can come if they want to, or they can go to another shop and buy whatever they want for their children," Sahlberg said. But what if all the schools in the United States were clearly excellent, as they pretty much are in Finland?

Herein lay the real surprise. As Sahlberg continued, his core message emerged, whether anyone in his American audience heard it or not. Decades ago, when the Finnish school system was badly in need of reform, the goal of the approach to education that Finland instituted, resulting in so much excellence today, was not actually excellence.

Instead the goal—a goal that makes perfect sense in terms of the Nordic theory of love—was equity.

To help explain what Finland did more than four decades ago, it's useful to jump ahead for a moment to consider some recent research on education. A few years ago two MIT economics professors, Abhijit V. Banerjee and Esther Duflo, published a book called *Poor Economics: A Radical Rethinking of the Way to Fight Global Poverty*. In the book they sort through various solutions that are commonly recommended to solve the problems of poor countries in areas such as nutrition, health care, finance, and education. Education, in particular, is often seen as a miracle cure that can solve all of a country's problems.

Banerjee and Duflo discovered that experts who are tasked with solving a country's problems basically tend to think about education in one of two ways. The first, the "demand" approach, sees education as an investment like any other. Parents will pay for their children to go to school because it's an investment that will result in future earnings. Only when the benefits of education are understood to be high enough will parents either pay to send their children to private schools or, alternatively, demand that public education be improved. In this way of thinking, competition is the key to ensuring that parents get the level of quality of education they want for their children. Change will be driven by demand, not supply.

This view of education is widely accepted around the world and is popular in the United States. Even though the United

States has an extensive network of public schools, mainly run and financed by the states, one in ten American students attends private school, and practically all university education is tuition based. Even public education relies heavily on services provided by the private sector, including privately run—and increasingly for-profit—charter schools and testing programs created by multinational corporations.

The demand approach is behind the concept of "school choice," which usually means promoting further privatization of education. Often it goes hand in hand with other ideas that are fundamental to the global school-reform movement: more standardized tests to measure the effectiveness of teachers; more teacher accountability for the results of those tests; more competition between schools, teachers, and students; and more hours of study.

Some of these ideas have been embraced by one Nordic country, Sweden, which has opened its school system to private entrepreneurs. Britain has embraced standardized tests. India is experimenting with school vouchers that can be used in private schools. In the United States both Barack Obama and Mitt Romney embraced school choice in the 2012 American presidential campaign. Romney in particular showed unwavering faith that schools will improve only when parents have the opportunity to choose from a variety of options: public, charter, and private schools. The government's job, the thinking goes, is simply to enable this process of natural selection by giving parents vouchers to help pay for any school they'd like.

There is, however, a quirk to education that makes approaching it as a normal investment tricky, as the MIT professors Banerjee and Duflo point out. Here's the problem: Parents are expected to pay the price of investing in education, but children are the ones who reap the benefits—and usually that happens only many years or even decades later. This creates a major disconnect between the incentive and the reward, a disconnect that is seldom acknowledged. In a traditional or agrarian society, many parents would choose not to make this investment because there's no immediate payoff, compared with keeping the child at home or on the farm to help out. But even parents in a modern society can be stymied by this disconnect, especially when education is very expensive. What's more, the demand approach requires that parents actively manage their children's education. Navigating a confusing variety of educational options, tackling a competitive application process, and ensuring that your child gets into the right school requires not only money but also skills, time, and very often connections. The demand approach makes the child's destiny almost utterly dependent on the desires and capabilities of his or her parents. This is the exact opposite of what a society informed by the Nordic theory of love would hope to achieve. (I'll return to the matter of Sweden shortly.)

What about the second approach to thinking about education that Banerjee and Duflo identify? Their name for it may not come as a surprise, but the content might. In what they call the "supply" approach, education is not seen as something that comes into play only when parents demand it; rather education is seen as a basic human right. This goal stands regardless of what individual parents would choose for their child, or what a family's particular circumstances would allow them to afford. Banerjee and Duflo summarize this view as follows: "A civilized society cannot allow a child's right to a normal childhood and a decent education to be held hostage to a parent's whims or greed. . . . This rationale explains why most rich countries simply give parents no choice: Children have to be sent to school until a certain age, unless parents can prove they are educating them at home."

At the end of the 1970s, when education administrators in Finland were ready to lay out the goals and methods of their new unified school system, it was indeed this supply approach to education that seemed to best reflect not just the Nordic theory of love, but also the realities of the fast-changing modern world. The supply approach seemed the best way to achieve Finland's goals for a strong knowledge economy, and to ensure Finland's success as the twenty-first century approached. Finland's administrators committed Finland completely to the principles of the "supply" approach, and the country has never looked back.

In short, Finland has achieved its spectacular success with an approach that is, in just about every way, the diametric opposite of the approaches to education reform that are trending in America today. It will hardly come as a surprise that such very different approaches also have very different consequences.

It's an unfortunate fact that the United States remains astonishingly backward compared to almost all other advanced Western countries when it comes to education, because in America, what predicts how well a child will do in school is not a child's aptitude or hard work, but the status of the child's parents— which is to say, their own levels of education and wealth. Other countries suffer from this condition too, but the United States is especially anachronistic. And it's getting worse: The influence of this wealth predictor in the United States today has only been growing stronger in recent years. A Stanford professor found that in 2010, the gap in test scores between rich and poor students in the United States was about 40 percent larger than it had been three decades earlier.

Other statistics related to this fact are equally jarring. Take child poverty. A UNICEF report in 2013 looked at child poverty in twenty-nine developed countries. For this report UNICEF used a common technique that measures income inequality across societies with differing levels of wealth: A child is deemed poor if the disposable income of the child's household is less than half of the country's median. The results of the UNICEF study put Finland's child poverty rate at less than 5 percent, the lowest of all rich countries. By contrast, the child poverty rate in the United States comes close to a shocking 25 percent—nearly a quarter of the entire population of children. Out of all the countries that UNICEF surveyed, the United States was actually next to last. Only Romania fared worse.

One might argue that this rate is not significant since it is relative. In absolute numbers poor American children are surely better off than poor children in many poorer countries. However, the comparative poverty rate shows that in the United States, a much larger percentage of children than in other advanced nations lack access to the basic opportunities, activities, and material comforts that are considered normal by most people in society. You don't have to be dirt-poor, or living in Third World conditions, to fall drastically behind in American society.

These two American trends—(1) poor children in the United States fare worse in school than wealthy ones, and (2) the United States has more poor children than all other rich countries—together make crystal clear that America lags far behind other advanced nations, and faces a fundamental challenge in trying to improve the performance of its students as a whole.

Ironically the poverty rate itself has become a much-wielded weapon in the American education debate. One camp uses America's high child-poverty rate to defend America's public schools: It is not the schools that are the problem, but the circumstances of the students. The argument goes like this: If Finland had as many poor students as America does, it surely wouldn't be able to achieve such good results. In order to fix its schools, America must fix poverty, these critics say. The second camp thinks that poverty rates are just an excuse. There is no reason why a poor child should be less able to learn than a wealthy one, provided that the child and his or her teachers are held to a high standard. The United States has a long tradition of poor immigrant children excelling in school and becoming, eventually, better educated and wealthier than their parents, proving that a student from modest means can make it as long as they work hard. The conclusion here is that in order to fix poverty, one must first fix the schools.

Both camps are right in some ways. Studies have shown that child poverty is associated with a long list of risks, many of them related to education: problems with learning, behavior, health, teenage pregnancy, and drug and alcohol abuse. Clearly income inequality in the United States does make it harder for the education system as a whole to compete with the education systems in more equal societies like Finland. However, income inequality doesn't always or automatically mean that there will be big differences in learning. Many countries, such as Israel and Mexico, have greater income inequality than the United States, but show less variety in learning between students of different backgrounds. Even Finland has income inequality. While it's moderate compared with the United States, income inequality has grown considerably in Finland over the past few decades. Yet there's been relatively little impact on the educational performance of Finnish students.

Either way, however, American education reformers of all camps often tend to dismiss the example of Finland as having little to offer America, because Finland is such an equal society by comparison. This argument entirely misses the point of Finland's success. Overcoming the effects of poverty was precisely what Finland's education system was built to do, and it has succeeded in doing exactly that. All those decades ago, when Finland committed itself to its supply approach to education, it was doing so to help Finland progress beyond the kind of old-fashioned disparities that still so badly plague America today. What Finland has clearly shown is that creating excellence by focusing on equity is not only possible, but a highly effective strategy in equipping a nation for the future.

That said, some of the things that Finland has done to achieve this success can still come as a surprise. For starters, Nordics tend to be firm believers in not educating their children much at all—at least at first.

FREE-RANGE KIDS

While living in the United States, I got to know a Finnish couple named Ville and Nina. They both worked for big companies in New York, and they lived in a beautiful old house in Westchester, a wealthy county north of New York City with good schools. Their two sons, Sisu and Kosmo, both born in the United States, attended a small private day-care program housed in a homelike setting nearby that cost about $1,300 per month per child. At day care, Sisu, the older child, had already mastered the alphabet and numbers by the age of two. Ville was impressed by Sisu's new skills, and he felt inspired to read extra books to Sisu at home to further advance his progress. Nina, however, felt more conflicted. "I remember thinking at that point, Please stop, don't teach him. My two-year-old doesn't need to know all this yet."

If Nina's reaction to Sisu's early learning sounds strange, it's not—not in Nordic countries. A few years after Ville and Nina and their kids had moved back to Finland, I spoke with them in their home near Helsinki. By then their younger son, Kosmo, was three and a half and attending a good English-language day care in a nice suburb. He still hadn't been taught letters and numbers.

My Finnish friend Laura provides another example. When she spent a year outside Finland, at Oxford, with her family, she was astonished to discover that her four-year-old son's British play school kept a dossier on her son's learning goals, so they could report what he'd mastered each month. Laura, taken aback, told the play-school staff she'd be happy simply if her son was happy, and if he learned a little English and made some friends. Now it was the British play-school staff's turn to be surprised. They asked Laura how she could be so relaxed about education, considering that she was from Finland, the land of superlearners.

My Danish friend Hannah, a psychologist, found herself firmly opposed to a new fad in Danish day-care centers: measurements of children's progress. Even if the centers were only measuring whether a child could color inside the lines, Hannah told me she'd prefer that the staff just leave her children alone to play by themselves, discovering and expressing their inclinations and creativity.

Are these Nordic parents crazy?

If there is one belief shared by most education experts around the world today, it is that the first years of a child's life are crucial to later success. But on the question of how best to secure a foundation for a child's future success, views differ drastically. In the United States, public education—that is, compulsory, universal, and free education—usually begins at age five, with one year of kindergarten. However, ever since research suggested that early-childhood education offers clear benefits, especially to disadvantaged children, Americans have concluded that children should start school sooner. One of President Obama's most-talked-about policy proposals was to extend publicly funded preschool to all four-year-olds. In 2014, the newly elected mayor of New York City, Bill de Blasio, did exactly that for the children in his city.

People in Nordic countries, too, certainly consider early childhood crucial to a child's later success. In Denmark and Sweden, virtually all three- to five-year-olds attend day care, with the other Nordic nations following close behind. In Finland, three-quarters of children in that age range attend publicly funded day care. But in the Nordic countries there is a very clear distinction between day care and school. Education proper does not begin until children are six or seven years old. In Finland most children have begun with one year of voluntary kindergarten when they're six; at the beginning of 2015 this one-year kindergarten was made compulsory. But actual school starts late by American standards: not until children turn seven. If you ask Finns, their day-care centers for younger children are not schools at all, and are not meant to be. In fact until a few years ago, Finland's public day-care system fell not under the jurisdiction of the Ministry of Education but under the Ministry of Social Affairs and Health.

So why are Nordic parents so seemingly delinquent when it comes to giving their toddlers a head start? The answer is disarmingly simple: Childhood should be childhood. Finnish day-care centers have no specific goals when it comes to teaching the alphabet, or numbers, or vocabulary. Instead they follow each individual child's interests and create a foundation for later independent learning by supporting children's social skills and curiosity. Mostly this is done according to a well-known Finnish proverb: "A child's job is to play." A typical daily program in a Finnish day-care center involves not just recess but several hours of outdoor play throughout the day—no matter what the weather—along with quiet time, games, napping, and crafts. Field trips are taken to forests, sports centers, theaters, and zoos, and activities might include swimming or baking. All Nordics are great believers in the benefits of fresh air and exercise, starting with putting babies outside to nap in their prams, even in winter—of course, they are bundled warmly. Danes and Norwegians have day-care centers called "forest kindergartens," where children spend their entire days almost completely outdoors in nature—even in cities like Copenhagen, where a bus might pick the kids up in the morning and bring them back in the afternoon—and other day-care programs might take three-year-olds out for a nice long hike.

In Finland day-care staff typically read books aloud, and children learn to sit still and complete small tasks—eating hot meals together, helping each other pour milk, or clearing their dishes. If the children are playing shop, the staff might help them use numbers in their transactions, or offer other bits of knowledge to enrich other games, and some children may pick up some reading skills. But no child is expected to learn to read before first grade.

Finnish day-care staff members meet with parents once or twice a year, but the conversation usually revolves around things like toilet training and cooperation with other kids, or the need for unified rules at home and at day care when dealing with tantrums. Finns' most persistent concerns about the quality of day care have little to do with educational achievement. Instead the questions that tend to consume Finnish parents are: Can families secure a spot at the day care closest to their home? Are the play-group sizes too big? Are the meals and hygiene top-notch, or just pretty good? Are the children allowed to nap too long? (Parents don't want kids to be so well rested they won't fall asleep at bedtime.) Does the staff have old-fashioned ideas about gender roles, or are they more progressive? When it comes to questions regarding academic learning in day care, Nordic parents tend to be adamant: Less is more.

Compared to child care in many other countries, Finnish day-care centers are remarkably consistent in quality and spirit—there are no confusing and expensive options for Finnish parents to navigate. The centers also tend to have universally excellent facilities with well-equipped playgrounds. Such reliability and consistency aren't just quirks of Nordic culture. As with family policies, they result from a clear policy commitment in Nordic countries, at the national level, to equity at an early age for all children. A UNICEF report has commended Finland in particular for spending considerably more than the OECD average on early-childhood care, and for setting the highest standards of staff-to-child ratios of any advanced economy: one adult for every four children under three years old, and one adult for seven children over the age of three. (Because of long parental leaves, Nordic day-care centers usually accept only children older than six or even nine months.) Staff members must have at least a bachelor's degree in early-childhood education, or a specialized degree in social work or nursing. Finnish children may just be playing, but even then, Finland's national day-care policies ensure that their caretakers are skilled professionals who know what they're doing—and who keep an eye out for any signs of issues that might hinder a child's learning further down the road. When children do get to kindergarten, the UNICEF report also notes that Finland has set stringent minimum qualification requirements for kindergarten teachers, most of whom have a bachelor's or master's degree in education.

By comparison the realities that worry American parents at typical day-care centers can be quite different, as I was reminded when I heard Sam Kass, who at the time was the White House's senior policy adviser for nutrition policy, explain that First Lady Michelle Obama's fight against childhood obesity often involved simply trying to persuade day-care staff to take the children outdoors—instead of planting them in front of a television all day. At the opposite extreme, my American acquaintances who have children in academically competitive preschool programs worry about their children being forced to sit still and study too much at too early an age. In Nordic thinking, letting children play, letting them get creative in solving the problem of their own boredom, is a head start on future learning that potentially goes much deeper than memorization and early technical mastery.

But there is another big piece of the puzzle that allows Finnish children the luxury of a true childhood. Unlike American parents, Finns don't have to start worrying about their child's future educational path the moment the child is born. As Pasi Sahlberg puts it, "school readiness" doesn't mean that families and their children have to get themselves ready to succeed in school. It means that schools have to get themselves ready to receive children, and that schools are there to help every child make it. And ready they are.

GROWING GOOD TEACHERS

Some time ago I watched a movie called *Blue Is the Warmest Color*. It's one of those French films about young women and sexual discovery that have something of a history of shocking American audiences. Having grown up in a Nordic culture, where nudity and sexuality are treated in a more blasé manner, I wasn't particularly focused on the movie's much-discussed sex scenes. Instead it was a moment around a dinner table that lingered with me. In the scene the protagonist, Adèle, is dating a new girlfriend named Emma, and meets Emma's mother and stepfather for the first time. Whereas Adèle's family is working class and conservative, Emma's family is artsy and upper class. Over oysters and white wine, Emma's parents ask Adèle what she wants to do in life. "I'd like to be a teacher," Adèle responds. "Ah, yes," says the mother, clearly not impressed. "Why would you like to do that?" Adèle explains that school has taught her many things she wouldn't have learned from her parents or friends, and she wants to pass that on to other children. Emma jumps into the conversation, suggesting that perhaps Adèle will change her mind once she starts studying. Emma's stepfather strikes a conciliatory note: "At least you know where you are going."

The scene stayed with me because it illustrated so well what I had discovered was an enormous difference between Finland and many other countries: respect for teachers. It was hard for me to imagine a similar scene in a Finnish film; it would make no sense that an educated family would look down on a career in teaching.

Many American school reformers are convinced that the biggest problem of public education in the United States today is bad teachers, and that the reason for it lies with the teachers' unions. One common complaint is that the unions prevent schools from firing bad teachers. The documentary *Waiting for "Superman,"* a deeply touching film about the plight of poor American children in bad public schools, was widely watched and praised, and laid the blame at the door of the teachers' unions.

From a Finnish point of view, however, if you are worried about not being able to fire a bad teacher, the solution would be not to hire a bad teacher in the first place. The key to the debate over teacher quality—and respect for teachers—is actually a different, larger question. How should we be thinking about the profession of teaching? Is being a teacher like being a registered nurse, in which case an associate or bachelor's degree with some specialization is usually sufficient preparation? Or is it rather like being a journalist, in which case a college degree, a certain kind of attitude, some street smarts, and on-the-job learning are often enough? Or is being a schoolteacher in fact more like being a lawyer or even a doctor, requiring a significantly higher level of formal, postgraduate professional training?

In Finland teaching is not considered to be an innate talent or an easily learned skill, any more than being a doctor is. One of the most important policies introduced by Finland's school reforms was the requirement that all teachers from elementary through high school have a master's degree. Today teacher-training programs are among the most selective university majors in the country.

What does it take to become a teacher in Finland? The first thing to note is that in Finland, as in much of Europe, university systems are generally structured so that greater specialization occurs earlier in a student's career. An approximate analogy might be the way an American college student who wants to attend medical school might start specializing in premed courses as an undergraduate. In Finland students who are planning to become teachers must begin specializing in education from their first year of college onward. Even those who want to teach primary school must complete an undergraduate major in education, along with minors in the subjects included in the primary school curriculum. After that, prospective teachers must complete advanced studies that in the United States would be the equivalent of graduate-level training to earn a master's degree. Candidates for upper-grade teaching, meanwhile, must major in the subject they will be teaching, such as math or history, but they are also required to study education either in an integrated five-year program, or in a concentrated fifth year. Each candidate for a master's degree in education is expected to work some seven hundred hours preparing and teaching classes in a real school in front of real students under the supervision of a more experienced teacher, a system similar to university teaching hospitals. That amounts to about six months of six-hour school days, or almost 10 percent of the whole degree. Only eight universities offer these degrees, and the course work is similar in all schools.

In the United States teacher-certification systems vary from state to state. My home state of New York is one of the few states that do require public school teachers to eventually get a master's degree. In Texas, by contrast, a person with a bachelor's degree can become certified as a teacher through training that lasts only three months. Most states have introduced similar alternative routes to fast-track new teachers into the profession, creating a chaotic patchwork of certifications and training programs of different lengths and orientations. Several studies have found that even most of America's university-based education schools have low graduation requirements and fail to prepare teachers for the realities of the classroom.

The American idea that anybody smart and motivated

enough can be a teacher, without specialized and rigorous training, is reflected perhaps most clearly in the celebrated program Teach for America. Recent college graduates are put into teaching jobs without previous teaching experience or significant education course work. There is an appealing idealism to the program, but critics have increasingly been questioning the results. In the past it perhaps could have been said that teaching wasn't rocket science, but in the high-tech knowledge economies of today, it can actually come pretty close.

On the other hand, is there a danger in setting too high a bar for those who want to teach? The requirements in Finland may sound burdensome. And surely Finnish teachers who survive all that training must then demand higher salaries in return.

In fact, compared with other professionals in Finland who hold bachelor's or master's degrees, teachers' salaries are average, and considerably below those of lawyers and doctors. That said, in the United States teachers tend to earn clearly less than even the typical college graduate. As for Finland's exhaustive training requirements, the result has not been fewer candidates entering the field. Once ambitious young people discovered that teaching was a career path that could earn them admiration and respect, education programs had no trouble recruiting the best and the brightest.

But even if American attitudes changed, wouldn't draconian new standards for teacher training, and paying for all that training up front as Finland has done, amount to overreach for a taxpayer-funded education system? Not necessarily. Judging from Finland's experience, it is exactly that approach that solves many of the thorniest problems currently vexing education reformers, especially those in the United States today. The data are pretty clear: The countries that perform best in the global PISA survey are those that tend to invest the most in their teachers.

This simple prescription goes a long way toward fulfilling the goal of the Nordic theory of love: that individuals get the high-quality instruction they need to shape their own destiny, regardless of their family's fortunes or actions. In addition, once you've invested in training your teachers well, you can give schools tremendous freedom. Instead of micromanaging teachers, and monitoring them with ever more invasive methods, which is what many approaches to reform in the United States have tried to do, you can more or less sit back and let teachers do their job.

Finnish schools have no standardized tests. To Americans pushing school reform, this simple fact can seem shocking. Everyone from Barack Obama to Mitt Romney has assumed that standardized tests are required to ensure quality schools and quality teaching. In order to receive federal funds for their public schools, all American states are required to administer standardized tests in math and English, beginning in the third grade. Science tests are also given from time to time, and individual states may add other tests of their own to the battery.

America's standardized tests seem particularly weird from a Finnish perspective. These tests have not been primarily used to evaluate students. Instead, students have been used as fodder for evaluating schools, school districts, and teachers. In New York City, public school officials published the performance rankings of—not the students who took the tests—but the eighteen thousand teachers who taught them. The reports, which named individual teachers as well as their schools, ranked teachers based on their students' gains on the state standardized math and English exams over five years. Every student, parent, colleague, friend, neighbor, or random stranger was able to access the teachers' scores online. Schools have been shut down and teachers fired when their students haven't shown improvement on the tests.

When Finland's school reforms began in the early 1970s, the government dictated a strict national curriculum, monitored all textbooks, and even dispatched inspectors to ensure that schools and teachers were complying with the program—in effect using similar methods to what Americans are introducing now. Gradually, though, as more and more Finnish teachers went through the new, more rigorous training, the government relaxed its grip, and the public school system grew increasingly laissez-faire.

American critics of the Nordic countries like to rant about the evils of top-down regulation and big-government "socialism," but the reality is that the Finnish government has actually decentralized education and managed it with a light touch. Over the past few decades, the Ministry of Education has given more power to municipalities and to the communities that actually run the schools. While there is a national core curriculum, it has become much less prescriptive since my days in school. The government sets overall goals, as well as minimum hours for instruction in the major subject areas, but the municipalities and schools decide how to reach those goals, and whether they want to offer additional instruction in other subjects.

As a result all Finnish teachers from primary through high school have far more professional discretion and independence than do their counterparts in American public schools. Finnish teachers can decide how they will teach, when they will teach each particular topic, and which textbooks—if any—they want to use. Because of this autonomy it can sometimes be hard to say what a typical Finnish classroom is like. It depends on the school and the teacher. This freedom is not given lightly. It is a direct consequence of the rigorous training that all teachers must undergo, which in turn lets parents and the government alike trust that teachers are up to the job.

The lack of standardized testing doesn't mean that Finns are hostile to evaluating students. The goal of the Nordic theory of love is to empower individuals, and that means holding them to high standards. Finnish teachers are trained to assess children in the classroom during daily activities, as well as by using tests they create themselves. In practice many teachers simply modify tests that come with the teacher's manuals that accompany their chosen textbooks—which are also generally produced by teachers. And unlike on American standardized multiple-choice tests, Finnish students are usually required to provide written answers at some length. Periodically the Ministry of Education tracks national progress by testing a few sample groups across a range of different schools.

There is one exception to Finland's general rule of no standardized testing. It's called the National Matriculation Exam. Compulsory education in Finland goes through the ninth grade, when students are fifteen or sixteen years old. After that most students attend another three to four years of voluntary high school, either at an academic or a vocational institution. Students who attend the academic high schools must, at the conclusion of their studies, pass the National Matriculation Exam in order to receive their high-school diplomas, as well as to qualify for entrance to a university. The exam is renowned in Finland for its rigor and scope, and I remember well my own efforts to prepare for this intense, daunting test. Students write essays or solve equations for hours on end, and not just for a day or even for several days, but for several weeks, during the biannual testing period, which occurs at the same time throughout the entire country.

How, then, does Finland hold its teachers and administrators accountable, if not through standardized testing? The Finnish education guru Pasi Sahlberg put it this way during his talk at Teachers College: "In the Finnish language we don't have the word *accountability*. It doesn't exist," he said. "In Finland we think that accountability is something that is left when responsibility has been subtracted."

For Sahlberg what matters is that in Finland all teachers and administrators are given prestige, decent pay, and a lot of responsibility. If a teacher is bad, it is the principal's responsibility to detect the problem and address it. Firing a tenured teacher is difficult in Finland, too, and nearly all Finnish teachers are unionized, but that's not seen as a terrible problem, since the preferred solution is to figure out what a particular teacher's weakness is and then offer him or her additional training. In extreme cases, if repeated attempts to help the teacher do not succeed, and several warnings are issued, the teacher can be fired. But it's telling that such measures are rarely necessary.

When Finnish education authorities have, on occasion, considered the possibility of instituting standardized tests, the aim has been not to monitor teacher performance but to ensure all students are graded fairly on their final report cards at the end of their compulsory education. So far Finns have concluded that the problems with standardized testing outweigh its benefits. Testing takes away teachers' independence (one of the reasons people are drawn to the profession); standardized tests are expensive—American spending on testing is estimated to reach $1.7 billion per year; and if a school's funding or teachers' careers are tied to the tests, some schools are likely to start fudging their scores.

Worst of all, standardized tests can misdirect schools away from what really matters: learning. But what, exactly, should learning consist of in the twenty-first century?

The question may sound simple enough: What is the purpose of education? In practice all societies debate this question, revising their answers on the fly. Should children be educated to fill the roles that a society most needs at any given time— manufacturing, say, or engineering, or software development, or nursing—or should they be educated to reach their fullest potential as human beings, whatever that may be? Should they be taught the arts and creative thinking, or should they be taught concrete skills and diligence? Should they be taught self-esteem or self-control? Should they be taught math or music? In the United States now, much of the talk swirls around the idea that schools are not preparing students for the jobs crucial to the twenty-first-century economy—high-tech jobs that tend to require mathematics and science.

The Finnish education system does embrace math and science; they are subject areas in which Finnish students perform exceptionally well, and they've helped Finland achieve economic success. The company that propelled Finland to a new level of prosperity in the early 1990s, Nokia, was a high-tech engineering behemoth that designed and built mobile phones. Finland's economy has long relied on other engineering-based industries as well: shipbuilding, elevator manufacturing, pulp and papermaking, and forestry—so much so that you often hear Finns with more artsy inclinations bemoaning Finland as a "land of engineers." Recently Finland has taken pride in a new generation of Finnish start-ups that have created some of the world's most popular mobile games and apps. So you might think that schools in Finland, like those in the United States, have primarily emphasized STEM subjects—science, technology, engineering, and math—over the arts. But the reality is more intriguing.

Finns still see the basic goal of public education as preparing children not for standardized tests, not for college applications, and not for specific jobs or industries, but more generally for life, although a life that takes place in the twenty-first century. Schools aim to graduate well-rounded human beings who are creative as well as technically skilled. To this end, physical education, arts, and crafts remain crucial elements of the permanent curriculum, alongside more academic subjects. All students—girls and boys—must even study carpentry, sewing, and cooking.

The contrast with American trends in education couldn't be greater. In my neighborhood in Brooklyn in New York City, for example, storefronts started popping up over recent years offering after-school arts programs for children. It's rare to see such a thing in Finland, and at first I admired this blossoming of passion for the arts in the United States. But then I realized the reason: Local public schools had simply been dropping arts from the curriculum entirely, as they have been all across the country.

On the same day back in 2012 when New York City was busy publishing the scores of its teachers based on students' standardized tests, the Finnish National Board of Education was busy, too: with an announcement that it was adding *more* lessons in arts, crafts, civics, and Finnish language to the curriculum. One might legitimately ask how necessary it is to sustain such subjects in a public school system with limited resources in a high-tech age. This was exactly the question that the well-known American news anchor Dan Rather posed to Linda Darling-Hammond, a professor of education at Stanford

University and a frequent visitor to Finland herself, in a documentary about Finnish schools. Darling-Hammond pointed to the benefits across the curriculum of teaching arts and crafts: "These things that we think of as frills are at the core of building an active, able mind that not only can enjoy other people and communicate and have artistic abilities but also can do the core subjects in more flexible ways." Darling-Hammond called it "building the cognitive muscle."

To be sure, there are areas where Finnish schools can and should improve. The world is changing constantly, and schools must as well. Finnish educators do their best to downplay international comparison tests—after all, Finns don't believe in standardized testing—but Finland's ranking in the PISA education survey has started to slip, and this has spurred some urgent conversations about the future.

One of the big questions in the mix is whether competition is good or bad when it comes to helping kids learn and achieve. And here, too, Finland may offer some important lessons for America.

COMPETING BY COOPERATING

I spent three years of my life at the Tiistilä School in the town of Espoo, from grades seven through nine. The school had a different name back then, and the lower and upper schools used to be separate units, but the school's two low, red-brick buildings with floor-to-ceiling windows framing the cafeterias and lobbies still look the same. Today the school serves about seven hundred students from kindergarten through the ninth grade. One recent fall day, I pulled my old bike from my parents' shed and rode it back to school. Children swinging from monkey bars, teenagers giggling in hallways—it all felt so familiar. The energy, the excitement, and the tribulations of youth were the same as ever, even though much had changed.

American parents, teachers, administrators, and policy-makers debate how much involvement schools should have in the lives of their students. In Finland the Nordic theory of love provides some key guiding principles. In addition to providing a high-quality education, Finns also believe that their public schools absolutely need to be actively involved in securing children's health and safety—another crucial aspect of establishing every child as a self-sufficient individual, independent of the abilities and means of their parents. This starts with the basics. Finnish public schools offer all pupils free hot meals, health care, psychological counseling, and individualized student guidance.

More generally Finnish schools also try to be a place where young people feel comfortable. To visitors Finnish schools often look remarkably relaxed, much as Finnish day-care centers do. There are no uniforms or strict codes of conduct, and the youngest students even take their shoes off before entering classrooms. Most Finnish children attend schools that are small compared to those in many other countries; nevertheless, more than half of Finnish children are in schools with more than three hundred students. In grades one through six, the average class size is twenty students, but class size can sometimes rise above twenty-five students, which is a common cause for complaint among Finnish parents. Schooldays are short, and recesses tend to be frequent; most teachers send their students out to the yard for fifteen minutes every forty-five minutes, rain or shine, and for a longer period after lunch. And, as American observers often note with shock, Finnish teachers assign very little homework.

The law on basic education in Finland specifically states that after school and homework, students should still be allowed time for hobbies and rest.

Some of these policies were already in place when I went to school. But there have been new developments. When I was a student there more than two decades ago, the Tiistilä's student body was economically diverse, but there wasn't much cultural or ethnic diversity. Today a third of the students at the school come from an immigrant background.

In addition most schools today have new "pupil welfare teams" that typically consist of a teacher, the principal, a doctor or a nurse, a social worker, a psychologist, and a counselor. The team will convene to discuss problems, and meet with students and their parents. If the problems with a particular student persist, it is up to the parents to decide whether their child should switch to a special school for students with learning differences.

Students in Tiistilä, as in other schools, are also entitled to a flexible system of in-school tutoring, consisting of anything from a few extra hours of support to studying one or more subjects permanently in smaller groups. About half of Finland's graduating students have taken advantage of this tutoring system at some point during their school years, rendering the stigma associated with extra help almost nonexistent, and making private tutors almost unheard of—in sharp contrast to the United States, where private tutoring has become a profitable industry unto itself, and one that severely exacerbates the gap in educational opportunity between rich and poor. Finland's approach also stands in stark contrast to other education superachievers such as Korea, where exhausted students trudge off after school to another grueling evening shift at private tutoring centers. Instead most Finnish municipalities offer first-graders a spot in a subsidized after-school club so that they don't have to be alone until their parents get home from work. In the clubs students can eat, do homework, participate in sports, or just play. None of this existed when I went to school.

If you ask Finnish teachers how it's possible that Finland can excel in international surveys even as its students spend less time in the classroom than students in almost all other OECD nations, they offer simple explanations. The time in school is used efficiently. Teachers have the freedom to move their schedules around to suit their lesson plans. While there are no standardized tests, schools send clear signals to students that schoolwork is important. The schools almost never cancel classes during the school year—there are no American-style snow days, even this close to the Arctic circle—and teachers monitor students' progress vigilantly, providing help if they start falling behind.

Yet with so much support, it might sound as though Finnish students don't actually have to work that hard to succeed. Aren't they missing out on the positive effects of healthy competition and striving?

In his book Pasi Sahlberg quotes a line from a Finnish writer named Samuli Paronen: "Real winners do not compete." It's hard to think of a more un-American idea. In the United States today, the drive to reform schools is suffused with the language of competition. When schools and teachers are pitted against one another, the thinking goes, the best performers will emerge. Among students, too, competition is seen as bringing out the best in young people, spurring them to greater accomplishment, whether through academic rankings, sports events, or lists of the prestigious colleges and universities to which they've been accepted. And in many of the countries where students perform well on the PISA survey, high expectations also mean more competition.

When it comes to education, though, Finland's remarkable success suggests that the Finnish attitude toward competition—which is to say, avoiding it whenever possible—might have some serious merits. There are no lists of best schools or teachers in Finland, with the sole exception of rankings, compiled by the media, of academic high schools, which are based on the grades they require for admission and the performance of their students on the National Matriculation Exam at graduation. In Finland what makes the system work is cooperation. Teachers build courses, create lesson plans, and even teach classes together, and principals offer one another advice. Lately Finnish teachers have been discussing the possibility of sharing lesson plans online for colleagues to use freely.

In what may come as another surprise to Americans, Finnish schools have no sports teams. Physical education is included in the curriculum, but if students want to compete in sports, they do so on their own time. An extensive network of sports organizations, both privately and publicly funded, exist to facilitate youth sports teams. But at school, gym classes are designed not to teach competition but rather to introduce children to different forms of exercise so that they can build a healthy lifestyle. While living in the United States, I came to appreciate the way team sports at American schools foster community spirit, teach teamwork, allow poor kids to participate in expensive sports, and give students opportunities to shine in fields other than academics. At the same time I wondered if team sports also consume too much of education budgets, create unnecessary hierarchies within the student body (the world-famous jocks and nerds), lead administrators to give questionable leeway to athletes in their academic work, and overall, distract staff and students alike from the school's primary mission.

Finnish students compare their grades and compete against

one another as all humans do, and Finns love competition when appropriate—just visit Finland when the Ice Hockey World Championship is under way! But schools as institutions encourage students to focus on their own work rather than to compete against one another.

However, that doesn't mean that the work they are asked to do is easy.

When a journalist named Amanda Ripley studied the experiences of foreign-exchange students—both Americans going abroad, and students coming to America—for her book *The Smartest Kids in the World*, she found that most of them thought high school was more difficult outside the United States: Math problems were harder, exams more expansive, and grading more severe. One of the students Ripley interviewed was a Finnish teenager, Elina, who spent a year at a high school in Michigan. Elina describes the astonishment she felt when an American history teacher gave the class a study guide with the questions *and* the answers for an upcoming exam—something that would never happen in Finland. Not only that, but many of the students still managed to do poorly on the test. Elina got an A, which she didn't particularly take pride in; how could you fail if you had been given the answers in advance? In Algebra II, the most advanced math class offered at her American high school, she got a score of 105 out of 100 on her first test. Until then Elina had thought it mathematically impossible to score 105 percent on anything, Ripley notes wryly. In Finland Elina had been a good student, but not exceptional. American high school felt like elementary school to her; instead of learning to write long history essays, as she had in Finland, the assignments for her history class in the United States consisted mostly of making posters.

To be fair, Finnish exchange students usually come from

academic high schools, while their less academically inclined peers have at that point already switched to vocational schools, thus making comparisons with all-inclusive American high schools somewhat unjust. Yet when it comes to the question of how best to support students and help them perform better, Ripley's observations about academic expectations reminded me of a difference between Nordic and American parenting styles. Once a Nordic child starts school around the age of six or seven, parents and teachers start encouraging independence, and helicopter parenting is a rarity. American parents, by contrast, feel obliged to become hyperinvolved in their children's academic and extracurricular lives, helping with homework and arranging tutors, so their kids can get into good schools. This is exactly the sort of unhealthy dependence that the Nordic theory of love is intended to avoid.

Tellingly, when Amanda Ripley interviewed Kim, an American teenager studying for a year in Finland, Kim reported that what she loved most about her experience in Finland was the independence and autonomy she was given. Kim explained how Finnish teenagers were expected to manage their own schedules and workload without parental or teacher oversight, which she felt was entirely different from the expectations back at her school in Oklahoma. She was amazed to see eight-year-olds walking home from school alone—perfectly normal in Finland—and ten-year-olds hanging out without supervision, even in the big city of Helsinki. Kim concluded that in Finland teenagers are treated like adults.

A Swedish acquaintance of mine once described the differences in parenting styles between him and his British wife when it came to their two school-age children. "She is much more prescriptive in what they should do and what they shouldn't do, and what they should wear and not wear, and what they should study and so on," he explained. "From her British point of view, that is caring. She thinks Nordics are uncaring and not so engaged. From my view it's, 'Guys, you have to do this yourself. I'm not going to be around every day. I'm not with you in school. You have to organize this yourself.'"

What a Nordic parent sees as teaching children self-reliance can look to others like neglect. And what to others is caring, to a Nordic is hovering. Nordic parents spend a lot of time telling their children that school is important, and many parents will quiz their children before tests or ask if their homework is done. Overall, however, they rely on their children to handle their schedules and their work much more than Americans do.

In Finland, because schools are there to ensure the independence and self-sufficiency of students, parents can also trust the school to help their child if he or she is having trouble. Though some might criticize Finnish schools for "coddling" kids with warm food, nurses, lots of recess, short hours, and no standardized tests, in reality Finnish students are expected to learn complicated material, and their disappointments are not washed away or glossed over with compliments. Teachers are not their nannies. In Nordic thinking you absolutely give children the conditions they need to succeed. But then they have to work for it. And as it turns out, there is some evidence that this might be exactly the way to go.

Recent research by two American professors suggests that parents volunteering in school or helping children with homework does not help students do better in school, contrary to what is generally believed in the United States. "The essential ingredient is for parents to communicate the value of schooling, a message that parents should be sending early in their children's lives and that needs to be reinforced over time," write Keith Robinson, an assistant professor of sociology at the University of Texas, Austin, and Angel L. Harris, a professor of sociology and African and African American studies at Duke University. "But this message does not need to be communicated through conventional behavior, like attending PTA meetings or checking in with teachers. . . . What should parents do? They should set the stage and then leave it."

After all the evidence in favor of Finland's approach to education, though, a huge question still hangs over it all. In the end, could the Finnish model truly be applied to a country as diverse as the United States? Do Finland's policy choices—the supply approach, universal day care, ambitious teacher education, lack of standardized tests, in-school tutoring, short schooldays, and cooperation—really explain Finland's success?

Or is the reason for it actually much simpler: That Finns are all the same?

RICH, HOMOGENEOUS, AND UNIQUE?

Finland is a small, ethnically homogeneous, and rather quiet place. The United States is a vast and uproarious multitude. The differences are enormous, so it's perfectly understandable that many Americans doubt the relevance of Finland's experiences in education. The doubters say that Finland—like any Nordic country—is a poor example for the United States, not only because Finland has less poverty, but also because in Finland everyone is more or less the same. Frederick M. Hess, director of education policy studies at the conservative American Enterprise Institute, for one, thinks all this "Finlandophilia" is completely blown out of proportion.

Yes, Finland and the United States are different. But consider the fact that most American education is managed by the states. Finland's population of 5.5 million is easily comparable to many an American state. In fact, more than half of America's states—thirty of them—have populations *smaller* than Finland's. Solely on the question of size, there's no reason any number of states in the United States couldn't implement a system just like Finland's. As for diversity, it's true that Finland is a relatively homogeneous country—slightly more than 5 percent of Finnish residents have been born in another country, compared with 13 percent in the United States, and ethnically, Finland's population is far more uniform. But again, as of 2010, there were nineteen states in the United States that had a *smaller* percentage of foreign-born residents compared with Finland. Meanwhile, Finland has rapidly been growing more diverse, with the number of foreign-born residents doubling during the decade leading up to 2012. Did the country lose its edge in education as a result? No. What's more, immigrants have tended to concentrate in certain areas, so there are some Finnish schools that are extremely diverse. Have those particular schools lost their edge? No.

The argument that Finland's school success is based mostly on a homogeneous culture, rather than primarily on smart education policies, is also undercut by some rather interesting evidence within the Nordic region itself. Sadly, not all Nordic countries are education success stories. In fact, those whose educational policies and school systems are more like America's are not doing especially well—despite the cultural value they put on education, and despite the same sort of homogeneity Finland has.

An American former schoolteacher and current education analyst named Samuel Abrams, who has taught for years in both private and public schools in New York City, conducted research as a visiting scholar at Columbia University's Teachers College on the differences in education policy between Finland and one of its close neighbors, Norway. Unlike Finland, Norway has taken an approach to education that is more American than Finnish, using standardized tests and teachers who have received less rigorous training. The result? Mediocre performance on the PISA survey. Educational policies like Finland's, Abrams suggests, are probably more important to the success of a country's school system than a nation's size or ethnic makeup.

Nevertheless, in recent years even the Nordic countries have been experimenting with offering citizens more choice in general, particularly the option to use private providers for some government-funded services. Sweden, especially, has opened its school system to private entrepreneurs and for-profit schools. Today 14 percent of Swedish students attend a privately run school. Proponents of school choice in America and across the globe have hailed this school voucher system in Sweden. However, they have often misunderstood or ignored some of its critical features. Sweden allows parents to choose any government-approved school on the government krona, but Swedes, like all Nordics, are still very much focused on the equality of services. Thus Swedish independent schools are allowed to charge only the price that the voucher covers, and they are required to follow the national curriculum.

In reality, what Sweden's "free schools," as they are called, resemble is American charter schools. And frankly, the results are questionable. School choice has increased social and ethnic segregation in Swedish schools, and the country's PISA results have fallen more than any other country's from 2000 to 2012.

Sweden does have a significant immigrant population—in 2013, 15 percent of its population was born in another country, which is actually a higher rate than the United States—but immigration did not explain Sweden's declining performance. Finland's more direct approach of providing education almost entirely as a public service has so far generated much better results. All of which raises the question: Does money actually buy better education?

A few years ago I came across a startling headline in Finland's biggest newspaper. In the future, the headline declared, Finnish schools may be funded according to the level of education of a child's parents. Had Finland really decided to funnel more money to schools for children from privileged backgrounds? As I read the article, I realized that my years of living in the past— which is to say, in the United States—had made me jump to the wrong conclusion. In America the sad and anachronistic reality is that schools for privileged children *are* better funded than other schools. What the Finnish government had announced was exactly the opposite, a policy that would take Finland even further into the future. In municipalities where parents had *fewer* high-school diplomas, the schools would get more funding.

The way schools are funded is one of the most astonishing differences between the United States, which does not perform particularly well in global education rankings, and other more advanced nations that do. Consider Finland: Even though its schools have a lot of local autonomy when it comes to designing their syllabi and administration, strict rules are imposed from the top down that require all municipalities and the central government to cooperate in funding all the required operations for all schools. This means that Finnish schools are funded through more or less uniform tax rates and by a much broader swath of society than just the immediate neighborhood, town, or city where a school is located. Municipalities have some leeway in how they allocate funding across different schools, but they can't go against the Ministry of Education's requirements for the minimum hours that must be taught in each subject area. Cutting an arts program to save money, for example, would be strictly forbidden.

Indeed, instead of cuts that disadvantage certain students, Finns favor a much more forward-looking policy of "positive discrimination." The national government allocates *extra* funds to municipalities with schools that face particular challenges. Such challenges could include a higher proportion of students with learning differences or special needs, more immigrants, high levels of unemployment in the municipality or a lower level of education among parents—the latter being exactly the subject of that newspaper headline. For sure, wealthy municipalities might be able to offer students more electives, for example, foreign languages, but overall these differences are small.

In the United States, by contrast, the funding that different schools receive is allowed to vary across an enormous range, resulting in vast disparities in the amounts of money available to educate different children in different districts, and even children in different schools within the same district. As many Americans well know, the biggest problem with how schools are funded in the United States is the bizarrely old-fashioned custom of relying on local property taxes. The most obvious problem with this is the huge disparities that exist in wealth based on property ownership. According to one report, "local property wealth per capita in a given state's richest school district can be *50 times* that of the poorest, or more." As a result, schools in wealthy areas tend to be far, far better funded than schools in poor areas, with nicer buildings, better-paid teachers, more course offerings, and newer technology.

A United States federal commission of twenty-seven educa-tion experts chartered by Congress studied equity in education, and delivered a withering condemnation of America's system of funding schools through property taxes, a system that is entirely unsuited to an advanced country in the twenty-first century. In its 2013 report the commission declared that disparities in school funding are the biggest contributor to inequality in American ed-ucation today. The commission also pointed to an oft-overlooked injustice hidden in the property-tax system: the wealthy can raise more money while paying lower tax rates. "Imagine two towns," the commission suggested. "Town A has $100,000 in taxable property per pupil; Town B has $300,000. If Town A votes to tax its property at 4 percent, it raises $4,000 per pupil. But Town B can tax itself at 2 percent and raise $6,000 per pupil."

To a rather amazing degree, the American system of fund-ing education actually achieves exactly the antithesis of the Nordic approach. Instead of freeing each child from the cir-cumstances of his or her birth, the U.S. system of paying for education does the opposite: It firmly cements the dependency of almost every child, first and foremost, on his or her parents' wealth—or lack of it. This robs rich and poor students alike of the chance to develop autonomy and independence as they grow up, further wasting the talent that America needs to succeed as a nation. But that's not all; the American education system is also terribly inefficient. In 2011, only four other countries in the world spent more per student than the United States educating children aged six to fifteen. Most of the world's superachievers in education are not among the biggest spenders. Because of smart policies, Finland is able to spend less per student than do Norway, Denmark, Sweden, and the United States on all levels, with much better outcomes.

The good news for America, though, is that for precisely this reason, Finland is an encouraging example for any country that is facing diminished budgets. When Finnish school reform began in the 1960s and 1970s, times were tough; in the 1990s, the country faced a devastating banking crisis and recession. Public budgets for health care and family benefits were slashed without mercy. But schools overall survived the cuts and have remained on course. So how does Finland manage to spend less than the United States?

One area in which Finns excel is cutting administrative costs. School principals are teachers to begin with, and they continue to teach while on the job. Above individual schools, management occurs in the municipalities, without the complication of smaller districts. Above that, municipalities answer directly to the Ministry of Education. When Dan Rather completed his documentary about Finland's approach to education—the film was titled *Finnish First*—he compared school administration in Finland with school administration in Los Angeles. Rather reported that the Finnish government oversaw more than a million students, from primary school to university, and did so with about 600 administrators. In comparison, Rather noted, the city of Los Angeles oversaw some 664,000 students, and did so with about 3,700 administrators.

Many of Finland's other education policies also help save money, including integrating students with learning differences or special needs into normal classrooms, avoiding grade repetition, keeping class sizes relatively large, and skipping standardized tests.

So is there a beacon of hope for reforming American education in any of this? Clearly, for anyone truly interested in advancing equity of opportunity and educational performance for all American children, public education must be the focus, and Finland's example shows that it can be done even without ballooning budgets. Yet how could we possibly get there? What Finland has accomplished seems so distant from what the United States could do.

As it happens, there is more than a glimmer of hope. It turns out that Finns did not invent most of the education policies they are currently using. Americans did. Child-centered education, problem-solving-based learning, educating people for democratic life—these are all ideas introduced by American thinkers. While no country can import an educational system wholesale from somewhere else, Finland shows that it is certainly possible to import educational ideas and adapt them to another country. In fact Finnish educators continue to admire many aspects of the American education system: the way American schools interact with their communities; the way American teachers interact with students as individuals and nurture their self-confidence; the ambitious projects that students in many American schools undertake.

It doesn't seem, then, like much of a stretch to suggest that the United States could borrow smart ideas about education from Finland. On the other hand, it could simply take advantage of the best aspects of America's own knowledge on education reform—the ones that Finland has shown to be so effective.

There is also an area of education that I haven't discussed yet, and it is one that causes Finns to look longingly to none other than the United States.

LEARNING FROM . . . AMERICA?

On more than one occasion I've found myself hopelessly jealous as American friends have casually reminisced about their university years and the world-renowned economists, scientists, and artists who taught them. I could only dream of such star power among the faculty at my modest university back in Finland.

When the British *Times Higher Education* magazine conducts its prestigious ranking of the world's best universities on thirteen indicators that include teaching, research, citations, and innovation, along with the degree to which the staff, students, and studies have an international scope, America always comes out on top. In the 2015–16 ranking six out of the top ten institutions were American, three were British, and one was Swiss. The first Finnish university came in at a rather dismal 76th place: the University of Helsinki. Sweden did somewhat better, with Stockholm's flagship medical school, the Karolinska Institute, appearing 28th. How is it that Finland could have such a great basic education system but only mediocre universities? And conversely, how can the United States struggle so much with the basics, but dominate the entire world in higher education?

For starters, the PISA survey and university rankings are measuring totally different things. While PISA looks at the skills of all fifteen-year-olds in a country, university rankings look at the best universities in each country, not the skills of all students graduating from all universities. Kevin Carey, the director of education policy programs at the New America Foundation, was getting at this distinction when he pointed out in an article: "When President Obama has said, 'We have the best universities,' he has not meant: 'Our universities are, on average, the best'—even though that's what many people hear. He means, 'Of the best universities, most are ours.'" As Carey goes on to explain, this distinction obscures some important information: "International university rankings . . . have little to do with education. Instead, they focus on universities as research institutions, using metrics such as the number of Nobel Prize winners on staff and journal articles published. A university could stop enrolling undergraduates with no effect on its score."

The more appropriate comparison would be a PISA study for university graduates. In 2013, OECD did publish just such a survey for the first time, measuring the literacy, numeracy, and technology skills of adults with and without college education in different countries by asking them to solve real-life problems. Finland was again among the top countries, while Americans—even those with a college education—came in below the OECD average.

Just as we must ask what the purpose of education is, we must also ask what the purpose of universities is. Though Finland's best university, the University of Helsinki, may languish in rankings, Finland's population of adults with university degrees is clearly very well educated. Perhaps the more important question is, What are universities in the United States and Finland accomplishing? America spends more on higher education per student than any other OECD country. At the same time America's top universities, while brilliant, represent an exceedingly elite concentration of resources, and are hardly accessible to most ordinary citizens. Moreover, for the tiny number of students and their families who manage to get through the gates, an American college education comes with a breathtakingly high bill.

While one might expect college education to become cheaper and more accessible over time, as it becomes the norm, in the United States the opposite has happened; tuition costs have risen much faster than median family income, and state and local governments have cut funding to schools. Although there is always a chance that a child will qualify for grants, loans, or even scholarships, my American friends start saving for their child's college fund as soon as the baby is born, if they can. At a time when more and more employers are requiring a college degree, getting one has become less and less affordable for the average American.

Universities in Finland by contrast continue to implement society's assurance of equity of opportunity. All Finnish universities are public and charge no tuition. At Helsinki University the amount that students have to pay tallies up to an annual grand charge of about $110. This is simply to cover membership in the students' association. Meanwhile university students receive a stipend of about six hundred dollars per month; this helps them with rent and groceries, and in the process helps them become established as autonomous adults. Part of the stipend is taxable, and if the student works during a semester and earns wages over certain amounts, the stipend gradually decreases. Otherwise, though, because the Nordic system is dedicated to the independence of every individual, and discourages financial dependence on family, there is no means testing for the stipend.

Imagine, then, what it's like to be a Nordic parent. You can simply focus on raising a human being, in an age-appropriate way at every stage, without ever once feeling guilty that you're not saving enough money, or not making enough money, to secure them the college education they'll need to avoid ending up in the gutter. Rather than micromanage teenagers' lives, you can, for the most part, let them take satisfaction in their nascent adulthood by handling much of the college application process themselves. How different that is in every way—psychologically, financially, and academically—from the American college experience.

In America family wealth helps students get ahead in many ways, and as America relies more and more on anachronistic ways of arranging its society, that's only becoming more true. After the financial crisis, as colleges saw both their endowments shrinking and public funding diminished, admissions at some schools shifted to favor students whose families could afford to pay full price. And as everyone knows, alumni donations to competitive colleges may help, and certainly can't hurt, the chances of one's own children getting an edge in admissions. These practices, combined with ever-increasing tuition and an ever more competitive and complex application process, contribute to a brutally exclusive and deeply entrenched inequality in American higher education.

I'd be the first to admit that Finland could learn a lot from the best American universities. My Finnish friends who have studied in places like Berkeley or Yale marvel at the small class sizes, world-famous teachers, and the ambition and energy with which both the faculty and students conduct their work. Finnish universities can seem slow-paced and lackluster in comparison. But while Finland certainly should focus on improving its universities, the United States has a long way to go to improve the accessibility of higher education, as many American policy makers have realized. Ultimately, if the goal is to educate a nation's people, nothing is more important than equity of opportunity, and if the goal is to produce creative, confident, flexible, independent thinkers, nothing is more important than nurturing the autonomy of the individual.

PEACEFUL PARENTS

Comparing education systems can feel like a fool's errand. International studies only testify to whatever it is they are built to measure, and they cannot express the whole reality of any education system. As a Finn, I am keenly aware of the irony that the main claim to fame for Finnish education is an international standardized test, when standardized tests run counter to Finland's entire philosophy and approach. Finns themselves find many faults in their own school system: lack of innovation and creativity; bullying; class sizes that are too big; conflict and restlessness in the classroom; inadequate support for both gifted students and at-risk youth; and insufficient resources for health, counseling, and tutoring. To the horror of many Finnish parents, in recent years education administrators have tried to cut costs by combining small schools into bigger units.

Finnish schools need to keep evolving. The Finnish education expert Pasi Sahlberg is concerned about the lagging performance of teenage boys in Finnish schools, and what he sees as a lack of vision in Finland for the education system's future. He would like to cut the strictly programmed, shared classroom time in higher grades by half and use the time for independent study and group projects that would break down the traditional separation of students by age. He would add more focus on skills that Finnish schools now mostly ignore: social interaction, communication, and debate. Finally, and most significantly, he would make the most important task of a school helping students to find their own passion, and to channel that passion into learning all subjects better. This would require rethinking almost everything about the current Finnish model, including teacher education.

In Finland, too, some parents have started to send their children to schools that offer more electives or are considered otherwise better than the school closest to their home. This can happen for a variety of reasons: Parents may be afraid that other students in the school drink and are a bad influence, or that a significant immigrant population slows everyone's learning. At the same time schools have started to create selective tracks, to which pupils must apply through entrance exams. These are not gifted tracks the way they are understood in many parts of the world—students are not taught an accelerated curriculum in all subjects. But these special tracks can add extra lessons in music, dance, or science, for example.

However, taken overall, Finnish parents trust their neighborhood schools. And it's not just the structure of the basic education system that creates relatively peaceful parents and families. It's also the accessibility of higher education after the compulsory education system ends. As a society Finland has set a goal for itself that every graduate of junior high school will have a spot in a school at the next level waiting for them, whether academic or vocational, and that all youths under the age of twenty-five will be meaningfully occupied in either studies or employment.

And since most Finns do not need to worry about paying back huge student loans, they can choose a career with a lower salary without fearing personal bankruptcy. The system Finland has created allows parents like my friend Noora to trust that their children will do just fine. This affords everyone involved a tremendous amount of autonomy and freedom—the key values of the Nordic theory of love.

Finland's goal of equity has resulted in a system where each individual student, completely without regard to family background or wealth, gets the educational foundation he or she needs to succeed in today's global economy. By contrast, in America the state of education is breathtakingly sad: Educational choice and competition abound, yet in reality people's options are so limited that the notion of a "land of opportunity"—what America is supposed to be all about—is increasingly a fiction. Young people grow toward adulthood not with increasing independence but with debilitating dependence, on either the lottery-like vagaries of patchy public schools, along with a few charter schools, or their parents' ability to pay for private schools, expensive tutors, and fancy colleges. Either way American families are trapped by the inequities of the system, and the path of the individual is largely predetermined, robbing young people of independence and a sense of confidence and agency in the creation of their own fates. This is bad for rich as well as poor people. The levels of anxiety in the United States today about education are proof enough that instances of social mobility through education are the rare exception, even without all the data confirming that this lack of mobility is indeed the unfortunate truth in America.

When I moved to America, my own education was already complete and I didn't have children yet. Even so, the realities of education in the United States intruded into my life and dreams, contributing to the anxiety I was feeling. When Trevor and I talked about having kids, we focused on the most immediate worries: parental leave, child care, paying the bills. But if we let ourselves think further or talked to our friends or relatives who had children, our unease only grew more intense. We were living in a rental apartment in a nice area with good schools, but being able to buy a place in a good school district seemed utterly beyond our means, and with our income, paying for private school would be out of the question. Generally, at this point in our conversation, we concluded that we would just have to move to Finland if we had children. In fact that's exactly the decision that several Finnish American couples I know have made. But how sad is it that one feels the need to leave one of the wealthiest and most exciting countries in the world simply because it's such a hard place for your kids to get a decent education?

I'm sure many Americans in our situation would just quit whining, pick themselves up by their bootstraps, and start working to make the extra money it takes to provide for a child. But is it right that children suffer for the choices of their parents, and that society loses the contributions those children could otherwise make, if only they had a good school? At the national level, the goal of educational policy in the United States—as articulated by almost everyone from the president on down—is to preserve American competitiveness into the future by investing in a knowledge-based economy. Finland's experience suggests that to win at that game, a country has to prepare not just some but all of its population well.

If I could choose, I'd want my child to have the best of both worlds. From Finland I would take the affordable, relaxed day care, highly educated teachers, high quality of all neighborhood schools, and lack of tuition. From the United States I would take the diversity of student populations and the systematic and inspiring way that the best American schools encourage students to express their individuality, think for themselves, and communicate their opinions and skills to others without self-consciousness or unnecessary timidity. I keep thinking how different my own life might have been if I'd had access to the best American drama classes, science projects, or debate clubs.

Is that an impossible goal? Finland's experience shows that

it is possible to achieve excellence by focusing not on competition but on cooperation, and not on choice but on equity. The basic principles and policies that Finland has adopted are not complicated, and could be implemented almost anywhere. The principle of creating a level playing field that supports every individual—call it the schoolmaster's version of the Nordic theory of love—led Finland to commit to supplying an equally good education to everyone, free of financial considerations. In the end it was the commitment to educational equity that resulted in excellence, not the other way around, and this commitment has placed Finland in an admirable position as it faces the future—a challenge that America, too, must face.

The United States already possesses all the resources and knowledge it needs to improve its schools. The best American schools continue to infuse students with traits that people in other countries envy: energy, creativity, self-confidence, and entrepreneurial spirit. Combining the best of Finnish and American approaches would bring the United States into the twenty-first century and create an education system truly designed for the future. It would allow America to benefit from all its talent, and it would free children and their parents both from worry and unhealthy dependencies. Schools are not the only places that teach us what we need to know in life, but they are the beginning. That beginning needs to be open to all.

FIVE

HEALTHY BODY, HEALTHY MIND

HOW UNIVERSAL HEALTH CARE COULD SET YOU FREE

WELCOME TO BURKINA FASO

It was a sunny Saturday in late April in New York City. The weather was unusually warm, and Trevor and I were planning to head out to the park to enjoy the first taste of summer after a cold winter. But first I sat down and went through the day's mail. An official-looking envelope had arrived for me from Finland. Perhaps it should have worried me, but it didn't.

By then I'd been living in the United States for just under four months. Trevor and I weren't yet engaged, so I didn't know that I would eventually become a permanent resident of the United States. I was still paying taxes to Finland, and I was still enrolled in Finland's national health-insurance program. In addition I'd taken out a reasonably priced Finnish travel insurance plan to cover me for any emergencies in the United States. It seemed like a good situation for the time being.

When I tore open the envelope from Finland, everything changed. The letter inside, from a Finnish government agency, informed me that because I was now residing outside Finland, my benefits as a Finnish citizen were being suspended. As I stared at the letter, a tight knot formed in my stomach. My new life in America had already been taking its toll on me in anxiety, but the causes for my unease hadn't been entirely clear, even to me. Now I had a reason to worry that was crystal clear. My access to Finland's national health program had been cut off, and in the same moment, the supplementary travel plan I'd purchased had been invalidated, too. Essentially I had just lost my health insurance.

Relax, Americans would tell me. When I mentioned my new lack of health coverage to American acquaintances, several explained that they themselves had lived without health insurance for years—some because they couldn't afford it, but others just because they didn't think it was necessary. "You just have to go to your local free clinic," they advised me, and "you'll be taken care of."

Needless to say, that wasn't really the way it was supposed to work. People in the United States who do not have health insurance are supposed to pay for all of their treatment themselves: doctors, ambulances, hospitals, drugs, tests. Charity clinics might help, but they are no substitute for having health insurance. As a result, what tends to happen in practice is that Americans who lack insurance forgo some of the most important medical visits a person can make, like screenings for diseases such as breast cancer or prostate cancer. When sick, they also tend to put off going to the doctor unless they experience unbearable pain, at which point the illness may have progressed so far that they're already in serious trouble and require far more invasive and expensive treatment. I certainly didn't want to end up in that situation myself.

I started to harbor serious fears about ending up deeply in debt if I went to a doctor without insurance. Sitting at my kitchen table in Brooklyn reading the newspaper some mornings, I'd run across stories like the one about an uninsured young woman about my age who'd experienced sudden digestive discomfort, ended up in the hospital for a couple of days, and been stuck with a bill of over seventeen thousand dollars. I heard stories of people who elected to have a painful tooth yanked out, instead of getting it treated, because simply removing it was cheaper. Millions of uninsured Americans don't even take their prescribed medicines, or take only part of the prescribed dose, or self-medicate with random leftover drugs they get from their friends, all in order to save money.

Yet many Americans, including politicians who should know better, continue to repeat the reassuring mantra that no American dies for lack of health insurance. It turns out that even this isn't true. Victims of car accidents who lacked health insurance, for example, received less treatment and were significantly more likely to die of their injuries than victims who had health insurance, even when they were taken to emergency rooms, according to one study I read. Other studies estimated that uninsured adults in the United States had a 25 or even 40 percent higher risk of death than insured adults, even after adjusting for various factors such as age, smoking, and obesity.

In addition, one had to ask how many Americans were regularly risking death because they knew that seeking treatment was likely to be financially ruinous. Yes, American emergency rooms are required to take care of anyone in acute pain, or in a condition serious enough to require immediate medical attention, but they are certainly not required to do so for free, and they're not required to care for people with potentially deadly chronic conditions such as diabetes, which can kill you, too. The notorious bills that uninsured patients receive from hospitals for emergency-room treatment—thousands of dollars for just a few stitches—can be incentive enough to stay home and take your chances, even if you are seriously at risk. Hospitals might ask uninsured patients to pay for treatment in advance, pushing debt collectors on them even as they sit in the waiting room, and can sue them later if they don't pay their bills—and seize up to a quarter of their after-tax wages in payment.

In fact I learned that medical bills were the cause of most personal bankruptcies in the United States, which meant that hundreds of thousands of Americans were losing their property and having their credit scores destroyed every year as the result of being uninsured or underinsured for health care. In America the uninsured were reduced to begging for leniency from hospitals, and begging from friends and family for burdensome financial assistance in the face of their staggering medical bills. Many ended up dragging their family members into debt along with them.

I sat in my Brooklyn apartment and imagined with a shudder what a good impression I'd make on my new American boyfriend's parents if I suddenly required emergency surgery without insurance, and needed a quick fifty thousand dollars to cover the bill.

By now I'd developed great affection for many aspects of life in America, and I was impressed by the fantastically high-tech medical technologies that American doctors and hospitals seemed able to deploy routinely to improve health and save lives. The cutting-edge clinical trials and experimental treatments

American patients had access to clearly brought unique benefits, and I knew that American medical schools and research institutions were among the most advanced in the world. All the same, as someone from a Nordic society, I'd also had a hard time explaining to Americans, even to Trevor, what it was like to move from a country with a national health-care system such as Finland's to the United States.

To be sure, health care in the twenty-first century is a huge challenge for every nation, and no country has a perfect system. Today even the countries that score best on global health-care surveys struggle with continuously rising costs, overburdened hospitals, long wait times, and administrative nightmares. But there are several different ways of approaching these problems, and when you've experienced life with a Nordic health-care system, coming to America is a shock.

A few years ago an American journalist named T. R. Reid set out to catalog what the basic approaches to health care were around the globe. Reid identified four basic models that different societies use to manage health care for their citizens. One model is the approach that Finland uses today, along with the other Nordic countries—Sweden, Norway, Denmark, and Iceland, with some variations in implementation. It goes by the name "Beveridge model," after William Beveridge, the economist and social reformer whose 1942 report inspired Britain's National Health Service. The UK continues to use a version of this approach, as do countries like Spain and Italy.

The basic idea of the Beveridge model is simple: Health care is provided and paid for by the government through taxes, just like other public services such as public education. As with public schools, users of public health care pay nothing or small copays when they go to see a doctor, and like teachers, many doctors are full-time salaried employees of national or local governments. Doctors can also be private providers paid directly by the government. In addition, there may be other private doctors, hospitals, and insurance policies that users can choose, if they are willing to pay for these themselves. Because the government is paying most doctors' salaries, the expenses of the hospitals, and most of the medications, it can negotiate good deals, which in turn keeps costs down. This is also the model that is often presented in the United States as something to be terrified of, and which is frequently labeled with the scary-sounding term "socialized medicine."

The second basic model Reid identified is the "Bismarck model," named for Germany's late nineteenth-century chancellor and used in that country as well as in Japan, Belgium, and Switzerland. There health-care providers such as doctors and hospitals are private, as are the health-insurance companies. Employers and employees share the cost of insurance, and the government picks up the tab for the unemployed. However—and this is a big "but"—the system is not-for-profit; the private insurance providers are essentially regulated charities. They are required by law to cover everyone, and the government controls costs by regulating medical services and fees.

The third basic model is the "National Health Insurance model," used in Canada and to some extent in Australia. The providers of health care are private, but the national or local government runs a single, unified health-insurance program that all users pay into and that in return pays the bills—which is why it's also often referred to as a "single-payer" system. This arrangement allows the government to negotiate lower prices with doctors and hospitals.

In his book *The Healing of America: A Global Quest for Better, Cheaper, and Fairer Health Care* Reid points out, however, that most of the world's countries are too poor and disorganized to offer any of these three models. Instead these countries rely on a fourth model, if it can be called a "model" at all: Patients simply pay for whatever medical care they can afford themselves, with no insurance or government plan to help. This is the ugly reality for many in countries such as Cambodia, India, and Burkina Faso, to name a few. The results of this system are, as Reid writes, predictably straightforward and brutal: "The rich get medical care; the poor stay sick and die."

The American health-care system occupies its own peculiar niche, because it's a hodgepodge of all four models. According to the U.S. Census Bureau, in 2014, 55 percent of Americans had employer-sponsored health insurance, 37 percent were covered by some form of government health-care program, 15 percent paid for private insurance themselves, and 10.4 percent (or 33 million people) had no health insurance at all.

Most Americans under the age of sixty-five live in a mercenary version of Germany. Employers negotiate health insurance for their employees from private insurance companies, and the employer and employee share the cost. The insurer, in return, is supposed to pay for treatment provided by private doctors and hospitals. Unlike in Germany, however, the insurance companies and medical providers in America are largely for-profit businesses, with every incentive to charge as much as they can and give out as little as possible. Moreover, the United States government does not pick up the insurance tab for the unemployed, and does not regulate prices of medical services to manage costs.

For those over the age of sixty-five, meanwhile, the United States is a confusing and inadequate version of Canada. The government runs its own health insurance program—Medicare—and pays most or part of the bills. Then there's Medicaid, for the very poor. The federal government and the states fund health care for particularly impoverished citizens, especially children, pregnant women, the disabled, and the elderly, but the eligibility requirements and exact provisions vary from state to state. You might conclude—especially if you come from a nation that has one of the first three models mentioned above—that Medicaid in the United States is rather like a national health-care system. However, you have to remember that in America "poor" actually means "extremely destitute." Many adults in the U.S. who are struggling financially are nowhere near poor enough to qualify for Medicaid, and many states do not offer Medicaid to childless adults at all.

American military veterans, meanwhile, actually live in an increasingly underfunded version of Britain or a Nordic country. The government pays the salaries of doctors and the costs of facilities, which belong to the Veterans Health Administration. But because of America's prolonged military campaigns in the Middle East since 2001, the VA as a whole has been flooded by an enormous influx of veterans that has been straining the system. The federal government has been trying to improve the service by adjusting funding and reforming management.

Finally, for uninsured Americans, who are usually either young, self-employed, unemployed, or working part-time or for small businesses that don't offer health insurance (or only offer insurance that is prohibitively expensive), the United States is not that different from Cambodia or Burkina Faso. The uninsured have to pay out-of-pocket to get medical care. If they can't, they get emergency care, but a bill will follow, causing many to rack up debt, lose their credit ratings, or end up in personal bankruptcy. For small or chronic conditions that aren't life threatening, they must either find a charity clinic, pay up, or keep suffering.

On that sunny April day in New York City, when I opened that letter from Finland, I joined the ranks of this last group of Americans. Now, when I looked down from our apartment to the bustling street below, I no longer saw Brooklyn. All I saw was Burkina Faso.

It's hard to exaggerate how fundamentally the loss of health insurance destroyed my sense of personal security and well-being. In most other modern industrialized societies, including Finland, health care is considered a basic human right. I couldn't wrap my head around the thought that in my new home country, it was really considered okay for people not to get care, or if they did, to be forced into bankruptcy as a result. I went from incredulous to frustrated, to scared, to weepy, to angry, and back again. It didn't matter that for the time being I was perfectly healthy. Each irritation in my throat meant pneumonia, and every twinge of my knee or elbow signified surgery. A lump on my neck meant cancer. And everything meant insurmountable bills.

Considering that millions of people around the world lived without health insurance for their entire lives, it was true that I was fortunate. If things got really bad, I could always move back to Finland. In addition I had some savings, and Trevor and I did both have families who might be able to help us out, at least a bit, if things got rough. By American standards I was still relatively privileged. But by Nordic standards, and by the standards of most other advanced nations, I was in fact in actual danger of becoming destitute.

And so it was that I joined the ranks of the haggard, overworked Americans who spend countless hours of their lives researching their options, trying to find a less-bad health-insurance arrangement from among many confusing, expensive, and downright terrible alternatives. And I soon discovered that I couldn't do it alone.

UNHEALTHY DEPENDENCIES

When I first moved to the United States, I struggled to understand what Americans meant when they discussed whether or not a job came with "benefits." I envisioned subsidized gym memberships or lunch vouchers, and wondered what all the fuss was about. After I learned that buying health insurance on your own was so expensive that mostly it had to be bought through a group of some kind—an employer, a union, a professional association—and that employer-sponsored health insurance usually covered that employee's entire family as well, I started to understand: Securing a job with benefits, or at least this one benefit, could literally mean the difference between normal life and bankruptcy, or even life and death.

It also struck me as peculiarly un-American that private businesses would be saddled with such a profound social duty. It sounded so, well, socialist. Wasn't the purpose of a business to make profits, not to arrange the medical treatment of its employees? Meanwhile American citizens were dutifully paying their taxes—so wasn't it the purpose of their government to provide essential social services in return for those taxes? And wasn't it completely twisted that when people lost their jobs, they lost their health insurance as well, right when they might need it the most?

From the perspective of any society that claims to value and support the autonomy of the individual, the fact that at least half of all Americans depend on their employer for what is perhaps life's most essential social service makes no sense. It severely curtails one's freedom. People cannot choose what kind of work life they want without weighing the financial and medical risks for themselves and their families of becoming, say, an entrepreneur rather than a salaried employee, or of pursuing their dream rather than taking a mind-numbing desk job. Not to mention that if you succeed in establishing a small business, and you're fortunate enough to grow, you're then burdened once more when you have to shoulder the administrative and financial burdens of health insurance for your employees. Entrepreneurs in the Nordic countries don't have to worry about their own health insurance at all. They already have it, they always will, and they can choose to follow their dreams at least free of that particular worry. Business owners in the Nordic countries can offer their employees extra health coverage at a private clinic as a perk, and many do, but this is nothing that even remotely approaches the administrative and financial burdens with which American businesses struggle on a daily basis.

Relying on employers to arrange health insurance makes no sense in other ways as well. Every time an American considers changing jobs, he or she faces a complete upheaval of his or her health-care situation, and often the frightening prospect of a gap in coverage. A typical example: One of my acquaintances in the United States changed jobs and found himself uninsured for three months. The insurance from the new employer didn't kick in immediately, and the so-called COBRA insurance meant to bridge such gaps was too expensive for him and his wife without the substantial employer contribution they'd been getting. So for ninety days they just lived their lives unprotected, hoping for the best. Americans go on churning in and out of various health-insurance plans as their jobs, finances, location, and eligibility change, but doing so is exhausting, bewildering, and an inefficient use of everyone's time, energy, and money. Worse, insurance companies know that many of their customers will leave them for another plan at some point. As a result insurers have little incentive to cover preventive care that could save costs in the long run. For private insurers offering plans through employers, the best strategy is to pay as little as possible now—people's future health be damned.

Later in life, Americans have their personal freedom and independence curtailed in yet another way, again courtesy of their health-care system. A survey of working Americans revealed that more than half the respondents reported that they planned to work longer than they would like to, just so they could continue receiving health insurance through their employer.

In any Nordic country these kinds of curbs on personal freedom would be considered totally unacceptable. Nordic people believe that everyone should work, just as Americans do—the level of workforce participation in the Nordic countries easily matches or exceeds that in the United States. But it would be unbelievable in a Nordic country that your career choices should be dictated by health care. This is especially true in today's twenty-first-century economy, in which people increasingly work on short-term projects, as part-time employees, or as self-employed freelancers. In our hypermodern world, which requires a nimble society with a flexible, healthy workforce, separating health care from the nature of an individual's employment is smart.

And what about ObamaCare, the much-discussed, -defended, and -maligned Patient Protection and Affordable Care Act that took effect in the beginning of 2014—didn't it solve many of these problems? It did attempt to address some of them, at least in theory. The new law required practically every citizen and legal resident to buy private insurance, or otherwise pay a tax penalty. It helps people with low incomes lacking affordable employer-provided insurance by giving them tax credits to pay for insurance. It makes it easier for individuals to buy insurance directly through online Web sites—the infamous "exchanges" that suffered so many problems when they were rolled out—thus enabling freelancers, the unemployed, and owners and employees of small businesses to get insurance. It is, in fact, created with people like Trevor and me in mind. In practice, however, it still has many problems, as I quickly discovered.

Once Trevor and I got married, I got my American "Green Card," the coveted residence permit that would allow me to work freely for American employers. In theory this would allow me to get a job with employer-sponsored health insurance. In addition I'd now have the option of joining Trevor's health plan for freelancers, as his official spouse. I started hunting for a job but my résumé, which consisted mostly of editing and writing articles in Finnish, along with the worst economic recession in the United States since the 1930s, did not exactly have employers in New York rushing to hire me. Trevor and I sat down and pored over our finances, and the latest health-insurance plans offered by the Freelancers Union. We were making money, but our sad conclusion was that the health plans for freelancers that included a spouse were much too expensive for us. We were stuck.

And thus I experienced, firsthand, another type of unhealthy dependency that the American health-care system pushes people into: not just unhealthy dependencies on employers, but unhealthy dependencies among family members. Since my prospects of finding a decent job were so slim, I now did what many Americans do: I told my spouse that he'd better get a job that provided us both with health coverage.

By then I'd already encountered quite a few American couples who lived with such arrangements. Although one spouse might want to change careers or become self-employed, nevertheless they'd agreed that he or she would stick with the job they had. The main reason, of course, was that the entire family relied on the health insurance that went with that job. Having grown up with the Nordic theory of love, with its basic principle that healthy relationships between people are built on the true independence of each individual, financial and otherwise, such arrangements felt to me dangerously conducive to resentment. When one person has to put part of their own potential or dream on hold, or quash it altogether, while their spouse and children rely on that person's sacrifice, everyone is being subtly held emotional hostage. It is just this sort of arrangement, and the tarnishing of otherwise loving relationships, that the Nordic theory of love is intended to avoid.

For many Americans arrangements like these do not appear problematic on the surface. The family is seen as a unit that works to the benefit of all its members, and if one person in the family is happy in a job that provides health insurance, there doesn't seem to be any problem at all. And even if that one person would prefer to become self-employed, or make other decisions that would complicate the family's access to health care, isn't it only right that they put their family first? Making sacrifices is part of being in a relationship and having a family. Certainly on a basic level that's just as true in Nordic countries as anywhere else.

Yet such dependencies in relationships are a slippery slope. Sacrifices and resentments can accumulate silently, even subconsciously, and undermine the interactions of people who otherwise love one another. The goal of the Nordic theory of love is to prevent this corrosion of relationships, and to do so by creating social arrangements that allow everyone to give love as freely as possible, without strings attached. Calculations of who owes whom what, or who makes what sacrifices, should not be part of the emotional equation. That way the family becomes a team with each individual contributing to the whole from a position of independence and personal strength. Today our modern expectations—in the Nordic countries as well as in much of the United States—are that individuals should have this basic independence, while still being part of families and communities. But the outdated American approach to health care undermines that ideal, and this seemed especially tragic to me because it was so unnecessary.

Despite all of my qualms, however, if I wanted to stay in the United States and have health insurance, I had no choice but to become dependent on Trevor. In the process Trevor would have to make career choices and sacrifices that he might not otherwise have made, complicating our relationship with potential resentments, and deepening my psychological dependence on him. Fortunately Trevor did manage to land a teaching job that offered health benefits for both of us. I was relieved—until he came home from a meeting with his new employer and told me what it would cost.

Having heard so much about "employer-sponsored health plans," somehow I'd assumed that they would be cheap, or even practically free, for employees—wasn't that why it was called a "benefit"? I hadn't yet understood that a wide range of plans and costs existed, and that one had to be savvy enough to navigate them. I also hadn't yet realized the extent to which Trevor's new profession of teaching wasn't the highly respected profession in the United States that it was in Finland.

Later I would research the average costs of employer-sponsored plans in the United States. According to a report by the Kaiser Family Foundation, the total average annual premiums for employer-sponsored health insurance in 2015—in other words, the combined amount paid by the employee *and* the employer for the insurance—came to $6,251 for single coverage and $17,545 for family coverage. If you looked only at the amount that just the employee had to pay, from his or her own salary, the average annual share was $1,071 for single coverage and $4,955 for family coverage. But I also learned it is not unheard of for families to pay up to $15,000 of their own money every year, even for employer-sponsored health insurance.

In addition to premiums, of course, most employer-based plans have an annual deductible that requires patients to pay a certain amount of their costs themselves first (on average, $1,318 for single coverage). The majority of American workers also have to shell out copayments for office visits with physicians, as well as part of the cost of their prescription drugs. Gradually I came to realize that when an American says how much they pay for their insurance each month, it tells you nothing until they clarify their deductibles, copays, coinsurances, the extent of the coverage, and all the other terms I had never heard of before in my life. Mostly, the bigger the employer, the better the deal for employees.

Trevor's new employer was, unfortunately, not big, and teaching in America, especially at a small institution, could provide some awfully small "benefits." With Trevor's new salaried job, our only option for health insurance was a family plan—there was no spouse-only option—that would cost $790 a month for the two of us. And that was after the employer had kicked in around half of the total cost. Granted, our payments would be a bit less than the freelancer's plans we'd been looking at, but this was not at all what I'd been expecting. In fact, it was more than double the national average for a family plan at the time, and we didn't even have kids.

I did my best to take this latest blow with grace. But nine and a half thousand dollars a year sounded like an enormous sum, and there were copays on top of it. This was another of those moments when I felt I really wasn't cut out for life in America. Tears started to stream down my face. Trevor watched me silently for a while, and then softly asked, "Have I told you lately that I'm insanely in love with you?"

We hugged each other tightly. Two lovers, tortured by the American health-care system. I almost laughed through my tears. So this was the drama of romance, American-style. Life had been so different for me before.

WHO'S THE BEST?

Living my life in Finland, I'd received my primary medical care from a variety of sources. When I was a kid I'd visited either the school nurse, a public clinic, a public hospital that specialized in treating children, or sometimes a private doctor paid for by my parents. In college I used a publicly funded student health center. Later, when I was a working adult, I usually just went to my local public clinic. Occasionally I saw the private doctor offered to me for minor illnesses by my employer. And at other times I chose to see a private dermatologist or gynecologist outside either the public system or my employer's plan.

So what would all this cost me? When I went to the public clinic, I might owe a copay of some twenty dollars for the first few visits of the year. Once I'd reached a cap, there was hardly anything more to pay out of pocket. In 2016, the combined annual out-of-pocket maximum for most services—public clinics, emergency rooms, tests, operations—for every person in Finland was about $750, no matter what kind of treatment you'd received or how expensive it was. If I'd had to take pre-scription drugs, my out-of-pocket copays for those would also have been capped; in 2016 the annual maximum was about $660. And if I'd been poor, Finland's social services program would have helped me with the copays, too. Many medications for serious long-term illnesses such as diabetes, multiple sclero-sis, or cancer are covered at special rates, with the patient paying less than five dollars per prescription.

Meanwhile, if I went to see a doctor who'd been made avail-able through my employer, the visit was simply free. On the other hand, if I went to a private doctor outside my employer's plan, I paid most of the bill myself, although the government generally subsidized these visits as well.

I usually made my choice about where to go for primary care based on little more than which location was most prac-tical and could give me an appointment fastest. I didn't really worry about differences in the quality of care, because there isn't much difference between the private and public primary care physicians in Finland, apart from the question of who pays the bill. Many doctors split their time working for both the public and private sector. Municipalities sometimes buy services from private providers, while employers sometimes buy services from public clinics. Private clinics can often offer an appointment faster, while public clinics are cheaper or free.

Should something serious turn out to be wrong with you, though, all these primary care providers will send you to one ad-dress: the public hospital. Private clinics and hospitals in Finland mainly offer care for conditions that are not life threatening, in such specialties as ophthalmology—say, cataracts—gynecology, dermatology, and dental care, or surgery for sports injuries. The more involved and expensive care for more life-threatening issues, such as cancer treatments or cardiac operations, is almost completely the domain of the public sector. When it comes to the big stuff, the country simply takes care of you, at negligible cost to you. Period.

Finns and some other Nordic citizens have legitimate grievances with the current state of their health care. In the public hospital system, if you require nonemergency or elective surgery, the waits can be long. For example, in 2014 the average wait for cataract surgery was only about thirty days in the Netherlands, but almost three times that in Finland (the same wait existed in Portugal). The average wait for a hip replacement was about forty days in the Netherlands, but 116 days in Finland.

Americans might assume that long waits for these sorts of surgeries are the inevitable result of having a health-care system run by the government. But that's not the case. A study in 2014 by the Commonwealth Fund, a private foundation specializing in health-care research, ranked Britain, which also uses the Beveridge model, as fourth in the world in access to specialists, right after the United States. Britain has also shortened its wait times dramatically from the past—all it took was for the government to commit the right additional resources. So for Finland this is a solvable problem, and the Finnish government has already taken steps to address it. Patients in the Netherlands, Germany, and France, all of which have national health-care systems of one kind or another, have faster access to nonemergency and elective surgery than do patients in the United States.

Even so, the next thing I can imagine an American saying

about all this is: America has the best doctors and the most advanced medical treatments in the world. Americans are willing to put up with their system because no public health care can compete with that. Right?

It's hard to make any unequivocal statements about the quality of care between health-care systems in wealthy nations, but two things can be said for sure. One: Wealthy people tend to get more care than the poor almost everywhere. And two: Of all the developed nations, the country that has the most severe extremes of this sort of inequality is the United States.

Everyone agrees that the United States is home to some of the world's best medical schools, highest-skilled doctors, most productive research institutes, best-equipped hospitals, and most innovative treatments. If you have the money in the United States, you absolutely can get world-class care. But here's the thing that somehow escapes American awareness in this discussion: *Everyone* else in *all* the other wealthy industrialized countries—absolutely including all the ones that have universal national health-care systems—is also getting world-class care. And they get it whether or not they have a fancy insurance plan and a huge reserve of personal wealth.

In addition to conducting surveys on education, the OECD—the joint organization of wealthy nations—studies health care in different countries. According to its research, the United States as a whole does not actually outshine other countries in the quality of care. The United States has shorter life expectancy, higher infant mortality, and fewer physicians relative to the population than most other developed countries, including the Nordic nations. When we look at outcomes in some dramatic illnesses, such as cancer, the United States does have some of the best survival rates in the world—right after or ahead of the Nordic countries. The rankings vary marginally here and there, but overall the United States and the Nordic nations achieve very similar results in how long patients live after a cancer diagnosis.

However, there is a particularly important respect in which the United States has performed considerably worse than the Nordic nations. A Commonwealth Fund study from 2011 concluded that in comparison with fifteen other industrialized countries, Americans under the age of seventy-five were the most likely to die of conditions that are at least partially preventable or treatable. These include bacterial infections, diabetes, heart disease, stroke, or complications of common surgical procedures. As many as 91,000 fewer Americans would die prematurely if the United States could achieve the rate of the leading country, which was France—a nation with a strong national health-care system using a variation of the Bismarck model, with public and private providers and regulated, nonprofit insurance plans. Sweden, Norway, Finland, and Denmark all performed better in this regard than did the United States. When the Commonwealth Fund compared American health care with ten other nations on criteria such as quality, access, efficiency, equity, and healthy lives, the United States ranked dead last.

American patients skip care because of costs more often than do patients in other countries, and American doctors are more embroiled in what the Commonwealth Fund calls "administrative hassles." So despite America's strengths in the kind of high-tech and dramatic emergency hospital care that you see on TV—I have been addicted to the show *Grey's Anatomy* for years—American health care also has severe weaknesses. The American cardiologist-turned-author Sandeep Jauhar summarized the state of health care in the United States in an interview about his book *Doctored: The Disillusionment of an*

American Physician on National Public Radio. "American medicine," Jauhar told NPR listeners, "is the best in the world when it comes to providing high-tech care. If you have an esoteric disease, you want to be in the United States. God forbid you have Ebola, our academic medical centers are second to none. But if you have run-of-the-mill chronic diseases like congestive heart failure or diabetes, the system is not designed to find you the best possible care. And that's what has to change."

And compared with Nordic citizens, Americans are losing their freedom and independence in yet another way: financially. When it comes to health-care costs, the U.S. system means that Americans are getting robbed.

THE PRICE WE PAY

One fine spring day in New York City I was having coffee with an American friend whose wife had given birth in the previous year. He mentioned they had recently received a number of unexpected bills from the doctors involved and from the hospital, six months after the fact, related to the delivery. The bills ran into the thousands of dollars. He and his wife had insurance, and he hadn't been aware that these bills would be coming, but he assured me it wasn't a huge problem. He'd called the hospital, and the collections office had agreed to lower the amounts based on the couples' earnings. Now they were paying fifty dollars a month toward the remaining bill of a thousand dollars or so. He also mentioned that overall, he felt his insurance had been good. A few years back he'd had surgery on the same plan. The cost of the surgery had been more than ten thousand dollars, but his share had been only around fifteen hundred dollars.

I had just returned from a trip to Finland, and I was speechless. It wasn't that I hadn't heard a story like his many times before. One friend in New York had to pay $950 for the extraction of a wisdom tooth, since she didn't have dental insurance. Another acquaintance's wife went to the emergency room to have a glass fragment removed from her foot. The hospital took X-rays that revealed nothing, and the doctor told her to see a specialist. Then they sent her a bill for $1,244. One friend with an affordable corporate insurance plan, including dental, found that none of the doctors who specialized in fixing the particular problem she had with her jaw took any insurance, so she had to pay $1,600 out of pocket. What rendered me speechless was not the bills and costs themselves, although I did find them outrageous, but the fact that my American friends didn't seem to realize there was anything strange about all this.

For sure, many Americans with good jobs and high-end insurance don't end up paying much extra for their care. But even for many middle-class Americans, underinsurance that results in extra medical bills is a terrible problem. A Harvard study surveyed people who were being forced to declare personal bankruptcy as the result of an illness. The majority of them turned out to be middle aged, middle class, and college educated, and they'd had health insurance at least at some point during their ordeal. Their financial troubles resulted from a combination of copays, prescription drug costs, and bills from doctors and hospitals rising into the tens of thousands of dollars, as well as from lost income during their illness. Even when Americans have health insurance, they mortgage their homes and borrow money to pay medical bills.

ObamaCare was partly intended to solve some of these problems. For example, the Affordable Care Act put limits on copays for preventive services, and it capped annual out-of-pocket maximums for most policies. In 2016, these caps were

$6,850 for an individual, and $13,700 for a family plan. That's still a lot of money. And ObamaCare didn't solve the problem of insurance companies sticking patients with humongous bills for services that the insurers decide they're simply going to refuse to cover, not to mention costs for out-of-network treatment that is often impossible to avoid. All this would be utterly unheard of in Finland.

Americans tend to assume, of course, that people in Nordic countries are also getting a rotten deal. Nordics, after all, have to fork out so much in taxes over the years to pay for their public health-care system.

Before I discuss the very interesting question of taxes—which I'll get to in the next chapter—here are the comparative statistics specifically on health-care spending. Regardless of how health care is paid for—through taxes or private insurance or direct payments from patients—each country spends a certain amount on health care for every citizen. Finland's per-person spending is, along with Iceland's, about average among the OECD countries. How about the United States? The quality of the medical care in the United States is, as we've seen, pretty much identical to, or in some areas slightly worse than, Nordic medical care. Yet Americans are paying, per person, two and a half times what citizens of Finland and Iceland pay. In fact the United States now spends more on health care than any other country in the world by a wide margin.

How come?

In 2013 the normal delivery of a baby in the United States cost on average $10,000—four times as much as in Spain. An MRI fetched more than $1,000, compared with $140 in Switzerland. American bypass surgery cost $75,350, or almost five times as much as in the Netherlands. The average cost of a hospital day in the United States was more than $4,000, as opposed to $480 in Spain. How is it possible that Americans end up paying so vastly much more for exactly the same services?

Several American investigative journalists have set out to answer exactly this question, and their discoveries have been stunning. To begin with, American hospitals routinely charge such high prices for even the smallest items that the practice could be called fraudulent—if it weren't perfectly legal. Steven Brill's extensive report "Bitter Pill: Why Medical Bills Are Killing Us" in *Time* detailed hospital billings of $1.50 for a generic painkiller that you can buy a hundred of on Amazon for $1.49, $18.00 for an individual diabetes-test strip that Amazon sold in boxes of fifty for $27.85, or 55 cents each, and $13,702.00 for an injection of a cancer drug that costs the hospital less than $4,000.00

A series of articles in the *New York Times* by Elisabeth Rosenthal, tagged, "Paying till it hurts," also showed how Americans are systematically charged more for drugs, scans, and procedures than are patients in other developed countries. "Americans pay, on average, about four times as much for a hip replacement as patients in Switzerland or France and more than three times as much for a Caesarean section as those in New Zealand or Britain," Rosenthal revealed. "The average price for Nasonex, a common nasal spray for allergies, is $108 in the United States compared with $21 in Spain." Drawing on a report by the Commonwealth Fund, Rosenthal went on to compare hospital stays in the United States with those in other developed countries. She found that while hospital stays in the United States were no longer than those in other countries, they nevertheless cost three times as much.

There are a variety of reasons for the high cost of health care in the United States, and a lot of them are related to the fact that it's an old-fashioned, free-for-all of private arrangements, rather than a modernized, rationalized, national system with clear regulations. American insurance companies negotiate prices down as much as they can, but often their bargaining power is limited. There are only so many hospitals in most areas, and those hospitals have also been consolidating to create more powerful private entities. By buying up doctors' practices and forming in-house labs, hospitals have managed to form near monopolies, increasing their leverage against insurers, which allows them to charge more.

In addition American hospitals treat many health issues with heavy-handed and expensive methods, whereas their European counterparts will often choose a less intrusive solution that's just as effective. When it comes to delivering babies, for example, the American rate for C-sections is much higher than in other developed countries, and needless to say, each American C-section costs more than it does elsewhere. Pharmaceutical companies, for their part, keep gouging Americans with higher drug prices than they charge elsewhere in the world. American insurance companies, hospitals, and doctors also all spend extraordinary amounts of money on administration, because the complexity of America's private system has created multiple layers and separate areas of management as well as various middlemen. Not to mention the huge sums that American health-care companies and providers spend on advertising to drum up more business.

A lot of these drivers of excessive cost simply don't exist in other countries. There are far fewer bills, forms, and disputed claims when care is provided by a public hospital, or paid for by a single public insurance provider, nor is there any need to advertise. As the *New York Times* has noted, many of the typical professions that soak up consumer dollars in the American health-care industry—medical coders, claims adjusters, and care navigators, to name a few—are unnecessary and unheard of in other countries.

Then there are American doctors. They order more tests than do doctors in other countries, and Americans are charged more for those tests, as well as for their medical devices and drugs. American doctors also take a much bigger cut of all these charges for themselves than do their European counterparts, and they often have extensive financial arrangements with laboratories, device makers, and drug companies that can skew their incentives and entice them to choose a more expensive form of care, beyond what is medically necessary.

I have family members in Finland who are doctors and dentists. They earn a comfortable income, but their homes are normal homes in ordinary suburbs or in apartment buildings, and no one is driving Porsches. Based on an OECD report, Finnish doctors who are general practitioners earn twice the average Finnish salary, which is pretty darn good. Specialists in Finland do even better: They earn two and a half times the average salary. But for American doctors the earnings premium is dramatically higher. In the United States general practitioners earn three and a half times the average American salary. American specialists take home five and a half times the average.

American doctors do work longer hours than Finnish doctors, but this doesn't wholly explain the higher earnings, since doctors in Canada and France work similar hours but make less. One of the biggest justifications American doctors tend to give for their high salaries is that they have to pay off the debt for their very expensive educations themselves. It's true that this is not an expense doctors trained in Finland have to worry about, since medical school in Finland—if you can get in—is free. Another justification for the high incomes of doctors in the United States is the expensive malpractice insurance they're forced to buy. In Finland such costs are negligible.

In all fairness, though, it is not the doctors who earn the most in American medicine. That dubious honor goes to the real bosses of American health-care profits: hospital administrators and insurance company executives.

Who pays the price for all this? The average American.

Not long ago a man in the United States known as "Steve H." needed a neurostimulator implanted in his back. He had health insurance, and he went to an American hospital for the one-day surgery. The tale of Steve H.'s operation, which is both remarkable and totally commonplace, was one of the stories reported by Steven Brill in *Time*. The operation went well, but afterward Steve H. received a bill, despite having insurance. The bill included, as Brill puts it, "all the usual and customary overcharges." For example, among the many itemized entries was "STRAP OR TABLE 8X27 IN," for $31. Brill explains: "That's the strap used to hold Steve H. onto the operating table. Just below that was 'BLNKT WARM UPPER BDY 42268' for $32. That's a blanket used to keep surgery patients warm. It is, of course, reusable, and it's available new on eBay for $13. Four lines down there's 'GOWN SURG ULTRA XLG 95121' for $39, which is the gown the surgeon wore. Thirty of them can be bought online for $180. Neither Medicare nor any large insurance company would pay a hospital separately for those straps or the surgeon's gown; that's all supposed to come with the facility fee paid to the hospital, which in this case was $6,289." The total for Steve H.'s one-day operation came to $86,951. Steve H.'s insurance only agreed to pay out $45,000. The total amount that Steve H. himself now owed the hospital to pay for all those inflated charges was still $40,000. And that didn't even include the doctors' bills.

Compare this with the case of an acquaintance of mine in Finland. He had been suffering from numbness, pain in his back, and a burning sensation in his hand. After a few weeks of waiting to see if the pain would go away, he saw a doctor and learned that he would need surgery. He had the option to have the surgery in a private hospital, but he elected to use a public hospital that was part of Helsinki University. Afterward he spent a few hours in the ICU, followed by an overnight stay in the regular wing of the hospital. He was home the next day, and then got six weeks of paid sick leave. He, too, received a bill for the operation. His reaction to the bill was strong enough that he decided to post it on Facebook: "Just received a bill from the hospital. MRI pictures of the neck and the following neurosurgeon's appointment €29. Removal of two prolapsed vertebral discs by the most experienced neurosurgeon on neck problems in Finland + one night stay in the hospital €69.60. Total cost €98.60."

Forty thousand dollars, versus ninety-nine euros, which comes to about $105. My acquaintance was very happy with his care. Especially with the price.

How do Nordic countries keep costs so low? Many Americans believe they know the reason: death panels.

DEATH PANELS

What many Americans fear most about public health care is the idea that in countries with public health-care systems, the government unfairly—and maybe even secretly—limits the medical treatment that people can receive. This fear was infamously given voice by former Alaska governor and vice presidential candidate Sarah Palin. Health-care reform in the United States, Palin claimed, would lead to "death panels" of bureaucrats who would decide which people were "worthy of medical care." Palin's claim was quickly debunked. America's new Affordable Care Act—ObamaCare—included no provisions that would cause any individual to be judged worthy or unworthy of medical treatment. Later the fact-checking outfit PolitiFact actually named Palin's false claim the number-one "Lie of the Year."

Nevertheless many Americans continued to believe that Palin's statement was true, the assumption being that part of the way that Finland and the other Nordic countries reduce the medical bills of their citizens is in fact by having something like what Palin was describing—if not "death panels," at least committees of government number crunchers who rule out lifesaving procedures that are too expensive. This is simply not the case. As in the United States, in the Nordic countries there are no committees that pass judgment on whether or not a patient will get care. Such decisions are left up to individual doctors in consultation with patients. That said, doctors and patients in Nordic countries do face limitations, of course, exactly the same limitations faced by doctors and patients in the United States in dealing with private insurance companies—namely, whether or not certain treatments or drugs are covered. The difference is that in Finland and the other Nordic countries, the process for deciding which treatments and drugs are covered is reasonable, transparent, and accountable to citizens. That goes for pricing, too. Nothing could be further from the American way of doing things.

Absurd as it might seem, in the United States it is nearly impossible for anyone—consumers and experts alike—to actually find out in advance what a medical test or procedure is going to cost. When I finally got my first American health-insurance plan through Trevor's new job, I read the thick benefits book the insurance company sent, but I could understand little of it. The terminology was confusing, the rules more so.

Asking around, I discovered that my bewilderment was not at all unusual. In medical matters big and small in America, patients will mostly discover the price of their care only after the fact, even if they are stuck paying for it themselves. When a group of researchers from Iowa University telephoned more than a hundred American hospitals—two from each state, as well as Washington, DC—to request the lowest complete price, including hospital and physician fees, for a hypothetical hip replacement for a sixty-two-year-old grandmother, only one in ten hospitals was able to provide the full price, and even then the prices ranged from $11,000 to $125,000.

Patients aren't the only ones entangled in America's confounding, chaotic, and outdated patchwork of medical and insurance providers, and losing their precious time and resources trying to manage costs and plan their care. Increasingly, so are doctors.

An American acquaintance of mine who works as a genetic counselor described the problem of medical pricing in the United States from her perspective. Since each patient has a different insurance plan, a doctor often has no idea what a test or treatment is going to cost the patient, and the doctor can't spend all day on the phone calling everyone's insurance companies. Even when they try to figure it out, she said, often they can't. "I stood around for ten minutes on Friday with a cardiologist and a cardiology fellow debating whether or not to send a genetic test on an inpatient or wait until they were an outpatient," she wrote once in a Facebook post. "We were trying to figure out how to keep the family from getting a huge bill, but to answer that question would have required knowing if they had met their deductible for the year, if they had met their out-of-pocket maximum for the year, and what percentage of the testing their insurance would cover if they hadn't. There is NO WAY we could answer those questions on a Friday night—plus it's a really lousy use of our time."

Nonetheless many American doctors do spend countless hours calling insurance companies to get prior authorization for expensive drugs that the insurance companies would prefer not to cover. A Commonwealth Fund report found that more than half of American doctors report that the time they have to spend trying to secure drug or treatment coverage for their patients is a major problem—a bigger percentage than in any of the other ten countries that were surveyed.

As a patient, if you don't know what a treatment is going to cost you, sometimes it may not matter all that much, especially if your employer has done a good job at picking the plans they offer. But sometimes it does matter. One friend's doctor had recommended what the doctor described as a routine heart test for my friend's new baby, just to make sure everything was fine. The parents agreed—who wouldn't?—thinking "routine" meant covered. Only later did they discover that their insurance did not cover the exam, and a bill of a thousand dollars followed.

Many Americans have come to believe that the reason you can't really know what anything is going to cost is simple. With for-profit hospitals loading their bills with "all the usual and customary overcharges," as Steven Brill put it, what for-profit insurance companies do is first deny every claim they can, and then wait to see whether, and how much, you're going to fight back.

Let's be frank: This sort of behavior has no place in a modern civilized nation, not when we're talking about providing citizens with a service as essential as health care. Health care in the United States has regressed to such a Wild West state of affairs that patients, who in most cases are already suffering from an illness or other health problem as it is, also must additionally endure frustration, anxiety, and anger as they are forced to spend vast amounts of time and energy just fighting for the basic right to have their care covered.

No Nordic citizen has to put up with anything like this.

Nordic societies today have all decided that health care in a modern nation should be a fundamental human right, and as such, it makes the most sense to provide health care as a basic social service. Along with just about every other wealthy industrialized nation—except the United States—this means that the Nordic countries regulate the cost of medical services and drugs in a centralized manner, which prevents all of the pricing insanity so commonplace in America.

Take prescription drugs in Finland, for example. In this case there is indeed a "panel," and because it's a very important one, its decisions are open to public scrutiny. The panel consists not of death-dispensing bureaucrats but of medical experts— doctors, professors, and pharmacists—and its job is to review applications from pharmaceutical companies to have new drugs covered by the public system. The panel bases its decisions on studies of the drugs' effectiveness, and determines a maximum wholesale price as well as reimbursement rates for approved drugs. If the drug is approved, the public health-care system will pay much of its cost. In 2013 the committee's negotiations with pharmaceutical companies ended with 95 percent of applications accepted.

None of that, by the way, prevents patients in Finland from paying out of their own pocket for a drug that the national system doesn't cover. Once a drug has been approved for sale either by the European Union or Finland's agency overseeing medicine—the equivalent of the FDA in the United States—the drug company is free to sell it at any price and anyone can buy it, as long as he or she has a prescription and the money. This is exactly the same as in the United States. The price is restricted only for drugs covered by the public system.

Finland's system for evaluating and regulating the effectiveness of drugs and treatments has several key advantages over the laissez-faire approach in America. The most obvious advantage is that it helps the country control health-care costs by weeding out expensive yet ineffective treatments, or drugs that have a more affordable alternative. The downside is that there are cases where a drug that serves some part of the population is deemed too expensive to be covered.

However, since the decisions are open to public scrutiny, they can be challenged by taxpaying citizens. Compare this with the United States, where calculations over what to cover, and by how much, are most often made by private insurance companies, usually in secret. Reimbursements vary widely, for no reason that patients or even doctors can discern, leaving patients with no recourse, wondering why their plan covers one treatment but not another, and why the patient next to them with different insurance might get access to both. It's ironic that Americans so often dislike the idea of public health care because they think government will force decisions on them. Yet, unlike the private sector, in a democracy it is government services that are the one area that must be transparent, and that can be openly examined, explained, and questioned. A perfect example is the United States Veterans Administration, whose health-care system has recently been scrutinized, and as a result is now undergoing reforms. While governments make mistakes and might try to obfuscate their failures, it is private providers in the United States that, as we've seen over and over with "all the usual and customary overcharges," can't be trusted.

The fact that the current approach to health care in the United States generally avoids cost calculations up front may sound good at the outset. Naturally people want their doctors to choose the most effective care for them, even if it is expensive. Not considering costs, however, is causing Americans to get less value for their money, because expensive options are used even when cheaper ones would be just as effective. Some Americans have even started to plead with their doctors to take cost into account when making decisions about treatment, because more and more patients are realizing that they are likely to be the ones stuck with the impossibly high bill.

Pleading with one's doctor, however, is itself also becoming an exercise in frustration—and an exercise in suspicion—for many Americans. Out-of-control costs and the many other injustices that have become endemic to medical treatment in the United States are starting to undermine the very bedrock of the American health-care system: trust in one's own doctor.

The recent spread of the anti-vaccination movement is one of the more visible symptoms of this trend. However, I also encountered this mistrust among many of my American acquaintances in a more everyday way. More and more I noticed them voicing their suspicion that their doctors were pushing excessive diagnoses, expensive tests, and invasive operations on them in order to make money, rather than out of medical necessity.

Many had turned to the Internet instead, in search of alternatives such as dietary regimens or other noninvasive treatments. A Harvard study from 2014 showed that while the majority of Americans were satisfied with their most recent physician's visit, trust in the medical profession as a whole in the United States had plummeted since the 1960s. Of twenty-nine countries surveyed, the United States came in twenty-fourth in the proportion of adults who trust doctors.

To doctors this type of suspicious thinking can be frustrating. They've studied for years, maybe decades, to master their trade, they work exceptionally hard, and they aim to heal their patients, not to harm them. But no matter how unfair doctors feel such accusations to be, the suspicions held by growing numbers of Americans are not unwarranted. The United States does, for example, clearly have a more medicalized approach to pregnancy and delivery than many other countries, with unusually high rates of C-sections. Some patients might think this a good thing. But as the OECD has noted, approaches to birthing that rely on midwives instead of obstetricians are just as effective. In fact a review of studies found that births led by midwives resulted in fewer complications than ones led by obstetricians.

Similarly, American doctors order far more tests than do their counterparts elsewhere. They order more MRI tests per capita than any other OECD country. On the surface this, too, could seem like a good thing—more tests, better care. But according to the OECD, evidence suggests instead that Americans simply overuse CT and MRI exams. "Many studies have attempted to assess tangible medical benefits of the substantial increase in CT and MRI examinations in the United States," the OECD notes in a report, "but have found no conclusive evidence of such benefits." American doctors also prescribe far more antibiotics than Nordic doctors do, despite extensive studies showing that the more antibiotics are prescribed in a community, the more resistant bacterial strains will take root there.

Not that the Nordic countries are entirely immune from some of this. The vast new troves of health information that are becoming available online have created a new trend of patients second-guessing doctors in the Nordic countries just as in the United States. However, in the Nordic countries, patients are not usually suspicious that their doctors might be putting profits ahead of ethics. In a country such as Finland, patients certainly might worry that cuts in health-care budgets could be leading to longer wait times, or to doctors whose schedules are too rushed. But rarely would a Finn have any cause to suspect that a doctor working in the public system could be personally benefiting from a particular care decision. Most doctors are simply salaried employees, and their compensation does not primarily depend on the number of tests or operations they perform. It's hard to overstate what a difference this makes compared with the way the American system is structured, and how much better Finns and other Nordic citizens are served by their health-care system as a result.

Given the growing distrust of doctors in the United States, perhaps it's no wonder that Americans place so much emphasis on being able to find a doctor they like. In fact, perhaps being able to choose one's doctor is one of the few redeeming qualities of the United States approach. Surely Americans would lose that freedom with a public health-care system like Finland's.

Or would they? And what does it even mean to have the freedom to choose who provides your health care, and the freedom to choose how it's provided? Does that freedom actually set you free?

THE RIGHT TO CHOOSE

About a year before I moved to New York, my brother Mikko married his girlfriend, Veera, in a lovely little town in the Finnish countryside. An American family who were close friends of my mother's since her student exchange year in Ohio almost fifty years earlier had come all the way from the United States for the ceremony. In a fragrant orchard at a long table, I sat talking with two sisters from the American family. The possibility of my move to the United States was looming in my mind, and there were so many things I felt I still needed to understand. At some point our conversation turned to going to the doctor, and I asked the sisters how much it mattered to them that they be able to choose their own physician.

"I absolutely want to choose my own doctor," one of them said instantly. She then went on to describe how, when faced with a serious illness, she'd launched into an intensive program of discovery for herself, researching everything she could about the condition online, cataloging possible treatments, calling friends and relatives for advice on securing the best doctor, and advocating strongly for the treatments she felt were most appropriate for her. She wanted to be in control of her own destiny, she told me firmly.

I had never thought of doctors that way. If I were suddenly seriously ill, the last thing I'd want to have to do, on top of dealing with my fear and discomfort, would be charging ahead with the onerous task of researching doctors, treatments, hospitals, and prices. I'd want the doctors to take charge. They were the experts, not me.

Immediately, my own attitude made me feel weak and pathetic compared to this visitor from America. Apparently, I was willing to surrender my life thoughtlessly into the hands of strangers, without standing up for myself. I admired the way Americans seemed so consistently to take responsibility for themselves, no matter what the situation, without ever expecting anyone else to do it for them. Certainly much of what has made America great has been this attitude of self-determination.

Losing the capacity for self-determination is one of the things that many Americans worry about the most. A few years after that conversation, I ran across an online comment on an American newspaper's Web site, written by a vocal Internet commentator by the name of Guy Thompto. The comment struck me deeply, especially as someone who had grown up, as I had, on the border of the Soviet Union. "Sometimes freedom is taken away in large chunks, such as when the tanks rolled into Eastern Europe," Thompto wrote. But then he went on, and now he was talking about health care: "Sometimes freedom is scrubbed away, one layer at a time—such as when your freedom to freely choose the physician you want, what you are willing to pay, and what coverage you deem necessary for yourself and your family is taken away. People sometimes tell us that taking away these freedoms is for our own good, or sometimes for the good of the less fortunate. . . . We are told that if we disagree, we are greedy—or more often, ignorant."

Had I been coddled by the state back in Finland to such an extent that I'd developed a childish trust in the choices the government had made for me—whether in schools or health clinics? Worse yet, was I such a brainwashed underling that it simply had not occurred to me that I had the right to demand which doctor I saw? How did this fit in with the Nordic ideals of personal autonomy, individualism, and independence, and with the Nordic theory of love? Perhaps I should celebrate the ability to choose my doctor in America, and see what this new-found freedom was all about.

It turned out to be more complicated than I had expected. Soon enough I was lost in the mysterious maze of physicians, clinics, and hospitals throughout New York City, desperately asking friends for recommendations, calling various offices only to learn that they didn't take my insurance or didn't take new patients. Over the next several years, as Trevor's employer changed insurance companies, or Trevor changed jobs, we were frequently forced to leave whatever doctor we'd been using. Every time, we pored over plans, costs, doctor reviews, and paperwork. Choosing a doctor became an exhausting burden that yielded few, if any, benefits. Many Americans may be fortunate enough to have found a good doctor they like, and fortunate enough to live a settled-enough existence that they can build a relationship of trust with that doctor over time. But that is often not the way it goes.

When I lived in Finland, who my doctor was hadn't much mattered to me because all the doctors I encountered in the public health-care system struck me as quite good. However, let's say I had wanted to choose a particular doctor at the public clinic, and to see that same doctor every time. Over the past decade it has become much easier to choose your own doctor even in the public system. Norway and Denmark have already opted for the British model, in which primary care physicians are private providers, but the taxpayers foot the bill for everyone's visits. Patients can choose any doctor they want to sign up with, and doctors get paid partly based on the number of patients on their rosters, and partly on actual visits. Hospital care is still mostly a public service, and a referral from the primary care physician is usually needed for visits to a specialist. That said, many Danes have additional private insurance offered by their employer, which gives them other options. In Sweden patients can also choose their primary care physicians, whether private or public, and the taxpayer money follows them where they want to go.

In Finland options to see private doctors who are partly subsidized either by the government or by employers have existed for a long time. Today Finns can also choose their public doctors, health clinics, and hospitals freely, with only some limitations—for example, you can switch which public clinic you use no more than once a year, which helps prevent costly administrative churn in the system. Moreover, there has been talk in Finland of moving closer to the Swedish model, which would give Finnish patients even more fully taxpayer-funded options.

After comparing my experiences with doctors in Finland and America, I came to this conclusion: In some ways I got more care in the United States than in Finland. My American insurance typically covered an annual physical exam and all manner of routine tests that had never been performed on me in Finland, since no doctor there had ever considered them necessary. At the same time, having to arrange so many aspects of health care myself, while also having to navigate the ever-changing maze of employers, plans, prices, and the scarcity of openings with good doctors, I was thrown into a state of constant stress—and I wasn't even sick or injured yet. I longed for a different kind of freedom—the freedom of knowing that the Finnish health-care system was always there for me regardless of my employment status. I wanted the freedom of knowing that all the doctors were good and that their goal was whatever was in my best interests, rather than generating profits. I wanted to know that the system would automatically take me in and give me excellent care without my having to exhaust myself with self-advocacy in my moment of weakness and need. That was real freedom. So was the freedom of knowing that none of it would bankrupt me.

AN AMERICAN IN FINLAND

Everywhere in the world people have complaints about their health-care system, and even the best-performing nations still need improvement. The journalist T. R. Reid, as he describes traveling the world studying different approaches to health care, quotes a Princeton policy analyst named Tsung-Mei Cheng. Having observed the difficulties of creating effective health-care systems around the globe, Cheng came up with what she calls her three "Universal Laws of Health Care Systems." They are as follows: "1. No matter how good the health care in a particular country, people will complain about it. 2. No matter how much money is spent on health care, the doctors and hospitals will argue that it is not enough. 3. The last reform always failed."

Many Finns consider the Finnish health-care system a disaster. The health-care perks that salaried Finns get from their employers allow them to visit primary care physicians without any wait. This leaves the unemployed, the self-employed, or retired Finns to face longer waits at public clinics. In addition private care that is subsidized by the public system has ensured that Finns with money can buy their way into immediate elective surgery more quickly than the less well-off. By American standards the prices of private care in Finland are not outrageous, but Finns who can afford them do get better access to care than those who can't.

An American might think that it is only right to reward people for their hard work, and to give people incentives to get a job with benefits, not to mention to earn a salary good enough to be able to pay for better health care if they want to. In Finland today, however, the fact that such trends might be starting to emerge is generally considered a disgrace. While there are

Finns who think a more libertarian and private-sector approach would serve Finland better in health care, as in other areas of life, most Finns believe that their success as a nation in the twenty-first century demands that real equality of opportunity be extended to every member of society no matter what, including in the form of a strong national public health-care system.

To ensure that access to health care in Finland remains equitable, the Finnish government has instituted rules shortening the amount of time patients might have to wait before seeing a doctor. Now all nonemergency cases must be evaluated within three days of a patient contacting a public health clinic, and access to a general practitioner or specialist for nonemergency care must follow no later than ninety days after the initial evaluation. Elective surgery must be scheduled within six months. Needless to say someone who needs emergency care or is suffering from acute pain can always walk into an emergency room anywhere in Finland, for a copay of less than forty-five dollars. In addition the Finnish government is in the process of pushing through changes in health-care administration and funding that would create a more centralized system, in an effort to improve both efficiency and equality.

Still, if you've grown up with the American health-care system, you might wonder why any American would go to all the trouble to think about having a Nordic-style system instead. Maybe the devil you know is better than the devil you don't?

That's what Pamela might well have thought, until she was diagnosed with multiple sclerosis.

The hour-and-a-half drive from Helsinki to Lammi, a Finnish town of about five thousand people, runs on roads winding through farmland and past bright-red barns. On a crisp October day, the fields were covered by a thin layer of frost, and the low-lying sun shone brightly on the yellows and greens of autumn. When I arrived in Lammi I rang the bell of an apartment at the end of a small row of houses, and a forty-nine-year-old American from Alabama named Pamela opened the door.

Pamela is a chatty brunette with bright eyes and an easy laugh, and much affection for her white-and-black cat, Yoda, as well as her big blue-and-yellow parrot, Sibelius—named after the famous Finnish composer. The pets kept us company while we talked.

The story of how Pamela got to this small town in rural Finland started decades ago in Altamonte Springs, Florida, where she was working her first waitressing job. One night a Finnish student came in with a friend, and soon enough Pamela and the student started dating. They got married and lived in the United States for two decades, with Pamela working an office job in a hospital in Birmingham, Alabama. When her husband was offered a job back home, they moved to Finland. When I met her she had been living in Finland for five years, but now she and her husband were both struggling to find permanent employment. The company her husband had first worked for in Finland had since gone out of business. They were thinking of moving back to the United States, but there was an obstacle— Pamela had recently been diagnosed with multiple sclerosis.

Unlike in the United States, the fact that she and her husband were both currently out of steady work didn't mean they had no health-care coverage. As soon as Pamela was diagnosed she was taken in by Finland's public health-care system. When I met with her the Affordable Care Act was about to take effect back in the States. Encouraged, Pamela had researched options for individual insurance plans offered by the new health exchanges, but she couldn't figure out if she could sign up before she knew which state they might settle in, or how the tax subsidies would work in her case. With her illness, she couldn't risk being without health insurance for extended periods of time.

In Finland none of that was an issue. Her coverage was close to 100 percent, and it did not depend on employment or where she lived. She paid copays of forty dollars here, twenty dollars there, but the low annual caps that apply to all Finns applied to her as well. She was seeing a neurologist, an ophthalmologist, a urologist, a nurse, and a physical therapist, as well as attending subsidized exercise classes. Getting appointments sometimes took longer than she would have liked, but mostly she was happy with her care. "I've been to see lots of people. I feel like I've been taken care of," Pamela told me. Rummaging through her kitchen drawers, she dug out a cheese slicer with a special handle designed for people who'd lost strength in their fingers. Pamela waved it gleefully in the air. "The occupational therapist gave me this, and a cool knife, and scissors, and a chair to sit on in the shower," she explained, "and I didn't pay for any of it."

Having worked in an American hospital herself, and having had her share of health issues even before the MS diagnosis, Pamela had considerable experience with the health-care system in America. Her stories of the twists and turns she experienced in dealing with American health insurance and hospitals unwind like many an American health-care tale—with so many actors, phases, and hurdles that keeping track is hard even for the protagonist. Based on her experiences, she has deemed Finnish hospital care top-notch. One time in Finland she stayed alone in a hospital room meant for two people, with minimal cost to her. "I was there for five nights, had excellent care, two ambulance rides, X-rays, CAT scans, follow-up visits, and the whole thing ended up costing me three hundred dollars," she related, still astonished. Similar care she had received in American hospitals had seemed just as good to her, but came—as usual—with a much higher price tag and far more hassle and stress.

When Americans imagine a hospital in a public health-care system, they often envision something out of the former Soviet Union—a barren, gray, old facility with lazy staff, dirty sinks, and lack of adequate equipment. The decor of Finnish hospitals actually did strike Pamela as somewhat sparse and utilitarian, with the chairs lined up in the hallways next to the appointment rooms, instead of having general waiting areas, and without the customary buzz of American hospitals with their volunteers, chapels, and gift shops. Visiting a rather sad-looking gift shop in a Finnish hospital, Pamela immediately envisioned how she could spruce it up, and her American can-do spirit bubbled up: "I thought, I wanna whip you guys into shape!"

Squandered gift-shop opportunities aside, Pamela would like to correct some of the misconceptions about public health care that she feels her fellow Americans have. Finnish hospitals are just as clean and modern as American ones, sometimes even more so. But what about the latest medical innovations? Didn't she think she might get better, more cutting-edge care if she were to move back to the United States? No, Pamela replied, she didn't think she was missing out. And she had something with which to compare her Finnish care—her sister in the United States has MS too. Imagining herself back in the States, Pamela mused: "I'd be getting more cutting-edge care than in Bangladesh, yes, but not more than in Finland."

Later I encountered another American in Finland married to a Finn, and this American was also suffering from MS. Michele's experiences were very similar to Pamela's. But her disease had already progressed so far that she required expensive medications that Pamela did not yet need. In the United States drugs for MS are much more expensive than in many other countries; when she lived in the United States Michele was paying six hundred dollars in copays every year for one drug she needed, even with her insurance. When I chatted with her, I sitting in Brooklyn and she in Finland, she had just been to a pharmacy to fill a prescription for the same drug. In Finland, she told me, the drug was costing her the equivalent of fourteen dollars a year. (This was before the Finnish government set a new annual deductible for all prescription drugs—fifty-five dollars in 2016.)

Pamela missed her friends and family back in the United States, and reminisced about many aspects of American life that were easier for her—abundant parking, big grocery stores, a bigger house, cities designed for people who have difficulty moving. But as far as she was concerned, the quality of the medical care in both places is fine. For her it is all about being able to *afford* that care.

Pamela's case can be considered somewhat unusual, of course, in the sense that she happened to develop such a serious, long-term condition. But even when people don't, there is one ailment that no one can escape.

AGING WELL

The hope for all of us in the twenty-first century is that we survive to a healthy old age, and lead independent lives, passing our days as we would like and giving our affection and attention to our loved ones without strings attached. The Nordic healthcare system helps make this hope a reality, while the American health-care system often shackles people instead into relationships of dependency.

In the United States, Medicare helps those aged sixty-five

or older pay for their health-care needs. But there are some enormous holes in long-term elder care that Medicare doesn't cover—in fact some of the biggest expenses of all: room and board in nursing homes or assisted-living facilities; twenty-four-hour nurse services; home health aides who deliver meals, help bathe the elderly, get groceries, and clean the house. In America the cost for all such services simply falls on the elderly themselves, until they've exhausted most of their assets and are destitute.

To pay for all this yourself, the conventional wisdom in the United States is that you need to have saved at least a million dollars before you can retire. Unfortunately most Americans are nowhere close to meeting the minimums they need. Based on a 2013 estimate, the median financial net worth of an American household headed by someone nearing retirement—aged fifty-five to sixty-four—was, excluding homes and cars, not much over sixty thousand dollars. Meanwhile, in 2013 the median annual cost for a private nursing-home room in the United States was more than eighty thousand dollars. If an American completely runs out of money in old age, Medicaid—the state-run program for the poor—will probably kick in, but it will often require relocation to a nursing facility of questionable quality. Some states have also been cutting their Medicaid funding and changing eligibility requirements, leaving people who once relied on the program to their own devices. Considering all this, perhaps it's no surprise that several studies have identified running out of money in retirement as one of the most pervasive fears among large swaths of the American public, even among the wealthy.

Since many elderly Americans cannot possibly pay for all the services they need, their grown children end up taking care of them—not just helping to pay their bills but literally becoming their nurses and home health aides, as well as their health-care coordinators and advocates. This, of course, is on top of the burdens these grown children are already shouldering—trying to take care of their own kids, managing their own family's health care, and paying their own bills. This requires adults and their elderly parents to negotiate a profound, intensely personal, and often discomfiting new role reversal, in which parents who have grown accustomed to their autonomy become dependent, sometimes painfully so, on their own children. Sometimes these new relationships between older parents and their offspring become a wonderful opportunity for renewed emotional connection. The reality of life in the United States, however, tends to be that younger families with kids are already stretched terribly thin, struggling to make ends meet in terms of both money and time. While they might be more than happy to spend some weekends and holidays with their elderly parents, taking care of them and paying their bills is an entirely different matter.

As I observed the lives of my American acquaintances and relatives, I was dumbfounded to learn that it was perfectly common for people with careers and children to take turns with their own siblings doing elder-care duty. Others were paying thousands of dollars each month to help their parents cope, and some women in the prime of their working years were dropping out of the workforce and giving up their careers in order to care for aging family members.

These sorts of arrangements might not come as a surprise in a traditional society where, for example, daughters-in-law might be expected to cook three meals a day for a three-generation household and wait on their husbands' parents hand and foot. But that's not the society that most people in the modern West aspire to in the twenty-first century.

Nordic families love their aging parents as much as those anywhere in the world. That's exactly why they want their love for the elderly to remain untainted by the sort of resentments that can arise when aging parents are stuck in relationships of dependency with their own children—relationships that destroy the autonomy, independence, and freedom of everyone involved.

The Nordic countries are among the nations around the world whose populations are aging the fastest. Many aging societies across the globe still expect children to help pay for their elderly parents' care, but the Nordic nations, informed by a view of contemporary life that draws on the Nordic theory of love, are not among them. They believe that it makes more sense in this day and age for society to provide complete elder care as a basic social service. This in turn allows families to enjoy one another's company, unencumbered. It also ensures the dignity and well-being of every individual, regardless of his or her personal wealth—and regardless of the not-insignificant question of whether or not he or she happens to get along with every member of their family. Just as Nordic societies believe that children should not be left at the complete mercy of their parents, they also believe that parents should not be left at the mercy of their children.

Because of this philosophy the Nordic countries have arranged elder care largely the same way they've arranged public health care, as a fundamental government service that is paid for through taxes and that is available to everyone. A chief goal is to help aging citizens remain in their own homes for as long as possible, with municipalities supporting them by providing home health aides, food delivery, housecleaning, and shopping services either for free or at an affordable price. When the elderly do move into nursing homes or assisted living, the cost is partly covered by contributions from each resident's own pension or retirement income—to the extent that such income is available. But there is also a reasonable cap on these contributions, allowing each resident to preserve some financial independence as well. The rest is funded by the public system. As a result the assets of nursing-home residents are not touched, nor will their children be charged. Tellingly, many of my acquaintances in the Nordic countries—including those who see their elderly relatives quite frequently—remain unfamiliar with the details of their care and its costs. Much of it is arranged directly by municipalities, so there's no need for other family members to get involved in managing the logistics.

It must be stated, though, that Nordic elderly care—and Finnish elderly care in particular—has many problems. The quality and costs of such care are debated constantly, and the Nordic media have exposed poor practices in both privately and publicly operated nursing homes. Finnish politicians have begun to suggest that as the population continues to age, wealthy baby boomers can't continue to expect to get their care fully covered. In addition the Finnish eagerness to help the elderly live in their homes as long as possible has lately led to accusations that even those who cannot cope at home anymore are having trouble getting into nursing homes. Despite these issues, international studies have consistently found the Nordic countries, particularly Norway and Sweden, to be some of the best places on earth in which to grow old.

As with Nordic health care more generally, there is a fair amount of choice for the elderly. They can choose to pay for private services themselves, or to live in private assisted-living facilities. And many grown children do spend countless hours helping their aging parents. But instead of paying for and arranging the care from scratch, their burden consists of discussing the best solutions available with their parents and the municipal caretakers. In cases where family members prefer to care for their own relatives, the state will fill in where necessary.

For example, municipalities can provide a home health aide who might take over from the family members on weekends or during a vacation period, to give the main caregiver a break. Municipalities will also often pay a family member a stipend while that person stays home to care for an ailing loved one.

When comparing the American and Nordic approaches to elder care, it might still sound as if the Nordic approach breaks families apart by weakening the bonds between family members. However, research suggests that the opposite is true. Tine Rostgaard, a professor at Aalborg University in Denmark who specializes in Nordic family policies, explained it to me this way: "Because we have such a big public provision in place, you could also say that people dare to go in to give informal care because it's realistic for them. It's not too time consuming, and they don't stand alone with the biggest care tasks."

In other words, Rostgaard continued, having a public system that will take care of the fundamentals, and the most difficult aspects of care, actually frees up family members to provide truly loving care for their aging relatives in ways, and amounts, that are not overly taxing or exhausting. This leaves everyone more satisfied, and prevents resentments from poisoning relationships. Again the Nordic approach improves everyone's quality of life.

ENVISIONING A HEALTHY NATION

When ObamaCare took effect at the beginning of 2014, some people in Europe had the impression that America's health-care system had actually been rebuilt. I was chatting in New York with a friend visiting from Finland, and at the mention of my health-care woes, he brushed me off brightly, with impressive naïveté: "But now you have ObamaCare!" From the perspective of Europeans, the state of American health care has been such a strange anachronism for so long that it's perfectly reasonable to assume that it should have been fixed by now. But of course it hasn't.

The Affordable Care Act did address some of the problems. It has extended coverage to millions of Americans, required insurance policies to cover more people than before, and put some limits on insured people's expenses. What the law didn't do is make it simple to buy insurance, or address the overall problem of skyrocketing costs. I happened to be one of those frustrated people in America whose deductible and copays shot up after ObamaCare, even as my out-of-pocket maximum went down. And despite the lower out-of-pocket max, ObamaCare did nothing to ease my fears that if I had serious medical expenses, no matter which private insurance company I was stuck with, it would deny half of my claims anyway. As American commentators have pointed out, ObamaCare is a ridiculously complex, inefficient, annoying, and fundamentally compromised way of trying to do something simple—provide health care for all.

Setting aside the political influence of the private health-care industry, are there legitimate reasons why the United States can't accomplish what most every other wealthy industrialized nation has done, and create a true public health-care system?

As far as I can see, there are three main reasons why the United States arranges most of its health care through employers and private insurance companies. First, doing so doesn't require new taxes. Second, it allows people to choose for themselves the insurance plan and doctor they want. And third, many Americans assume that if you allow a number of profit-driven private insurance companies and private health-care providers to compete with one another, it's good for the consumer.

The thing is, Americans are already paying for much of their health care one way or another through taxes. Taxes finance Medicare, Medicaid, and all health care for military veterans through the VA system. The new subsidies created by ObamaCare work through tax credits. And even private employer-sponsored health care is being supported by taxes. Contributions to health-insurance plans by employers and, in most cases, by their employees are tax-free, which in effect means that employees are actually getting a big chunk of their compensation before taxes. This exemption makes employer-sponsored health care one of the biggest tax breaks in the federal tax code—which is to say, it's public spending in the form of tax dollars not collected. And as such it's a terribly inefficient use of tax dollars, because it directs the biggest benefits to those with the highest incomes and the most generous health plans. People with lower incomes and less generous plans, and those who are uninsured altogether, get a much smaller break or none at all. Overall these policies are a hodgepodge of measures created at different times that have ended up treating Americans very differently depending on how they get their coverage.

And when it comes to buying and selling health care, when a buyer in any transaction is desperate—as most of us are when we need medical treatment—the seller has a huge unfair advantage, and this can distort an otherwise rational free market. In holding on to its private, profit-driven model, the United States is way behind the times, and average American citizens are increasingly getting stuck with the enormous price tag for this completely outdated and unconscionably unfair system.

If a society had limitless funds, constantly running expensive tests on everyone and paying doctors and health-industry executives gigantic salaries would not be a problem, as long as the treatments were justified for medical reasons, and as long as the poor didn't get left behind. After all, that's what most of us think of as good medical care—the more the better. At the same time the issue is more complex than that. Health spending is growing everywhere in the world as populations age, as expectations rise, and as new technologies and drugs generate more tests and treatments for ailments that used to go undetected or untreated. In a sense no matter how much money a country spends, health care will always be a bottomless pit. There is always something more you can do, and indeed, we are doing much more now than just a few decades or even years ago. But that's also precisely why a modern nation in the twenty-first century needs to ensure that its money is spent wisely—that society is paying reasonable amounts for health care that is effective, and that the criteria for doing so are clear and transparent.

If America's reckless spending were actually creating incentives that dramatically increased the quality of care, then perhaps it could be justified. But the experience of the Nordic countries, along with other advanced societies that have national health care, shows that this just isn't the case. The care in the Nordic countries is equally as good as, or even better than, the care in the United States.

Because spending on health care in the United States has been growing much faster than the overall U.S. economy, and much faster than the family income of most Americans, Americans can essentially no longer afford it. This is sadly ironic: Futuristic new technologies and drugs are being introduced constantly, while most Americans are falling backward into a state reminiscent of the distant past, when only the well-off could afford medical treatment. As a Commonwealth Fund report explained in 2015: "In an effort to reduce their own cost of providing health insurance, employers have increased the amount that workers contribute to their premiums and also to their health care, through higher deductibles and copayments. The result has been a rapid increase in employees' out-of-pocket costs for premiums for plans that provide less financial protection."

In the decade leading up to 2013, employer-sponsored insurance premiums rose three times faster than wages. Employees' premium contributions and deductibles doubled. As a result Americans are being asked to spend a much bigger part of their wages on health care than just a decade ago. The system that is meant to benefit consumers is strangling them, often to within inches of their lives.

Sadly, many Americans only discover this when they get sick.

In 2014 a forty-eight-year-old nurse from Austin, Texas, named Genny was diagnosed with stage III colon cancer. Her doctors immediately signed her up for a complicated course of treatment that ended up requiring her to be hospitalized for nearly two months. She underwent radiation and several surgeries, and after that twelve rounds of chemotherapy. The treatments were painful, and she endured long periods of excruciating discomfort. The threat of death hung over her and traumatized her husband and their young daughter. On top of all this was the nightmare of her health insurance.

When Genny discovered she was sick, she was insured through her husband's employer. The insurance company was a large corporation with a nationwide presence, the coverage had been good, and over the years the family had diligently monitored their health, getting their teeth cleaned every six months and taking their daughter for annual checkups, without ever experiencing any serious problems. Now, as Genny started her treatments, everything seemed fine at first. The couple paid out-of-pocket copays and other small charges, but the insurance plan covered most of the costs.

After Genny was discharged from her long hospitalization, and after her several surgeries, she needed follow-up care on an ongoing basis. She still had several open wounds that needed to heal, as well as a catheter and an intravenous line, and she was still suffering severe pain. Her husband had already taken time off to care for her, and had to get back to his out-of-town job. No one in her immediate family was available to help her manage all this either. So she contacted a home health-care agency, gave them her insurance information, and started receiving care. Three months later her insurance company informed her that while home care was generally covered, in this case the provider had failed to get a prior authorization, and the company was thus refusing to pay for it.

Around the same time Genny started her chemotherapy. Partway into the months-long treatment, Genny noticed something odd: The forms from her insurance company were now stating that she was responsible for fifteen thousand dollars for each round of chemo. Suddenly—without warning, it seemed— for the past several treatments Genny had been incurring bills from the oncology center that now totaled some sixty thousand dollars.

Stunned, Genny put two and two together. A month into the chemo, her husband's employer had decided to switch everyone to a different plan with the same insurance company. Genny and her husband had received a notification of the change from the employer, but because it was still the same insurance company, and their coverage had always been good, given everything else they were dealing with they hadn't gotten around to checking whether there had been any changes to the specific doctors in the new plan. As it turned out, the oncologist and infusion center Genny had already been using had been in-network on the old plan, but not on the new one. No one from the oncology center had pointed this out to her, and she hadn't figured it out herself until after she'd already incurred tens of thousands of dollars in fees.

Then Genny's husband was laid off. The couple was left with no income, and now faced losing medical insurance altogether. Her husband's employer had agreed to keep paying the premiums for another six months, but after that they'd be on their own.

When I spoke with Genny, almost a year after the initial diagnosis, she was nearing the end of her chemotherapy, and as far as her health went, I was glad to hear that things were looking up. Her husband had also gotten a new job, and it came with new health insurance, though from a different company. But Genny was still struggling to figure things out with the old insurance company. "Every time I see one of their envelopes in the mailbox my heart seizes," she told me.

By now she had received dozens of statements from the insurance company, filled with inexplicable codes and confusing charges. "Just to give you an idea," Genny told me, "every chemo treatment has fourteen or fifteen separate charges. They're all for the same dates of service but they're different charges that are covered differently. Frequently they'll assign duplicate claim numbers, or they'll assign different claim numbers for the same date of service." When Genny had the strength, she spent countless hours going through the paperwork, and more countless hours on the phone trying to deal with the astronomical charges that had piled up. She shared some of the paperwork with me, and just looking at it seemed enough to make my head explode.

To avoid any breaks in her care, Genny was now paying the

oncology center monthly installments, and charging thousands of dollars' worth of bills to her credit cards. A patient advocacy group was trying to help her reach some sort of agreement with the insurance company. She still had no idea how much she would owe in the end, and she avoided tallying up all the expenses because it was too devastating. "It's frustrating, it's scary," she said, "and it seems completely arbitrary what gets covered and what doesn't. Nobody knows how much anything costs, and none of it makes any sense. As if cancer and unemployment weren't enough."

Some time after I spoke with her, Genny received both good and bad news. In response to her appeals the insurance company had finally agreed to treat her provider as if it were in-network—for certain dates. That meant that at least part of her chemotherapy would be covered after all. But her home care still wouldn't be covered. While this freed Genny from some of the most outrageous bills, she remained exasperated by the whole ordeal—and no wonder! This sort of thing is not supposed to happen to people fortunate enough to be living a modern life in a wealthy nation.

The husband of a close friend of mine in Finland had also been battling colon cancer. His Finnish doctors in the public healthcare system did everything they could to save his life, including a series of complex surgeries, hospitalizations, and chemotherapy over the course of several years. They were blunt with him about his chances, which were not good, but they never stopped trying; at one point he even underwent brain surgery at the hands of Finland's top neurosurgeon, who is a legendary specialist with an international reputation. When needed, the municipality sent health aides to care for him at home, and toward the end of his life also paid for his care at a private nonprofit hospice. Even with all the care he received, his approaching death and the exhaustion of enduring the operations and chemotherapy were devastating to him, to his wife, and to his two young children.

In his case the family's finances were also a concern. Although my friend—his wife—works, he himself was able to work only intermittently after his diagnosis. After they did the math, however, they realized that they could still cobble together enough income from her earnings, his salary when he could work, and from the cash benefits the Finnish public system sent them to continue to afford the middle-class lifestyle they'd previously paid for with two incomes. Never once did they have to worry about being left with huge medical bills.

Instead they could focus their energy on cherishing every additional day that the treatments brought, and on loving each other while he was still alive.

The experience of Nordic health care suggests that there is actually no good reason the United States can't switch to a similar approach, and offer high-quality care for less cost. Universal public health care could begin in a variety of ways. The federal government or state governments could operate public insurance plans on the new health exchanges. Such "Medicare-for-all" plans could offer a transparent, fair benefit package to anyone who wanted to buy it, and as these plans grew in participation, they could negotiate better and better prices with providers. This idea is not new. In fact, a public option has been proposed in the United States many times, notably during the early stages of the Affordable Care Act. Several polls have indicated that a half or even a majority of Americans are in favor of creating just such an option.

Some states and counties are already taking matters into their own hands. Vermont, for example, has been preparing to move to a Canadian-style single-payer option. The most recent plan was to create publicly funded insurance that would offer coverage to all residents starting in 2017, but a few years before the deadline Vermont's governor announced he was abandoning the plan for the time being due to cost concerns. Bills to advance similar plans have been introduced in several states, including Massachusetts and Ohio. Some counties in California are continuing efforts to create public plans or expand the functions of existing ones. Having every state create its own system is messier and more complicated than having the federal government offer public health insurance for all, but in Canada, for example, public health insurance is arranged by the provinces. Similarly, a variety of efforts by American states could hasten change and serve as a laboratory for nationwide reform.

What else could the United States do in the short term? The fact that the United States still does not regulate the prices of most medical treatments and drugs, or consider their effectiveness when determining coverage, is starting to look like a major national embarrassment. Today many nations continue to base their health-care systems on private providers and private insurers, but they set rates just as they do for any other public utility—as they would for an electricity company, for example—or they negotiate fees and basic benefit packages with providers and insurers. In Europe, where prices are regulated, American pharmaceutical companies still happily sell products, clearly deeming that business to be worthwhile. Drug companies warn, of course, that if their profits in the United States were curtailed it would reduce their ability to innovate, but the research and development costs of major American drug companies are but a fraction of their vast profits. Drug companies spend much more on advertising than on product development. As it happens, the United States is also one of the few countries that allows advertising of prescription drugs directly to consumers. As Steven Brill noted in his exposé for *Time*, there is no reason Americans should be subsidizing these companies with higher prices than in the rest of the world.

There are many ways to change the current American system. President Obama asked Congress to let Medicare officials negotiate prices with drug manufacturers, an utterly sensible practice that is, astonishingly, forbidden by current law. Several states have considered bills that would require drug companies to report their costs and justify their prices to public agencies. With costs continuing to skyrocket, the United States actually has no choice but to catch up sooner or later with the rest of the advanced world on cost control, and these measures could be a start.

The benefits of bringing public health care and more regulated health care to America would likely be huge. For employers, universal coverage would level the playing field and make everyone more competitive, at home and abroad. Currently U.S. employers that offer their employees health insurance, like those that offer parental leaves, are at a disadvantage compared with those who don't. They're also at a disadvantage when competing with companies in other countries with public health care. Many American employers have already hinted that they'd be more than happy to drop the burden of providing health insurance and instead offer their employees higher wages, or support for purchasing their own health insurance. ObamaCare forced big employers to keep offering health insurance, whereas a public option would free both employers and employees from the absurdity of health care that's tied to employment.

For doctors a more unified public system with set prices and clearly defined benefit packages would make their work easier. They wouldn't have to spend time figuring out what their patients' different insurance arrangements cover or don't cover, and they could be relieved of much of the paperwork that results from dealing with a multitude of companies and plans. While Nordic doctors complain about having to deal with bureaucracy and not getting paid enough, I've never seen them work the kind of factory line that several of my American primary care physicians and dentists do. Nurses and dental hygienists do most of the work while the doctor or dentist pops his or her head into room after room for a few minutes each, keeping up the pace in order to pay all the administrative assistants needed to handle all the insurance claims.

For individual Americans public health care would bring tremendous improvements in freedom, autonomy, and independence—freedom from employers, freedom from unhealthy dependencies within families, and freedom from countless hours spent arranging health care and figuring out how to pay for it. In a nation that purports to champion freedom, the outdated disaster that is the U.S. health-care system is taking that freedom away. But that's not all. There's another casualty of this system: community.

During a Republican presidential debate in 2011, Representative Ron Paul, a physician as well as a famous libertarian who at the time was running for president, was asked who should foot the bill if a healthy thirty-year-old man with a good job had chosen not to buy health insurance but had suddenly gone into a coma and required six months of intensive care. "That's what freedom is all about," Paul responded, "taking your own risks." The host of the debate, CNN's Wolf Blitzer, sought clarification: Should society really just let the man die? This time it was members of the audience who responded for Paul, shouting out an enthusiastic "Yeah!"

When I first heard about Paul's audience's "just let him die" approach I was outraged. How could any civilized human being think that way? A few years later I understood how. After I had been paying for insurance for a few years while constantly teetering on the brink of personal financial insecurity, I happened upon an article about a self-employed man who could have afforded to pay for health insurance but hadn't, only to find himself later suffering from advanced prostate cancer; ironically, the cancer had not been detected earlier because he had avoided doctors for fear of the costs. He confessed in the article that he had been an idiot, and expressed profound gratitude for the hospital that treated him and forgave most of his bills, which had already reached half a million dollars.

Just like that, I found myself empathizing with Ron Paul's audience. Unpaid medical bills fall either on taxpayers, as government money flows in to subsidize hospitals that provide charity care, or they fall on other individuals, when hospitals raise their prices to cover their losses, and when insurance companies raise their premiums to cover those higher prices. That man had made his choice. Why should I have to bail him out? In Finland I had never felt that way. The current system in the United States, even though we may not notice it, isn't just bad in terms of getting health care; it also literally tears apart the social fabric of the nation.

A health-care system funded through progressive income taxes ensures that everyone contributes according to ability. It also makes health-care decisions part of the nation's democracy and gives people ownership of the system. If the government were to raise taxes significantly to pay for health-care costs without improving care, people would be up in arms. But if a private insurance company raises its prices dramatically every year, people grumble but mostly can do nothing about it. And in America it happens all the time.

As I interviewed Nordic citizens about their health care, I was struck by how understanding they were of the need to keep costs at bay and to offer care to the neediest cases. Since they felt they were paying for a system that aims to treat patients fairly, they seemed to embrace the need to be responsible in their own demands as well. In the United States the prevailing feeling seems quite the opposite: that insurance companies are the enemies of common people, and thus should be squeezed out of every penny possible. One health-care researcher described a focus group of ordinary Americans in her study as having an "almost vengeful" attitude toward insurance companies, and a clear determination to go for the most expensive care that their insurance would pay for. If you feel the system is treating you unfairly, you feel no need to be fair in return.

It is difficult for Americans to realize what they're missing. Europeans can feel enormously proud of and even patriotic about their health-care systems because they pay for them with their taxes, and they genuinely feel that the system has been created by them and for them. If the system is not working, they are fierce in their criticism and their demands for change. Success in creating an excellent public health-care system is on a par with any other great national achievement, whether winning Olympic gold medals or landing a man on the moon. Such pride is within reach—especially since public health care actually seems to be what a majority of Americans, particularly the younger generations, want for themselves. According to the Pew Research Center, more than half of millennials believe it is the federal government's responsibility to make sure all Americans have health coverage. There is no reason a country as great as the United States cannot achieve this. Even Burkina Faso has since passed a tentative law on univeral health coverage.

These differences between nations remind me of an Internet meme that made fun of the premise of the hugely popular American TV show *Breaking Bad*. The story begins when the main character, a high school chemistry teacher named Walter White, discovers that he has cancer, but that his insurance won't pay for his treatment. Needing one hundred thousand dollars for his care, Walt hatches a plan to make money—by cooking crystal meth. The joke making the rounds online depicted how the TV show would go in a country with universal health care. Walt and his Canadian doctor are pictured as the doctor delivers the news:

"You have cancer. Treatment starts next week."

The end.

SIX

OF US, BY US, AND FOR US

GO AHEAD:
ASK WHAT YOUR COUNTRY
CAN DO FOR YOU

WELFARE OR WELL-BEING?

Before I arrived in the United States I had never heard of "big government." I know—someone from one of those "socialist" European countries where government arranges everything from child care to education to health care who doesn't know what big government is?! But it gets even weirder. I'd also never heard of the "welfare state," a term that makes most Americans recoil in horror. A welfare state, I learned, is in the business of producing "welfare queens," people who survive in a state of unhealthy dependency, living off other people's work and never bothering to do any themselves. According to Mitt Romney, who was caught on camera in an unguarded moment during the 2012 presidential campaign, the portion of the American population that apparently fit this description was a staggering 47 percent. Another symbol of all this deprivation often seemed to be food stamps. During the Republican presidential primary, Newt Gingrich was apparently only expressing a commonly held view when he offered to speak to an African American association on the theme: Demand paychecks, not food stamps.

Romney, meanwhile, took the idea a little further in a critique of President Obama that seemed to question whether Obama was truly American. The United States, Romney said during one of the primary debates, had a president who "wants us to turn into a European-style welfare state and have government take from some to give to others." Romney went on: "That will kill the ability of America to provide for a prosperous future, to secure our freedom, and to give us the rights which have been in our Declaration of Independence and our Constitution. I believe in an America that's based upon opportunity and freedom, not President Obama's social welfare state." Such comments were mystifying to me, and only after a while did I begin to understand that in the United States the term "welfare" refers to the idea of being *on* welfare—in other words, being poor, without a job, and becoming a burden to society.

By comparison, in my own language of Finnish—which, let me warn you, is a crazy-looking language when it's written down—the closest thing we have to the term "welfare state" would be the term *hyvinvointivaltio*. Literally, however, this term means "well-*being* state." To be on welfare would be expressed with entirely different words, such as to "get support for getting by" (more fun in Finnish: this would be written as *saada toimeentulotukea*). In 2013 the proportion of the Finnish population that received this benefit of last resort was only 7 percent. The programs are not entirely comparable, but by contrast, in 2013 the proportion of Americans who received some form of food stamps was more than double this, at 15 percent. In Finland, meanwhile, a larger share of the working-age population was actually employed than in the United States. On the basis of these percentages, it's a bit difficult to tell which country here is actually the "welfare state."

For a Nordic citizen, then, what we call a well-being state doesn't bring to mind things like getting free money without working. Our well-being state is there to make sure that citizens, all citizens, have equal opportunities for well-being—to pursue happiness, enjoy freedom, and achieve success. An overwhelmingly positive reference, it is not something that is handed down by "big government." It is something that we attain for ourselves through our own efforts—and through paying our taxes.

Talk of taxes, of course, immediately strikes terror in the hearts of most Americans, because European tax rates are supposed to be so much higher than in the United States, especially in the Nordic countries. Let's look at that. During the last year that I lived in Finland and worked a regular full-time job, as a magazine editor, I made the equivalent of $67,130—well above the median Finnish salary. After some standard deductions my taxable income was $61,990. So how much did I pay in taxes? The figure came to $18,973 in national and municipal taxes, or 30.6 percent.

Before drawing a conclusion about that figure, keep in mind that I didn't have much else to pay beyond that. For example, property taxes in Finland have a much smaller impact than in the United States. Here are some of the things that paying my Finnish taxes bought me: smoothly functioning and comprehensive health insurance, a full year of partially paid disability leave, nearly a full year of paid parental leave for each child and a smaller monthly benefit for an additional two years (should I or the father of my child choose to stay at home longer with our child), affordable high-quality day care, one of the world's best K–12 education systems, free college, and free graduate school. My taxes in Finland were not used to hand out money to some lazy moochers living on welfare; instead they were used to pay for high-quality services for *me*. As far as I was concerned, it was a bargain.

And here's the secret of this system: This is the bargain that everyone in a Nordic country gets, so the system is clearly in everyone's self-interest. Unlike in some bogeyman welfare state, participation in a well-being state does not require you to bow in submission before the altar of altruism, sacrificing your own advancement to help the unlucky. It supports your own personal freedom, your own autonomy, and each individual's ability to determine his or her own fate, since we don't need to depend on the financial largesse of parents, spouses, or employers for the fundamental services—health care, education, and aid during times of crisis—that each of us requires to fulfill our potential. On top of that there's a less tangible benefit: the pride and satis-faction of participating in a society that truly enables equality of opportunity for all.

While Americans tend to see their government and the ser-vices it provides as something separate from them, and often opposed to them, Nordic people see the government and its ser-vices as their own creation. The well-being state is from each of us, to each of us, for each of us, and by each of us. Even though Finns constantly debate how the well-being state can work best, people stick with it because they can see that on the whole, they come out ahead—not just as a group but also as individuals. People who are well off join the pact not out of unselfish desire to help those who are less fortunate, but out of a desire to make life even better for themselves and their immediate friends, col-leagues, and families.

From a Nordic perspective, citizens of the United States have actually made similar choices, particularly about how to maintain aspects of a social safety net, yet many Americans seem unaware of having signed on for them.

In early 2012 the *New York Times* investigated a mysterious phenomenon. In U.S. states where citizens were clearly benefiting from government programs, voters supported Republican candidates who, for the most part, promised to reduce government spending. One might conclude that it was the wealthy residents of those states who were opposed to government spending, precisely because they didn't want to support freeloaders. But in fact it was the very people whose lives were being improved by government spending who were voting to remove it.

When the reporters interviewed low-income residents of Chisago County in Minnesota, many interviewees said they were angry. Why? Because the government was wasting money and giving it to people who didn't deserve it. Even though these were many of the same people who were actually getting the money through programs such as Medicare, Social Security, and free school lunches for their children. They seemed to resent their own dependence on government, yet didn't know how they could get by without it.

What is the real problem for the residents of Chisago? Americans have the idea that government benefits are only for the poor and the lazy, even though the reality has changed dramatically. Back in 1979, more than half of all government benefits—54 percent—were going to households in the bottom 20 percent of the income scale. By 2007, however, that share had declined to 34 percent. Today the people whom the American government is helping the most are members of the middle class.

Why does the American middle class need so much help?

Over the same twenty-eight years, the after-tax income of the highest-earning 1 percent of Americans grew 275 percent. The same figure for the middle class was only 37 percent. For the bottom 20 gains were even scantier at 18 percent. It is no wonder that many hardworking Americans can no longer make ends meet. What's worse, however, is that despite this entrenched inequality, middle-class Americans, working people, and the poor are still told that America is an equal-opportunity society. As a result they are made to feel guilty that they need government involvement to stay afloat.

In the self-portrait that America paints, society is perceived as fair and just, and a failure to make it on your own is shameful, but in reality the cards are stacked against the poor and the middle class. The result is a system everyone hates. A lot of money is spent supporting the middle class, but the stigma associated with that support makes it hard to appreciate, or even acknowledge, what's being provided. Instead people understandably resent the system and the support, because society makes you feel ashamed about it. The only way out is to vote against it, even though that ends up being a vote against policies that have actually been helping the person who's casting the vote.

To make matters worse, Americans have perfected the questionable art of what Suzanne Mettler, a professor at Cornell University, calls "the submerged state"—making government policies invisible by administering them through private companies, or through the tax code, instead of just sending recipients government checks. In reality tax deductions, credits, and exemptions are government support for specific groups of people, in the form of tax dollars not collected, just as cash benefits are. However, many people don't perceive or acknowledge that reality, and wrongly assume that they're not benefiting from the government at all, even when they are. Taxes in America are extraordinarily and unusually complicated, and very few people are capable of truly understanding them and grasping how much each break has helped them in real dollars—not to mention that many Americans pay professionals to file their taxes, putting even more space between them and the details of the accounting.

These perception problems are exacerbated by the fact that people tend to consider taxes as money taken from them, and tax breaks as a rightful, if inadequate, correction of the situation. Cash benefits, by contrast, are seen as money received. There is no difference in reality, but the difference in perception is enormous. Consider an example from Finland: When the Finnish government sends every single Finnish family in the country a payment of more than a hundred dollars every month for each child, the families are clearly aware of the support they are receiving. But when the United States offers families with children the Earned Income Tax Credit—if they qualify—or the Child and Dependent Care Tax Credit, many recipients fail to understand that they are receiving a direct cash benefit from the government.

This sort of misunderstanding is pervasive in America. In a study Suzanne Mettler asked 1,400 Americans whether they had used a government social program. Fifty-seven percent said they had not. Then she asked if they had used one of twenty-one specific federal policies, including child-care tax credits, the Earned Income Tax Credit, employer-sponsored and thus tax-exempted health insurance, Medicare, Social Security, unemployment insurance, mortgage-interest deductions, and student loans. It turned out that 96 percent of those who had denied using government programs had in fact used at least one, and the average responder had used four. This clear disconnect between Americans' perception of who benefits from government programs and the reality makes it easier to keep demonizing the "welfare state."

In the Nordic countries, citizens know much more clearly what it is they are paying their taxes for. That translates into a clearer notion of why they have a government in the first place, and what the government's job is. In Finland when I went to the doctor at a public health-care center, I never felt I was receiving a benefit from the government that I hadn't earned. On the contrary, I had paid for it in the course of filing my taxes, and I also knew that if I became seriously ill, I would have earned the right to be treated by the system at virtually no additional cost to me, because my taxes had chipped in to help pay for the care of others. It was the very universality of the public health-insurance program that made it so fair and so positive for me. In other areas of life as well, Nordic policies are designed and executed for the explicit universal goal of creating a society of well-being for everyone. I have never felt ashamed about participating in a system that so clearly creates equity—and, crucially, that so clearly lets people succeed on their own merits as a result.

This makes the American critique of the supposed horrors of the European model strange. From a Nordic point of view, it's the current American approach that creates relationships of dependency. In Finland the goal is not to subsidize certain people or groups, but to equalize the basic support structure across the broad expanse of society. By comparison, many of the most visible American programs as they exist today look surprisingly targeted, selective, and, in many cases, stigmatizing—Medicare for the elderly, for example, or food stamps, school lunches, and Medicaid for the poor (now including many in the former middle class). Meanwhile childless young people and the reasonably well-off get few advantages out of the bargain at all, and when they do, they fail to see it. And then the very rich get tons of advantages—namely all the loopholes the tax code provides them to avoid paying taxes.

Contrary to American criticisms, the Nordic approach has also turned out to be good not only for most citizens, but for the entire economy.

Typically, American commentators and politicians dismiss the European approach as a whole by arguing that European nations are headed straight for bankruptcy. I want to address this criticism, but to do so I need to get a little bit technical for a few pages.

To be sure, the recent eurozone crisis that crippled the economies of Greece, Portugal, Spain, and other countries was devastating, and many European governments are certainly going to have to rethink their generosity to certain sectors of society—as well as the culture of tax evasion in some of their countries. Yet the three Scandinavian nations—Denmark, Sweden, and Norway (none of which are members of the eurozone)—came through both the global financial crisis and the European crisis in better shape than many of their peers. Iceland has had its troubles, but those were not created by bloated government benefits; the problems were caused by a lack of oversight for Iceland's privatized, deregulated, and—as it turned out—irresponsible banks, as well as mistakes in monetary policy. Apart from Iceland, none of the Nordic countries was felled by the global banking crisis.

Nordic economies go through cycles like all countries, and they make mistakes like everyone else. In the 1980s and 1990s they suffered debilitating recessions, thanks largely to blunders in the deregulation of financial markets. In Finland's case the collapse of the Soviet Union next door was also a factor. Later, as the euro crisis dragged on, Finland, which is a member of the eurozone, felt its effects.

On the whole, however, in the midst of the global financial crisis and a European meltdown, the Nordic region actually remained a haven of economic dynamism, freedom, and stability. With its strong foundation of basic services, the region has continued to generate highly educated workers, technologically advanced companies, and low barriers to trade, leaving the marketplace freer to focus on business. In international rankings of economic competitiveness or freedom, the Nordic countries remain consistently among the best, and even ahead of the United States.

To the extent that Finland has experienced financial troubles in recent years, have they been the result of too much government spending? Not at all. Rather, reports by international organizations have cited other reasons: weak demand for exports, Finland's aging population, loss of market share in the technology industry (the fall of the cell-phone giant Nokia), problems in Finland's forestry sector, and a relatively rigid labor market. In addition, some of Finland's recent economic challenges have been the result of something else entirely: Finland taking a "hit for the team," which is to say for all other Western capitalist democracies, in a standoff against Russia. The United States and other Western nations had imposed economic sanctions against Russia, to put pressure on Vladimir Putin. Simply because Finland happens to be next door, Russia was Finland's largest trading partner. Finland's economy suffered as a result of these sanctions. In addition, there's the more generic problem of the euro, the common European currency that, for better or worse, Finland adopted in 1999. American economists and experts have pointed out that despite doing everything right in putting its own financial house in order, Finland has suffered economic woes simply because, as a eurozone member, it's not able to devalue its currency. For sure, Finnish industry needs to revive itself, but the euro has made recovery that much harder.

As Finnish companies laid off workers and Finland's finances looked increasingly gloomy, the international praise heaped upon Finland only a few years earlier did, admittedly, start to look excessive. Finns themselves debated furiously how to get back to growth. This debate reflected a discussion under way all over the world: austerity or stimulus? Overall, Finns were veering toward austerity and cuts to some benefits, whose results remain to be seen. Yet these particular economic wobbles were not actually indicators that the Nordic model itself was in trouble—as shown by the economic health of the other Nordic countries, not in the eurozone and with different industrial structures.

Americans tend to assume that the Nordic nations are living beyond their means, but that's not the case either. Nordic governments are generally much better at balancing their budgets than is the United States. In 2014 the American government had accumulated a debt of more than 100 percent of GDP. Finland owed 70 percent, Denmark 60, Sweden 50, and Norway a little over 30 percent of GDP. In 2013 the OECD average was 109 percent. Over the past decade all the largest Nordic countries have been running regular budget surpluses. By contrast the United States has often accrued one of the largest deficits in the OECD.

The long-term financial health of the Nordic countries is also, in the end, a function of the Nordic theory of love. Faced with economic downturns or other problems, the Nordic countries have been willing to reform and cut their social programs, but they have always done so without abandoning the ultimate goal of supporting individual autonomy and equality of opportunity. By unburdening employers and workers of financial obligations to one another for things that aren't directly related to business—health care being the most obvious one—workers are better protected from the risks that accompany economic change, and companies are freer to operate. Preserving the freedom and independence of individuals this way has proved to be a good recipe for free-market dynamism. It's made workers flexible and productive.

In addition there's a surprisingly unsocialist aspect to many Nordic social benefits: They actually increase the incentive to work hard. This is because the generosity of many benefits is tied to an individual's income. This applies to benefits during periods of illness and unemployment, as well as to paid parental leaves and, as you'd expect, retirement benefits. The more you earn, the more you'll get while off the job. There are reasonable limits, of course, but the basic structure of the system provides a powerful motivation to work hard while you can, so that you can keep living reasonably comfortably even when you cannot. This is another reason why even well-off citizens in the Nordic countries tend to like the system: It benefits them, too.

Finally, one additional criticism is frequently used to slam the Nordic approach: Sure, it's easy for Nordic countries to give their citizens health care or education, since they are such rich countries with abundant natural resources and large GDPs. This misconception is mostly based on the unique situation of Norway today, which recently became awash in valuable oil and gas reserves. Finland, by contrast, has no significant natural resources apart from its forests and some metals. For the most part the people of the Nordic countries have acquired the wealth they possess today by working for it. They were not rich when they started building their well-being states—even Norway's oil was not discovered until the late 1960s.

In other words the Nordic middle class is not getting a free ride. Nordic citizens themselves pay for the services they get. Apart from Norway's oil and gas, there are no pots of gold showering Nordic citizens with unearned wealth, and neither are there evil communists robbing the rich of their due. The Nordic countries demonstrate that building strong public services can create economic growth, and that pooling the risks everyone faces in life—sickness, unemployment, old age, the need to be educated to secure a decent living—into one system funded by everyone is more efficient, and more effective, than each person saving individually to ensure security and survive misfortune, especially in today's age of global economic uncertainty and competition.

There is another way of saying this. Americans are right that big government isn't the best way to solve problems. The secret of Nordic success is not big government. It's smart government. And as many Americans themselves are already well aware, less big government, and more smart government, is something the United States desperately needs.

SMALLER AND SMARTER

After spending some time in America, I could well understand why many Americans hate anything to do with government. The post office is a disaster, the tax code is a mess, Amtrak trains rarely run on time, the roads are full of potholes, and the DMV is a nightmare. As Ronald Reagan famously quipped: "The nine most terrifying words in the English language are: 'I'm from the government, and I'm here to help.'"

The poor performance of American government services is just as shocking to anyone from a Nordic country as it is to Americans themselves. I watched, bewildered, along with the rest of the world, as the U.S. Congress failed to agree on funding for government operations back in 2013, and chose instead to shut down the entire federal government for more than two weeks, furloughing some eight hundred thousand workers. Soon after this debacle, I saw a survey indicating that Americans had a higher opinion of root canals, head lice, colonoscopies, and cockroaches than of Congress, and frankly, I'd begun to understand why.

For many Americans the solution is obvious: Get rid of as much of the government as possible. Americans draw on powerful political traditions when they argue that government just creates more problems than it solves. What do we actually need a government for, anyway?

Close to four hundred years ago the English philosopher Thomas Hobbes had one kind of answer to that question. Human beings are naturally in perpetual war against one another, Hobbes wrote in his famous book *Leviathan*, so therefore an autocratic ruler and a powerful state—a state as terrifying as the biblical monster known as Leviathan—were necessary simply to keep people safe by instituting law and order. Soon after Hobbes, however, the French philosopher Jean-Jacques Rousseau pointed out that while, yes, people had to give up some of their freedoms in exchange for law and order, that didn't mean they had to obey a ruler; people themselves could formulate the laws. Influenced by such ideas, America's Founding Fathers decreed the United States a democratic republic, a "government of the people, by the people, for the people," as Abraham Lincoln would later so eloquently put it.

So it was that in the late 1700s the United States arrived at a cutting-edge notion of what government was for, and what it should do. While the European nations continued to be governed by sovereigns who could be imperious and dictatorial, the brand-new United States of America was the most democratic and egalitarian country on earth—with one huge caveat, of course, which was the institution of slavery. Still, the United States became the leader in a worldwide democratic revolution that slowly overturned old governmental structures. In the 1800s, another philosopher inspired the United States even further, the British thinker John Stuart Mill. In his book *On Liberty*, Mill argued that as long as people have freedom of speech and trade, as well as freedom from other state interference, they can fail or succeed on their own merits. In the 1830s the Frenchman Alexis de Tocqueville glowingly described the U.S. contribution to modernizing government in his classic book *Democracy in America*. While many of the ideas of democracy came from Europe—home of ancient Greece as well as the Enlightenment and the French Revolution—the United States was the first modern nation to really put those ideas into practice. Today citizens throughout the world owe the United States an enormous debt for this enduring legacy of democratic self-rule and limited government.

Now that we are well into the twenty-first century, one might ask whether some new ideas about government are worth considering. Recently two members of the staff of the British magazine *The Economist*—a publication that has long advocated free-market policies and been a fan of the United States—

tackled the challenge of rethinking government today in a book called *The Fourth Revolution: The Global Race to Reinvent the State*. In it John Micklethwait and Adrian Wooldridge ponder, among other things, the work of that nineteenth-century British philosopher who has so inspired the United States, John Stuart Mill. Today Mill's ideas about freedom from state interference remain an inspiration for many Americans who want to dismantle as many government services as possible.

The irony, however, is that Mill himself realized later in life that his early ideas were faulty. Mill's reasons for changing his mind, based on his observations of the inequalities and social problems around him in Britain, are summarized by Micklethwait and Wooldridge as follows: "How could you judge each individual on his merits when dunces went to Eton and geniuses were sent up chimneys? How could individuals achieve their full potential unless society played a role in providing them with a good start in life?" And: "Wasn't a state that denied a poor man a decent education also restraining his potential happiness and freedom?" For Micklethwait and Wooldridge, the way Mill's own ideas evolved is representative of the debate between people who see certain government functions as an obstacle to liberty, and those who see certain government functions as essential to creating the basic foundation for liberty. Mill himself actually turned toward the latter view, as would the Nordic nations later.

Another favorite thinker in the United States when it comes to the role of government is the Scottish philosopher Adam Smith. Famously, Smith argued that if everyone acts in his or her own self-interest, resources will be divided optimally for everyone's benefit, as if guided by an "invisible hand." Today Smith's theory also remains beloved by those in the United States who argue that government services should be shuttered in favor of the superior workings of the free market.

The problem with Smith, though, is similar to the one with Mill. Smith devised his theory in the 1700s, but as time has progressed, many observers and societies have discovered that the "invisible hand" suffers from a substantial technical difficulty—it doesn't actually work the way Smith predicted. For example, as Micklethwait and Wooldridge remind us, the brutal era of industrialization demonstrated that to keep a free-market economy progressing smoothly—indeed, so that capitalists themselves could keep making money—factory workers needed protections, diseases needed a cure, and children needed an education. More and more nations turned away from oversimplistic interpretations of Smith's theory, and instead toward those that proposed that the state could be more of a referee and benefactor, helping to ensure progress. This idea has turned out to be a much better match for the complexities and challenges of the rapidly changing modern world.

Britain, the home of both Mill and Smith, has actually been one of the leading nations in the turn toward a more nuanced approach to governing in the modern age. At the beginning of the twentieth century Beatrice Webb, the daughter of a British businessman, became one of the founders of the now-famous London School of Economics, going on to write a landmark report for the British government. In order for Britain to succeed better as a society, Webb advocated a new idea: A state must secure a "national minimum of civilized life," including food and education for the young, care for the sick, income for the disabled and elderly, and living wages for workers. This idea would become a key element in Nordic thinking. (William Beveridge, who gave his name to the health-care model used in Britain and subsequently in the Nordic countries, was part of Webb's group.)

The United States began to progress along similar lines as

well. The so-called Gilded Age of the nineteenth century had created such gaping inequality and vast injustice that government clearly had to do something to prevent America from slipping back into the Dark Ages of aristocratic autocracy—which, after all, the American War of Independence had been fought to escape. Franklin D. Roosevelt's New Deal regulated financial markets, set maximum work hours and minimum wages, financed public construction projects, and set up programs like food aid to help the unemployed. (Later Lyndon B. Johnson's Great Society and the War on Poverty would advance the government's role in such key areas as education and some aspects of health care.)

However, as the twentieth century progressed, some governments in the West ran amok: Germany ended up with the Third Reich and Hitler; in the Soviet Union the excesses of Communism were an utter and unmitigated disaster. Even the United States, and to some extent Britain as well, went astray. The American government just kept getting bigger and bigger, and while some of its projects were successful—Social Security, to name one—many were too sprawling, too unwieldy, and involved micromanaging too many different projects in too many areas of life for too many targeted groups—all without the beneficial effects of increasing equality of opportunity. "Put simply," Micklethwait and Wooldridge say, "big government overextended itself." It's no wonder that when Ronald Reagan and Margaret Thatcher came along in the 1980s, promising to get rid of as much government as possible, they captured the imagination of many of their citizens. Ever since then "big government" has been a derogatory term in the American lexicon, and with good reason.

The trouble is, many Americans have come to believe there is no middle ground—no role for government services that might be "smart" rather than "big." Government, in whatever form, has come to be seen as the enemy. In one recent poll a third of Americans even believed that an armed rebellion might be necessary to protect their liberties from government intrusion in the near future.

So maybe it's no surprise that Americans don't take kindly to the government asking them for money.

PAYING THE DUES

When the U.S. presidential primary campaign began in 2011, I found myself cheering on one of the Republican contenders: the famously antigovernment former governor of Texas, Rick Perry, as he waved his proposal in the air to create a fantastically simple, postcard-size income tax form. I also wanted to tell him: That's Finland for you! As unbelievable as it may sound to an American, every year that I have to fill out my absurdly complex U.S. tax forms, I feel profoundly nostalgic about paying my Finnish taxes.

My tax form had been one page long, and came prefilled with my earnings and taxes paid, including the calculations for amounts owed or refunded. My job was simply to check that everything was correct and amend it if needed. During my years as a salaried employee, I mostly just looked it over and did nothing. As a freelancer I had to add my expenses and send the form back, but even then the process was incredibly simple. All individuals were taxed separately, regardless of their marital status, and shared deductions were split between spouses.

More surprisingly, having heard my entire life how much higher European taxes are than American taxes, I was stunned how high my total American tax rate turned out to be after paying federal, state, city, Social Security, and Medicare taxes. Not all Americans pay city taxes, of course, and some don't pay state taxes, but a great many do pay substantial property taxes, which in Finland are a small fraction of what they are in the United States. At the end of my second year of trying to build a business for myself as a freelance journalist in New York City, in 2011, my income after expenses had come to a not terribly impressive $33,900. Once I had all my financial figures for the year, I sat down and did the math. It turned out that I would owe more in taxes in New York than in Finland, while getting significantly less in return. In Finland, even as a freelancer, as I've noted, my taxes bought me hugely valuable benefits such as paid sick days and, if I had a child, maternity leave payments and affordable day care. Not to mention that for self-employed entrepreneurs, a Nordic country offers a far better deal for another reason—after I'd paid all my taxes in the United States, I still had to spend many thousands more buying my own health insurance. In Finland basic health care would already have been included in the taxes I'd paid.

Of course, someone with a different income stream (and better accountants!) might be in a different situation. The 2012 presidential campaign brought the quirks of the American tax code into focus when it was revealed that Mitt Romney and his wife, Ann, made $21.7 million in 2010 but paid a federal tax rate of only 14 percent, a rate more typical of households earning $80,000 a year. The Obamas, by contrast, paid about 26 percent on income of $1.7 million. These calculations don't include state or local taxes, but the Romneys' rate was low because much of their income came from investments, which are taxed at a lower rate than wages.

As with health-care systems, it's staggeringly complex to try to compare tax systems between countries, and between different people in different life situations within countries. Some countries tax wages heavily but levy almost no payroll taxes like the Social Security and Medicare taxes levied in the United States. Others do exactly the opposite. Some have one income tax rate for everyone—a "flat tax"—while others have progressive rates. Some focus on taxing wages, while others tax consumption or ownership. Some have only one national tax, while others add local taxes on top of that. Almost all countries tax families with children at lower rates than they do single people. Because of this variety, tax comparisons between countries and people are often incompatible, confusing, and even intentionally misleading.

For example, Americans often assume that ordinary Nordic citizens pay something like 70 percent of all their income in taxes. That is not true. Yes, Sweden's top marginal tax rate was at that level back in the 1980s, but those rates have fallen significantly since then, and they never applied to anyone's total income, only to income above a certain high threshold. However, simply comparing tax rates tells you virtually nothing without also comparing what a person gets in return for those taxes. A family in Country X might pay 40 percent in taxes, while a family in Country Y might pay only 25 percent. But if the family in Country Y has to spend another 25 percent of its income to pay for health insurance and school tuition, and the family in Country X does not, then the family in Country X obviously comes out way ahead, assuming that the quality of the services is the same.

So what income tax rates are people actually paying in different Nordic countries? The OECD has compared average tax rates for a single individual without children in thirty-four developed countries, including federal and local income taxes, along with an employee's social security contributions. In 2014

Denmark had the third-highest average tax rate at 38.4 percent, but this was still lower than in Belgium and Germany. Finland came in ninth, at 30.7 percent, and—here's a shocker—Sweden fell under the OECD average with a rate of 24.4 percent—less than the United States, which came in at 24.8 percent. It may seem hard to believe, considering how much more Nordic citizens get in exchange for their taxes, but average Finns pay income taxes and employee contributions at a rate only about 6 percentage points higher than the rate paid by average Americans, while average Swedes pay less than average Americans.

Overall the Nordic countries do collect more tax revenue in relation to GDP than does the United States. In Finland, Norway, and Sweden employers are required to contribute more to their employees' social security on top of their wages and employees' own contributions than in the United States. And it will come as no surprise that the Nordic countries tax the wealthy more than does the United States. The Nordic countries also tend to levy higher taxes on consumables such as food, gas, and electronics; this is partly related to a Nordic philosophy of using the tax code to achieve smart social goals by taxing practices or products that harm the environment or people's health, such as gas-guzzling cars and alcohol.

Once again, all this talk of tax rates is mostly meaningless unless we spell out what people get in return for their money. The very high-quality and reliable services that Nordic citizens get in return for their taxes—including: universal public health care, affordable day care, universal free education, generous sick pay, year-long paid parental leaves, pensions, and the like—can easily incur additional tens of thousands, if not hundreds of thousands, of dollars in after-tax expenses for Americans. Bottom line: For middle-class people, the amount of disposable income you end up with in the United States versus in a Nordic country can be very similar in the end, or even turn out to be a better deal in a Nordic country.

"I think I had a little bit more disposable income left after income and payroll taxes in the U.S., but our American property tax was a killer," said Ville, the Finnish father of two who used to live in Westchester, New York, but has since moved back to Finland. "And in the U.S. I should have saved for retirement, which I don't do in Finland because of the public retirement funds. After all that, I think I have more disposable income in Finland than in the U.S. If you add gas and food bills, it comes to about the same, since those are more expensive here. But then in the U.S. we paid a lot more for day care."

Keep in mind, though, how these calculations would change when Ville's two kids reach college age. When considering today's American college tuitions, the Nordic deal starts to look especially good. Overall the deal looks so good that many Nordic citizens living in the United States return to their home countries once they have children. Life is simply easier and cheaper for them back home.

The gap between Nordic and American attitudes toward taxes doesn't stem only from differences in how those taxes are used. It is also a question of fairness. The American tax code perversely favors the wealthy, a trend that makes absolutely no sense whatsoever for any nation trying to remain competitive in the twenty-first century, and a trend that has actually gotten worse and worse over the past few decades. The issue here isn't whether people should be allowed to get rich; of course they should. The issue, rather, is that in America people who have *much more* security than others are contributing proportionately *much less* of their income to the maintenance of the basic needs shared by everyone in society. In the Nordic countries it's a no-brainer that the rich are expected to contribute proportionately more. Top marginal income tax rates in the Nordic countries, including national and local taxes and employees' social security contributions, hover around 50 percent. Again, these rates apply only to income above a certain threshold, which in 2014 varied from the equivalent of about $63,000 in Denmark to about $115,000 in Finland—per individual. In the United States the top rate was somewhat lower than in most Nordic countries—although it was actually higher than in Norway and Iceland—and it applied only to income over some $400,000.

To an American ear these figures may start to sound scary, but let's pause to note whom exactly such tax policies would actually affect. It's pretty safe to say that around 95 percent of all Americans would not be affected if the United States had Finland's top marginal tax rate rules. Based on 2011 data, 96 percent of American individuals had income of less than $109,000, according to calculations by the Tax Policy Center.

A majority of Americans actually seem to agree with these Nordic attitudes. Many surveys have been conducted in which Americans say that taxes on the wealthy should be raised. And yet that hasn't happened; in fact the reverse has. "The effective tax rate for the wealthiest in this country—the rate actually paid after factoring in exclusions, deductions, credits, and other preferential treatment—has fallen dramatically," stated the Senate Budget Committee chairman Kent Conrad in 2012. "In fact, the effective tax rate for the 400 wealthiest taxpayers fell from almost 30 percent in 1985 to 18.1 percent in 2008."

It has gotten to the point today where even many wealthy Americans themselves agree with Conrad and are trying to figure out how to pay more. Such luminaries as the billionaire investor Warren Buffett and the novelist Stephen King have been writing op-eds telling the government to start taxing them at higher rates. If everyone in the country was getting the same low rates, that would be one thing. But that's not the case. President Obama has noted that both his and Warren Buffett's tax rates are lower than those of their secretaries.

The Nordic nations are living proof that even with higher taxes on the wealthy and on certain consumables, a country can remain competitive, rich, and happy. The dynamism and wealth of Nordic societies in fact give the lie to the argument so often heard in American political debates that higher taxes, especially on the rich, would discourage entrepreneurial activity, innovation, and the growth of businesses. What most motivates people is actually their relative wealth compared with others, not their absolute wealth, and other factors such as their status, sense of accomplishment, and relative quality of life. As there would be in any country, Finland has citizens who hate the tax system and try to avoid it, but on the whole, people in the Nordic countries see their system as being more or less fair. They get real value in return for their money—even the well-off do—and they can still pursue an income higher than their neighbor if they want to. There is no good reason why tax reform in the United States could not lead to similar results. All one needs to do is pair it with smart government.

GOOD-BYE TO "BIG GOVERNMENT"

If you had to boil down the difference between the United States and the Nordic countries to a simple phrase, one way to say it might be: The United States has an unfair tax system and big government, while the Nordic countries have a fair tax system and smart government. Another way to describe the difference is that the United States is stuck in the past and the Nordic countries are already living in the future. This is how John Micklethwait and Adrian Wooldridge of *The Economist* frame the conversation. They begin the final section of their book with a chapter titled "The Place Where the Future Happened First." They make no bones about it. It's clear to them that the place where the future has happened first is the Nordic countries, and it's in every nation's interest today to try to borrow the best from their example.

One of the reasons the Nordic countries have arrived in the future first is that after their 1990s financial crisis they set about reinventing their governments to nurture capitalism for the twenty-first century, making them less bloated, much more efficient, and more fiscally responsible. They did cut public spending and taxes, but they also invested in their people. In addition they added more choices to taxpayer-funded services, and created new systems to foster business. Denmark, for example, is famous today for its "flexicurity" system, designed to help businesses adjust to the fast-changing global economy—but without ruining lives. The system allows employers to fire workers easily, but it also guarantees the people who've been fired a decent benefits package for up to two years, as well as help finding a new job.

The Nordic country that Micklethwait and Wooldridge admire most is Sweden. For starters, the Swedish government maintains a strict budget surplus—at least 1 percent—over an economic cycle, and sets limits on what the government can spend in a given year. The model is flexible and allows for increased spending during a downturn, but the rules are stringent: The lost ground must be made up during the next upswing.

The assumption that Nordic government spending is

bloated, and must therefore be inefficient, comes from oft-cited statistics showing government expenditures in relation to GDP to be significantly bigger than in America. And indeed Nordic governments do spend much more in relation to GDP than does the United States. That's hardly surprising, considering that they use tax revenue and government spending to provide services such as health care, pensions, and day care, which obviously increases government spending, while the United States leaves citizens to make these arrangements with private providers. In addition this metric is generally a poor tool for comparing efficiency. It tells us how much money a government sends out to the world, but it doesn't say anything about the nature of that spending, since different governments pay for very different services.

A better way of comparing efficiency is looking at how much each country spends on a specific, comparable basket of services, regardless of who pays for it. The OECD has done exactly this, and found that when it comes to a specific array of social services, including items such as health care, pensions, unemployment benefits, child care, or credits for families with children, the United States ends up spending almost exactly as much as Sweden does in relation to GDP. Not only that, but Finland, Denmark, and Norway all spent *less* than the United States in relation to GDP for the same basket of services. This makes Nordic countries more efficient than the United States in producing these essential services—they pay less, but the quality and results of their services are in many ways just as good or even better than what Americans get.

Overall the secret to Nordic success is not complicated. Nordic societies have simply taken the job of government seriously. They make mistakes and have their troubles, but they keep tweaking their systems in search of improvements, and they work hard to balance the books. They prove that there is nothing inherent in government that automatically makes it less efficient for arranging social services than the private sector.

When it comes to technology, science, entertainment, and creating businesses, Americans are the smartest folks in the room. When it comes to government, it has to be said that they are, for the time being at least, the last in the class. Yet there is no reason why Americans couldn't get their house in order. Anyone who's ever read Alexis de Tocqueville's tribute *Democracy in America* knows how much the early American government got right.

What the United States needs is not bigger government but smarter government, government for the twenty-first century that is simpler and more transparent, that provides the basic social services and regulations that a government can best provide, and that then leaves the market free of all the targeted meddling that the United States is infamous for now. Despite the general atmosphere of frustration that has encircled government in the United States, this is an entirely realizable goal. In fact proposals and actions for smarter government are already percolating all over America.

New legislation and policies by state and local governments have already succeeded in many places in the United States in circumventing political gridlock in the federal government. Many states and cities have done wonders for their education systems, and several have already created their own parental leave, minimum wage, or even health-care systems. Proposals to restrict the role of money in politics through state or local action could change things further.

Handing over the drawing of congressional districts to independent commissions would stop politicians from manipulating the districts for their own gain and force them to appeal to a broader base. Limiting the veto powers of different actors in Congress would help spur the crafting of effective legislation. Technology can be used to make current government services more efficient. Even the federal government is running many services reasonably successfully already—Social Security, Medicare—and it is pushing through new policies, despite the challenges.

The idea that the American economy would be destroyed if the wealthy were asked to pay their fair share of tax revenue has been refuted many times; when the Clinton administration raised taxes in the 1990s, an economic boom followed. The government could start taxing investment income at similar rates as wage income, as it used to do under Ronald Reagan, or it could pass the so-called Buffett Rule—inspired by the billionaire Warren Buffett himself—that would ensure that all million-dollar earners and above pay at least 30 percent of their income in taxes. Or, the government could simply eliminate the copious tax breaks and loopholes that have crept into the tax code, which have made it so complicated, so unfairly beneficial to the well-off, and so burdensome to everyone else.

These are just a few examples and ideas. But in the country that experimented with perfecting freedom and democracy in the first place, shouldn't it be possible to rethink government in the twenty-first century? So go ahead: Ask what your country can do for you.

SEVEN

THE LANDS OF OPPORTUNITY

BRINGING BACK THE AMERICAN DREAM

A TALE OF TWO CITIES

The man was wearing several layers of clothing, including two pairs of pants, and his face was covered by a beard, strands of matted hair, and dirt. He was mumbling to himself, surrounded by tattered bags containing all his belongings. Then he peed in his pants. We got up and moved farther away, just as others had done before us. The stench, though, was inescapable, and I had to cover my nose and mouth to suppress a gag.

This could have been a scene from a Charles Dickens novel depicting the impoverished suffering of the nineteenth century. It could have been a scene in some dirt-poor Third World country. But it took place in an otherwise clean and orderly twenty-first-century New York City subway car, not long after my arrival in the United States, and it left me disturbed for days.

I had seen homeless people before, of course. But never in my life had I seen such an utter, complete, total wreck of a human being as that man on the New York City subway, and certainly never back home in Helsinki.

The Nordic countries have their psychiatric patients, alcoholics, drug addicts, and unemployed, but I couldn't imagine a person in a similar state roaming the streets of Finland's capital or any other Nordic city. Usually everyone has someplace to stay, if not in public housing, then in a decent shelter. And while you see the occasional person talking to themselves in public, the health-care systems reach more of the mentally ill than in the United States. Encountering the man on the New York subway was one of the moments that made it clear to me early on that in the United States you are really on your own.

Eventually I got so used to seeing the homeless that I stopped paying attention. Instead my attention was drawn to the other end of the spectrum.

As I began meeting people and sometimes getting invited to events or gatherings in apartments with roof decks, or gorgeous lofts with windows overlooking the Manhattan skyline, or brownstones with several floors and backyard gardens, I began performing a new calculation in my head. How were they able to afford it all? Some of these people were lawyers, doctors, or financiers, which easily explained their wealth, but some were artists, employees of nonprofits, or freelancers working on their own projects. Their well-appointed lifestyles mystified me, but I felt awe and cheer when faced with such uplifting examples of America's ability to remunerate talent. The American dream seemed to be alive and well, not to mention within my reach. If all these people were making it, surely I could, too.

Finally I realized that many of the people with an expensive lifestyle but a seemingly low-earning profession had family money supporting them. I hope it doesn't take someone from stuffy old Europe, like me, to point out that inheriting wealth, rather than making it yourself, is the opposite of the American dream. America became an independent nation partly to leave behind the entrenched aristocracy of the old country, to secure the opportunity for Americans to be self-made men and women.

I'd traveled the globe, and I'd lived in Finland, France, and Australia. Now in America I felt as if I'd arrived not in the land of Thomas Jefferson, Abraham Lincoln, and Martin Luther King, but in that proverbial nineteenth-century banana republic of extremes—entrenched wealth, power, and privilege on the one hand and desperate poverty, homelessness, and misfortune on the other. A cliché, yes. But that makes the reality of it no less brutal. Never before had I seen such blatant inequality, not in any other nation in the modern industrialized world.

For someone coming from a Nordic country, it's hard to comprehend the kinds of income inequalities one encounters in the United States. The twenty-five top American hedge fund managers made almost one billion dollars—each—in 2013, while the median income for an American household hovered around fifty thousand dollars. At the same time homeless shelters were overflowing with record numbers of people seeking help. It's telling that many of them were not drug addicts or the mentally ill, but working families. The United States has returned to the age of the Rockefellers, Carnegies, and *The Great Gatsby*, and the trend in that direction isn't showing signs of slowing. After the financial crisis, incomes for the wealthiest bounced back quickly, while the vast majority of Americans saw little improvement. Between 2009 and 2012, the top 1 percent captured more than 90 percent of the entire country's gains in income. This is not a problem that is only connected to the financial crisis. The share of income going to the richest Americans—the 1 percent, or even the 0.1 percent—has grown dramatically in recent decades, while the rest of America has faced stagnating incomes or even seen wages diminish.

The reasons commonly given in America for these changes are by now familiar. There's globalization, free trade, deregulation, and new technology, which allow the brightest talent to reign over larger realms and to amass more wealth. Today the most visionary CEO presides over a vast multinational corporation, instead of having fifty top executives running smaller companies. The best product is now sold everywhere, replacing local products. Because of advances in technology and the outsourcing of low-skilled work to poorer countries, workers in developed countries need increasingly specialized skills. The few who have such skills benefit. The many who don't suffer. At the same time arrangements at work have become less stable. Part-time and low-paying work has become more common, as technology has let employers optimize production, and as the power of labor unions has faded.

However, these oft-repeated reasons are not the whole story. Every wealthy nation is dealing with all these dislocating changes, not just the United States. Yet how different the experience has been in places like the Nordic countries, which have made serious efforts to adapt to this brave new future with smart government policies that fit the times. Rising inequality doesn't simply result from inevitable changes in the free market. Much of it follows from specific policies, which can direct change in one way or in another. Even though the times demand the opposite, American taxes have become more favorable to the wealthy. Partly as a result of this shortsighted change, American social policies have had to move from supporting the poorest to having to help prop up the middle class. Income inequality has increased everywhere, but in the United States it's particularly pronounced because taxes and government services do less to mitigate the effects of the changes in the marketplace than elsewhere in the modern developed world.

Observers from the Nordic countries like me aren't the only ones confused by America's anachronistic new reality—Americans are, too. When one study asked Americans to estimate the current distribution of wealth in the United States, the respondents dramatically underestimated the level of inequality. When asked to "build a better America" by constructing distributions with their ideal level of inequality, they came up with distributions that were far more equitable than even their erroneously low estimates of the actual distribution. Finally respondents were shown pie charts depicting distributions of wealth in unnamed nations and told to choose which nation they would rather join out of pairs of two, given what's called a "Rawls constraint" for determining a just society: "In considering this question, imagine that if you joined this nation, you would be randomly assigned to a place in the distribution, so you could end up anywhere in this distribution, from the very richest to the very poorest." Without knowing which countries the charts were based on, more than 90 percent of Americans passed over the chart portraying the distribution of wealth in the United States and chose instead the chart that portrayed Sweden.

It would seem that the average American is already far more sympathetic to the basic tenets of the Nordic theory of love than might be imagined. And yet, there are voices in the United States as well as in Europe that continue to insist that the vast inequalities of the twenty-first century are the new status quo, the unavoidable result of technological progress. In reality practically all studies show that in our hypermodern age, in which globalization, free trade, deregulation, and new technology have upended traditional relationships, the societies that are succeeding, and will continue to succeed, are those like the Nordic countries that enact smart government policies to ensure the health of their human capital. As more and more citizens need high levels of education, and then go on to work as freelancers, entrepreneurs, or on short-term contracts and projects in today's dynamic economies, Nordic-style government is the key to a nation's success.

Still, many Americans hold on to the idea that income inequality is an inevitable and perhaps even desirable state of affairs. This is understandable, considering that America has long been known as a place where everyone has a chance to improve his or her lot in life. That's what the American dream is all about: pulling yourself up by your bootstraps, rising from rags to riches. Naturally those who work hard earn more reward. It shouldn't matter if some are significantly wealthier than others as long as everyone has a fair chance at success. The trouble is, when it comes to opportunity, the United States has been moving further and further in the other direction. That chance at success is becoming smaller and smaller.

FROM FATHER TO SON

America has long defined itself as the land of opportunity. But what does this mean? The best way to quantify opportunity is to measure upward social mobility—the ability of people to raise their standards of living and have their children do better than they did. America does possess a proud and indelible legacy: It has offered a new life to millions of immigrants—myself included—throughout much of its history. But survey after survey reveals that upward social mobility has declined in the United States, while it has increased in other places, especially in northern Europe and particularly in the Nordic region.

There is no shortage of clear and convincing evidence for this. For example, take the correlation of a father's income with that of his son. A Canadian professor named Miles Corak found that in the United States and Britain, the *least* mobile societies, nearly half of the advantage that a father may have had in his time is passed on to a son in adulthood, and this was not the result of the son's own hard work and personal successes but can be explained by the advantages of belonging to the right family. In the Nordic countries, by contrast, there is far less of this sort of unfair advantage. Some of the most cited studies on this question have been led by Markus Jäntti, a Finnish economist at the University of Helsinki, who with his colleagues looked at inherited disadvantage—in other words, how much worse your chances are for success if you're born into a low-income family. They found that in the United States, 40 percent of men who were born into the lowest income bracket stayed in it. In the Nordic countries, that figure was only 25 percent.

There is a very clear and straightforward reason for the difference. As several studies have demonstrated, societies with less income inequality tend to have greater upward mobility for their citizens. The United States is stuck so far in the past when it comes to equal opportunity that President Obama's economic adviser Alan Krueger came up with the term "the Great Gatsby Curve" to describe the connection between the rising inequality and falling social mobility in America. It is certainly possible to start poor and end up rich in the United States, but research shows that doing so is much harder there than in other wealthy nations. America is no longer the land of opportunity—northern Europe is. This is the reality that led the British Labour Party leader Ed Miliband to make his surprising statement in 2012: "If you want the American dream, go to Finland."

The reasons for the crumbling of the American dream have been debated, but the most obvious culprits are American inequalities in income, health care, education, and resources available to families. It's no mystery why this is the case: The United States has simply not committed to basic public policies that ensure equality of opportunity the way the Nordic countries have.

In Finland the simple commitment that the nation made to unify Finnish education into one high-quality K–12 school system for all has made an enormous difference. Two countries may spend the same percentage of their gross domestic product on education, but as Miles Corak has noted, if this spending is directed to high-quality early-childhood education, and to primary and secondary schooling accessible for all, it is likely to create much more equality of opportunity than if it were directed to high-quality private university-level education that is accessible to only a few. Obviously Finland has deliberately adopted the former approach in order to meet the challenges of the twenty-first century, while America has been stuck with the latter approach, to the severe and direct detriment of millions of its children.

Affordable health care, day care, schools, and universities support equity of opportunities, but in the United States the availability of such services is not only severely limited, it has also been deteriorating in recent decades. Getting a good education is becoming increasingly difficult and expensive. American low-income families find more and more obstacles in their way, while the wealthy can buy their children all the props they need: books, hobbies, tutors, private schools, doctors, and connections. Time after time I admired some American superachiever only to discover that his or her parents, too, were outstanding in their own fields, and had money.

There's nothing wrong with a society in which parents who achieve success instill a similar drive for success in their children. But that's different from a society in which a relatively small number of families have vastly more financial and logistical resources than everyone else, and can provide many more tangible advantages to their children every step of the way. In the United States I was much less likely to discover that the successful person I'd met had succeeded despite his or her family background rather than because of it. A fantastic diversity of talents is born into children across all classes of American society. Yet among far too many of these children—the ones who aren't wealthy in particular—these talents aren't being discovered and nurtured. In other words they are being wasted.

The Nordic countries feel that they can't afford to waste the potential of any of their children, no matter what their fortunes in life.

Kaarina—the mother who'd told me about how liberating it was to have her husband take paternity leave and bond with their children—experienced a terrible family loss when her children were a few years older. Tragically Kaarina's husband died of cancer. He hadn't taken out life insurance, and unfortunately she didn't have much in the way of other family support. Kaarina was left to pay the family's mortgage and support her two young children all by herself.

This was a terrible emotional blow, and for an American middle-class family it might well have been a terrible financial blow as well. Yet in Finland, Kaarina managed to get through her husband's illness and death without incurring any debt. For starters, of course there weren't any significant medical bills for his cancer treatment. Then she and her children received a survivor's pension from the government, in addition to all the usual benefits available to families. Her children could, naturally, also continue studying for free in their high-quality public school, and could attend the subsidized after-school clubs. When her older son decided that he wanted to attend an English-language high school, located in a neighborhood dominated by diplomats and wealthy families, all he needed to do was pass the entrance exam. No tuition was needed, and public transportation took him there. The children continued to engage in hobbies they chose freely: swimming in the public pool, judo four times a week at a local club, gym at their school's facilities, and mixed martial arts at the free, publicly funded municipal sports center. None of their activities were expensive, because the operations were largely funded by the municipality and available to all. Later, should they want to go to college, that will be tuition-free as well. And since healthy parental leave policies for both Kaarina and her husband had allowed her to keep working at the same time that they'd raised their kids, she had a solid freelance career to fall back on after he died.

Kaarina's husband's death was still devastating, and needless to say she had all my sympathies. She also had my curiosity. At one point I asked her what she thought it had meant for her to have Finland's social policies in place when fate had dealt her such a difficult hand. "I'm a good example of what happens to a person who has no family and no employer to support them," Kaarina told me. "Anywhere else in the world, any-where outside of the Nordic countries, my family's life and my kids' future, not to mention my own economic and social status, would have changed dramatically and permanently. Now the loss is only personal, if you will. Any other time in history, my sons would have been struck by an immense tragedy also in light of their futures."

This is what it means to have deliberate social policies to support the autonomy of individuals, to secure the indepen-dence of children, and to ensure the development of children's talents for the future. In America, if you're lucky enough, you might have the private resources to keep you on track through life's challenges. You might also end up haunted by the knowl-edge that you may have gotten unfair advantages over others who are suffering. This can have the debilitating effect of un-dercutting people's sense that they are the master of their fate, that they've earned their own success.

Personally I was able to live my life in Finland not only taking pride in my own achievements but also taking pride in my participation in a social contract that went to extraordinary lengths to give every individual a fair shot at success. No one can shield children from the pain of a parent's death, or the trauma of dealing with mental illness, addiction, violence, or other trou-bles in a family. Children will always grow up in a variety of circumstances, some better than others. Still, I was able to take satisfaction in my own achievements exactly because I knew that my society did its best to offer everyone the same oppor-tunities—at least as much as any country in the world at the moment—and that in comparison with other people, my per-sonal achievements were my own, and not simply the result of being blessed with a fortunate family background.

In addition, I could reach for my own dream without having to focus solely on the one thing that most Americans today have to worry about constantly: money.

THE FUTURE OF THE MIDDLE CLASS

Here's a statement: The United States is one of the world's richest countries, and its middle class is the world's best-off middle class. The first part of that statement is still true. The second part was once true but is no longer. A study of income data in different countries over thirty-five years revealed that after-tax incomes of middle-class families in Canada—which were substantially behind those in the United States in 2000—now appear to be higher than those of their neighbors to the south. Median incomes in many European countries still trail those in the United States, but the gap in several, including Norway and Sweden, is much smaller than it was a decade ago. These trends shouldn't be surprising. Even though the American economy has grown significantly over the past few decades, the typical American family in 2013 earned no more than it did in 1988.

The poor in the United States fare far worse. A family at the lowest fifth of the income distribution makes significantly less money than does a similar family in Canada, Sweden, Norway, Finland, or the Netherlands. Thirty-five years ago the reverse was true.

But these figures only tell part of the story. From their shrinking share of take-home pay, middle-class Americans are also trying to cover rising costs for health care, child care, and education. In the Nordic countries, whether people make somewhat more or less than middle- or lower-class Americans,

Nordic citizens don't have to rob their own take-home pay to fund these other parts of life. The United States still offers some the chance to become fantastically rich, but for the vast majority of Americans, even just a comfortable middle-class life has become harder and harder to reach and maintain.

The means to restore the vitality of the American dream are well known and available. The OECD recommends three steps to counter the changes that have unsettled the labor market: investing in the workforce by offering easy access to education, health care, and day care; creating better jobs that pay more, especially on the lower rungs of the income ladder; and using a well-designed tax system to temper inequality and increase opportunity.

Americans are ready for these changes. In a 2014 survey by the Pew Research Center, U.S. respondents considered the growing gap between the rich and the poor the greatest threat to the world today, ahead of religious and ethnic hatred or pollution and environmental problems. States and cities have been raising the minimum wage on their own. Fast-food chains have started paying their workers higher wages—some even fifteen dollars an hour—while still making profits. And as the Nobel Prize–winning economist Paul Krugman has pointed out, the United States actually has a long tradition of letting the biggest earners and possessors of the largest fortunes contribute more in taxes.

The Nordic countries offer a clear road map for dealing with growing inequality in the United States. Another Nobel Prize–winning economist, Joseph Stiglitz, has noted that Sweden, Finland, and Norway have all succeeded in achieving about as fast or faster per-capita income growth as the United States, but with far greater equality. While class distinctions in the U.S. become more deeply entrenched and social mobility becomes more and more a myth, in Nordic countries upward mobility is a healthy reality.

Building this framework costs everyone a bit of money. And yes, those who do very well by it are asked to pay quite a bit more. That's because the lives of the very rich are already fantastically good, and there's an acknowledgement that additional wealth beyond a certain point has diminishing returns for personal satisfaction—something that should be obvious, but that is also increasingly supported by research. Walk around the streets of Helsinki or Stockholm for a few days, and you'll see rich people driving brand-new BMWs, Porsches, even the occasional Ferrari. What you won't see so much of is rich people who own four or five Ferraris. Frankly, Nordics would rather have health care and good schools.

On the whole, Nordic citizens support the arrangement because it is so obviously fair and generally works so well. What Finland and its neighbors do is actually walk the walk of opportunity that America now only talks. It's a fact: A citizen of Finland, Norway, or Denmark is today much more likely to rise above his or her parents' socioeconomic status than is a citizen of the United States. All this means that in the Nordic countries people actually end up being able to create wealth for themselves. Government in the Nordic countries tends to be like a referee who makes sure that the field is level and the rules are followed, but who then steps out of the way and lets the competitors determine who gets the highest score. If the referee were to stop the game and take points away from the winners and give them to the losers, which is what some Americans seem to think happens in the Nordic countries, of course no one would want to play. It's exactly because that's not the way it works that Nordic citizens find their system to be in their own best interests.

Although the Nordic theory of love may predispose the Nordic nations to the recipe for success that they've developed and put to such effective use, there is nothing inherently Nordic about it. Today many Americans actually see the issues of taxation, income inequality, and opportunity in ways that reflect the same core values as the Nordic theory of love, and are working toward policies more appropriate for the challenges of the twenty-first century.

The United States is still the country that people elsewhere in the world look up to. It has created a way of life that many people in the world can only dream of, a life steeped in individual freedom, material wealth, and a liberating degree of choice in everything from shopping to religion to lifestyle. It continues to welcome immigrants, and millions are drawn in by its promise of opportunity and a better life. It should not let those wonderful, essential features about itself be lost. Rather, it can and should do more to protect them. For the United States has strayed from its own ideals, and in reality, Americans today enjoy less opportunity than do people of other wealthy nations. The land of opportunity needs to bring the opportunity back.

EIGHT

BUSINESS AS UNUSUAL

HOW TO RUN A COMPANY IN
THE TWENTY-FIRST CENTURY

CLASHES OF CLANS AND ANGRY BIRDS

The October weather in Helsinki was at its worst. It was raining steadily, and the whole world seemed enveloped in a gray, wet, cold cloak. Walking toward the nondescript office buildings at nine in the morning, staring at the wet asphalt, I was reminded of why so many Finns struggle to get through the long winter.

On this day, however, I opened a door to a different world entirely—one of bright orange walls, canary yellow and forest green chairs, pink curtains, sneakers thrown in piles by the coatrack as if I'd walked into a house full of teenagers, and huge white blocks of letters in the middle of the space spelling "SU-PERCELL." The company had recently announced that the Japanese telecommunications giant SoftBank had bought a 51 percent stake in it for $1.5 billion—a huge sum for an online game start-up employing only around a hundred people.

In some ways Supercell's story is typical of start-ups all over the world. Six experienced game makers started the company in Helsinki in 2010. The first games Supercell created were failures, but in the summer of 2012 it published a game called Hay Day for Apple tablets and phones, and a few months later Clash of Clans followed. The games became phenomenal successes, topping app charts around the world and making Supercell more than two million dollars a day in 2013. The following year was even better: The company tripled its revenues and doubled its profits. Supercell's business model was praised in the media all over the world, including in the United States. By early 2015 the company had become such a high-profile player that it was able to splurge on a lavish Super Bowl ad for Clash of Clans, starring the movie actor Liam Neeson.

What was most interesting about Supercell for me, however, was that it dispels one of the most persistent myths that Americans believe about the Nordic way of life: that its "nanny state" kills initiative and innovation. Since Nordic governments hand everything to their citizens on a plate, this thinking goes, people become passive and uncreative—or worse, their spirits are crushed. After all, why would anyone bother working hard if they're too comfortable? And how can any company succeed, let alone be innovative, if it's constantly burdened by high taxes and by employees coddled with all sorts of rights?

While the Nordic countries may have created a secure life for the middle class, and equality of opportunity for their children, surely Nordic lands are little more than barren deserts when it comes to American-style entrepreneurial spirit. Indeed, according to this logic, Supercell should be the biggest failure in the world.

Supercell's employees are encouraged to go home at 5:00 p.m. All employees, not just the founders and managers, get stock options. They work in small teams—"cells"—that develop a game autonomously and have control over its fate. If they decide that the game they're working on is not turning out to be top-notch, and that they should kill it even though that means throwing away months of work, they can decide to do that. All that is asked is that they share what they've learned in the process with the rest of the company. Ilkka Paananen, a serial entrepreneur in his thirties, is one of the founders and the CEO of the company, and he believes that the keys to Supercell's success are a lack of bureaucracy, small and nimble units, sharing, and committed but independent workers—in short, collaborative relationships built on positions of autonomy. It's a bit like the corporate cousin of the Nordic theory of love.

Paananen doesn't see any problem with starting and running an innovative business in Finland. "Finland has a great education system and excellent health care," he told me when I met with him, checking off Finland's advantages. "The bureaucracy involved in starting and running a business is negligible. Basic infrastructure works really well. In my industry public funding is well developed, perhaps the best in the world. Finland has a strong, straightforward work culture, with ambition and a drive for quality. The workdays are maybe shorter than in the United States, but I'd claim that what we lose in time, we win in efficiency. And I believe that better work-life balance, as Americans say, contributes to that efficiency." Paananen smiled. "What else? Those come to mind first."

When Paananen talks about public funding, he's referring to a Finnish government fund that invests in research, development, and innovation in order to compensate for one of Finland's shortfalls: the lack of private venture capital. Of course today many Finnish companies receive significant funding from abroad. One of the early investors in Supercell was Accel

Partners, a Silicon Valley venture capital firm that counts among its other investments Facebook, as well as another Finnish game company, Rovio, the creator of the world-famous mobile game Angry Birds.

Even the supposedly high Finnish taxes fail to sour Paananen's view. He noted that Finland's corporate tax rate is in fact relatively low—20 percent in 2015 compared with the American rate of 39 percent—and after a company pays its taxes in Finland, it's done. It doesn't have to offer its employees health insurance or pension benefits, which both burden American companies with significant costs on top of their taxes. At the time I visited, logistical matters for Supercell's entire Finland-based operation of more than a hundred employees could be overseen by an administrative staff of just two people. Supercell had to employ another two administrators in the United States for its American office—for a staff there of only twenty employees. "That's what it comes down to," Paananen said. "If the society doesn't handle these things, the company has to take care of them." If the United States is so worried about crushing entrepreneurship and innovation, a good place to start would be freeing start-ups and companies from the burdens of babysitting the nation's citizens.

Paananen knows American realities well because he spent years working for an American game company, Digital Chocolate, after it bought his previous company. One of the problems he remembers the company having in the United States was the constant fight to keep employees. Not because he or the company he worked for were bad employers, but because American society forces people to put a premium on money. In Silicon Valley employees are always vying for a better offer, and when they get one they tend to jump ship. In Finland employees may have fewer options, but Paananen thinks that much of the difference comes from the fact that Nordic society makes it easier for people to have a good life without constantly worrying about money. From an employers' point of view, this means that employees tend to be more loyal; they're more likely to stay at a company for the long term, as long as they like their jobs. For the employer this makes planning easier and cuts costs for hiring and training.

Because of this long-term view, Paananen is not fazed by his employees' long paid vacations—five weeks annually—or parental leaves when they have kids, either. "I think about it this way: If you employ an incredibly talented person, it would be a real shame to ruin that relationship because they want to take a leave of one year at some point to see their child grow. In the long term, what difference does one year make, if our goal is to work together for twenty years?"

When it comes to taxes, Paananen and his Supercell colleagues might as well be spokespeople for the Nordic theory of love. There is perhaps no greater testament to what it means to belong to a society that invests in its people than what Paananen and his colleagues did after their hugely lucrative sale to SoftBank. After celebrating, they announced publicly that they planned to forgo any of the accounting tricks usually employed by the wealthy to minimize their tax burden. When the time came, Paananen paid $69 million in taxes, out of his 2013 income of $215 million, a tax rate of 32 percent. (Capital gains are taxed at a lower rate than wages in Finland too.) Most Americans in a similar situation—Warren Buffett aside—would probably think Paananen and his colleagues fools for letting the government take so much of their money without a fight. But Paananen's view of the matter was clear. They had gotten so much from their society—the same fair chance to succeed in the first place that all Nordics get, plus start-up funding and a steady pool of well-educated talent—that it was their turn to pay back. For them the ability to pay so much back *was* part of the success, and it felt good.

To be sure, Nordic countries have less noble members of the elite who try every trick in the book to avoid paying taxes, even going so far as to establish residence in other countries. But the civic-minded attitude of Paananen and his colleagues at Supercell is hardly unique.

Listening to Paananen, I thought of another successful Nordic entrepreneur I had spoken with earlier, the executive chairman and co-owner of the Swedish fashion brand Acne Studios, a man named Mikael Schiller. Acne's edgy apparel is sold around the world, and its influence on the young and trendy outstrips its size. The founders draw inspiration from American icons like Andy Warhol's Factory, while they themselves have perfected the skill of behaving like artists while making impressive amounts of money—the *Wall Street Journal* titled an article about them "How to Succeed in Fashion Without Trying Too Hard." For example, Acne shies away from advertising but publishes its own artsy magazine. Like Paananen, Schiller felt that it was the all-important job of government to provide the basic social infrastructure of good education, health care, roads, broadband, and so on. "That leaves us free to build our company around other values than just money," Schiller said when I met him at his company's stylish headquarters in a historic building in Stockholm's quaint Old Town. "In taxes, as in everything, simplicity is the key. Everyone should know what they are expected to do, and the rules shouldn't change all the time."

In terms of fairness, both Schiller and Paananen said, companies may be harming themselves if the owners of the companies are paying taxes at a lower rate than the managers they hire, as it undermines morale and is bad for the business. Both also said, independently, that they'd prefer greater fairness in taxes, even if it meant that their own personal tax rate would rise.

Not everyone is as positive as Paananen and Schiller when it comes to evaluating the role of the entrepreneur in the Nordic region. In Finland businesspeople in more traditional industries complain about the high costs of employing workers, and many entrepreneurs pine for the lower tax rates in Finland's next-door neighbor Estonia. Regular grievances include the perceived difficulty of firing people, union power, government bureaucracy, and of course taxes. But what Paananen was saying is undeniably true. While there is always room for improvement, the Nordic model does not stifle innovation or entrepreneurial spirit, it drives it.

In fact, history has proved that beyond a doubt.

INNOVATION IN THE AGE OF HAPPY FAMILIES

Companies and brands founded and run by Nordic citizens are famous all over the world. Think of such Swedish companies as Ikea, H&M, Spotify, Volvo, Ericsson, or Tetra Pak, the ubiquitous food-packaging company. Denmark has LEGO, Carlsberg, the shipping and energy giant Maersk, and one of the world's largest pharmaceutical companies, Novo Nordisk. The Internet video-chat company Skype was cofounded by a Swede and a Dane with the help of Estonian engineers. Finland is not far behind. The Finnish company Nokia was the world's largest mobile phone company for more than a decade—and, for a while, the largest company by market capitalization in all of Europe. Today Finland boasts companies such as KONE, one of the largest elevator manufacturers in the world, with 47,000 employees. KONE isn't just a manufacturing behemoth; it's also a high-tech innovator whose products are enabling the construction of new, record-setting skyscrapers a kilometer tall—3,300 feet, twice the height of the Empire State Building. Finnish pulp and paper manufacturers such as Stora Enso and UPM operate all over the world. Newer players like Super-cell and Rovio or Sweden's Mojang, the publisher of the hugely popular video game Minecraft (which Microsoft bought in 2014 for $2.5 billion), have been changing the face of online gaming. In fashion, small but influential companies such as Acne Studios, Denmark's Malene Birger, and Finland's Marimekko have stores and followers all over the world. Nordic design, furniture, and architecture are lauded around the globe, not to mention the recent huge popularity of Nordic crime novels and TV shows.

Nordic nations have produced what is, by any metric, an impressive quantity of successful international businesses and brands, especially for such small, out-of-the-way countries. As in any region, some Nordic companies eventually crash and burn, and others never get off the ground. Some continue to dominate their market for decades. This is all as it should be in a free-market, capitalist economy. But one thing is clear: Allowing employees to combine work and family, ensuring high-quality universal education, providing health care for all and day care for every child, and curbing income inequality have not destroyed the capacity for innovation, nor have they prevented Nordic individuals from building business empires, and in the process becoming wealthy, some enormously so.

When the World Bank ranks countries on ease of doing business, based on criteria such as starting a company, dealing with construction permits, getting credit, trading across borders, enforcing contracts, or paying taxes, the Nordic countries consistently rank among the most business-friendly nations in the world. In fact, on those criteria, American entrepreneurs would be better off in Denmark, which scored higher than the United States in the 2015 ranking. Sweden, Norway, and Finland followed closely, in the top ten.

The reasons for all this Nordic success in business are, once again, not complicated. They result from deliberate policy choices inspired by the fundamental values and goals of the Nordic theory of love: making sure that families are composed of strong and independent individuals who function well as a team, that workers are healthy and well educated and not overly dependent on their employers, that infrastructure is top-notch, that institutions are transparent, that the justice system works in the public interest, that corruption is low, that technology permeates society, that trade is free, that regulations are reasonable. Another way of saying all this is that the Nordic nations have cultivated the single most valuable resource a society can have in the twenty-first century: human capital. That dynamism, innovation, and prosperity result should come as no surprise.

In fact the Nordic model goes to extraordinary lengths to support entrepreneurs, whether all Nordic entrepreneurs recognize that or not. At the most basic level the Nordic approach reduces the risk of starting a company, since basic services such as education and health care are covered for entrepreneurs and their families regardless of the fledgling company's fate. And if the entrepreneur succeeds, he or she is rewarded by tax rates on capital gains that are lower than the rate on wages. It's true that entrepreneurs who hire employees in the Nordic countries face more protections for those employees than in the United States, making the firing of individual workers more difficult and guaranteeing some basic rights for all, including parental leaves and higher employer contributions to employees' social security. But in these cases it's once again the United States that is just way behind almost every other modern nation in affording workers basic protections. When the OECD compares countries on the ease of laying off employees, the United States stands alone as the one nation where, on most metrics, workers can be fired with the least consideration whatsoever. Nordic companies also have the advantage of being able to hire workers for trial periods—several months, or even half a year—while retaining the right to fire them for any reason during that time.

What about other difficulties that entrepreneurs and companies in the Nordic countries supposedly face, compared with the United States? It's true that Nordic labor unions are strong, but their relations with employers are mostly collaborative and civil. Unions and employers have traditionally negotiated labor contracts with their mutual interests in mind: that employers share the wealth with employees, in return for stable production schedules free from strikes or other problems. So what do the results of these negotiations look like—is treating workers fairly bad for business?

In recent years labor activists have been fighting to raise the American minimum wage from the federal $7.25 per hour to $15. At the center of this fight sits the fast-food industry, where workers typically earn wages barely above the legal minimum. The Nordic countries don't have national minimum wages; instead minimum levels are set by collective-bargaining agreements that all employers must adhere to. The result is that in Denmark, for example, fast-food restaurants pay their workers the equivalent of twenty dollars per hour. In Finland the average wage for a McDonald's worker was about fourteen dollars per hour in 2014. Not only that, fast-food chains in the Nordic countries must give their workers the same paid vacations and generous paid parental leaves as all other companies.

And what is the horrible cost to consumers of all this? A Big Mac in Denmark costs about a dollar more than one in the United States. In 2015 the Finnish and American Big Macs cost exactly the same. Surely this state of affairs must have crushed the Nordic fast-food business by now? On the contrary, all the Nordic countries have thriving fast-food industries, from McDonald's on down to local chains. From the Nordic perspective, it's not this Nordic approach that is unsustainable—it's the American approach that's eventually going to implode. For in the United States more than half of fast-food workers rely on some form of public assistance to get by, meaning that American taxpayers are actually subsidizing the fast-food industry in the United States, to the tune of billions of dollars per year. If we're hunting for countries practicing socialism, the United States appears to be a pretty strong contender.

Still, it's often hard for Americans to understand how you can run a competitive business if many of your employees are at any given time working shorter hours, on vacation, or taking their parental leaves, especially outside the admittedly unique world of billion-dollar start-ups like Supercell.

Are there challenges for Nordic companies? Sure. But with some clever organizing and a premium on efficiency, remaining competitive is not that difficult. Just ask the people who are doing it.

The headquarters of Denmark's Novo Nordisk, the world's largest insulin maker, with forty thousand employees in seventy-five countries, is tucked in a low-lying industrial park outside Copenhagen. The place looks unimpressive from the outside, but on the inside the lobby is shiny white and sleek, with curved, high tables and bowls of fruit for guests to nibble on as they wait. When I sat down with the company's senior vice president of HR at the time, Lars Christian Lassen, an assistant brought in a truly Danish lunch of *smørrebrød*—open-faced rye sandwiches—topped with gravlax and egg. I had come to ask one question of Lassen: How is it possible that a company like Novo Nordisk can compete against the famously dynamic and profitable pharmaceutical companies of the United States, considering that a Danish company must surely be burdened, to some degree, by the generosity the state requires it to give its employees?

"It is a challenge, but it can be done," answered Lassen, a lively man with thick, whimsical eyebrows and unruly hair. He believes that Nordic workers' commitment and independence make up for the time they are away on their various leaves. "I think that when our employees *are* at work," Lassen told me, "they want to deliver." He also thinks the company gains from being perceived as a desirable employer. He should know. He originally came to Novo Nordisk on a six-month research leave from his post at Copenhagen University, after completing his PhD in medicine. He ended up staying. When we met he had worked at the company for twenty years.

Lassen himself could easily leave the office at four o'clock if it was his turn to get dinner ready for his sons—as with most Nordic couples, his wife works as well. He would, however, catch up with work after dinner if needed. And while employees' long parental leaves do pose challenges for a company, not to mention to an individual's career, they do not prohibit business or innovation. One year of leave is actually easier to arrange than shorter stretches, Lassen said. It's not hard to hire someone else to cover a post for a whole year—especially since Nordic companies are not responsible for paying the absent employee's salary, since parental leaves are funded through taxes. As long as leaves are announced early enough, companies can plan for the future knowing exactly when their employees will return—and that they indeed *will* return, which is not always the case for women after their American maternity leaves, which are almost always too short.

"We don't measure people on their presence in the office, we measure them on the outcomes," Lassen said. "This is a company where people don't get fired because they leave at four o'clock to pick up the kids. They get fired if they don't deliver."

I heard similar sentiments from other business managers across the Nordic region. A Finnish woman I know named Veera Sylvius has a particularly high-pressure job. She's the CEO and co-owner of a company called Space Systems Finland, which performs a couple of extremely important tasks: writing software that runs satellites, and checking electronic safety systems for nuclear power plants, trains, and other heavy high-tech machinery. The company employs about seventy-five people from several countries and serves clients not just across Europe but in the United States as well. At any given time, she told me, a number of her employees, both men and women, are on parental leave or taking care of sick kids at home. Some take off a few days, others a month, and yet others a year. All are highly educated engineers, physicists, or software developers. Yet Sylvius didn't think their leaves threatened her ability to run a successful business.

"Having children and running your life outside of work is so important that people should be allowed to do it," she said. "Some employers claim that parental leaves are too much of a burden on companies, but I don't think that's true. Your business has to be in good-enough shape that it's not going to crumble just because someone is taking care of their children. If your business can't handle that, then you have a problem with either your business model or your management."

Sylvius herself has two children, and took about year and a half of parental leave for each. Her husband, who also works in the software industry, took care of their firstborn for another six months after she returned to work. Both she and her husband continue to have demanding and flourishing careers.

In Denmark, social policies have evolved further to help companies like Novo Nordisk remain competitive globally, while still protecting the rights of workers. Denmark's innovative "flexicurity" system makes hiring and firing people relatively easy, while at the same time guaranteeing up to two years of good unemployment payments for those who get fired, along with job retraining and placement assistance. Novo Nordisk's Lassen was frank about the costs and benefits of this approach to his company. "We pay a lot of taxes," he acknowledged, "but part of those taxes ensures that there is basic coverage for people who are unemployed. This is the social contract we have with labor unions, if you like."

When it comes to hiring foreign talent, the Nordic system can be an asset or an obstacle. Some foreigners balk at paying Denmark's high taxes, although the country allows foreign researchers and key employees to pay reduced taxes for several years. But the safe, relaxed, and family-friendly lifestyle in the Nordic countries can also be a big draw. Nordic executives earn less than their peers in other countries, but they are not rushing to get jobs abroad. It seems that most of them value a high quality of life over additional boosts in pay. There are, of course, notable exceptions. One of the most famous Nordic tax refugees is the founder of Ikea, Ingvar Kamprad, who fled Swedish taxes by moving to Switzerland in the 1970s, though he finally returned to Sweden in 2013.

Lassen also noted that Nordic social policies, because of the foundation of stability they provide, can actually encourage employees to take risks that lead to innovation. Workers, like entrepreneurs, can try out a new approach when the risk of ending up on the street is practically zero. Innovation can come from many types of environments. Obviously American companies are world leaders in innovation, which indicates that innovation doesn't necessarily require great employee benefits—even though one might note that Silicon Valley giants and pharmaceutical companies are known for their outstanding employee benefits, even in the United States. But when it comes to innovation Nordic companies are not far behind, which proves that a more humane pace, and flexible work practices, nurture it just as well.

The flexibility that Nordic workers enjoy goes beyond even what's envisioned by experts in the United States who advocate for more flexibility in the workplace. Swedes and Norwegians, in particular, have tremendous freedom, even more than Finns. It's almost dizzying to try to understand their work schedules. Swedish parents of children born before 2014 get to share and use 480 days of paid parental leave (approximately sixteen months) at any time in almost any increments until the child turns eight. The rules have since changed a bit, and today new parents can use their 480 days at any time before the child turns four, and a fifth of the days can be used until the child turns twelve. Both parents have to use at least three months or they lose that portion of the benefits. Most of my Swedish acquaintances have divided their parental leave days over several years by working only two or three days a week, or by taking a month off for several winters on top of their normal vacation time, or dividing the days in various combinations between the spouses instead of taking all the days in a row during the child's first years. They have to announce the leave they wish to take two or three months in advance, but if they do that, their employer can't deny them the leave.

How is it possible to run a company like that, I asked Kristin Heinonen, a Swedish acquaintance who at the time managed a small digital design company. "It's not really a problem," she said. She thought about it for a moment. "It's so ingrained in the culture here. In my company it usually works out well, so that as someone is coming back from a leave, another one is taking theirs. Sometimes it's also useful, like during the recent downturn when we had less work. A couple of my coworkers happened to be on partial or full parental leave at the time, and it was convenient since the company didn't have as large expenses for salaries as usual."

Americans are generally more productive in terms of GDP per hour worked, but Denmark and Sweden come very close to the United States in efficiency. (Norway, with its oil, is even more productive than the United States by this measure.) Finland, I'm a little embarrassed to admit, is the least efficient of the group. In some ways, however, the American view that working less is automatically a sign of laziness and inefficiency is misguided. When a company or a country does well and there is more wealth to share, workers can take their cut in either money or free time. Nordic workers often prefer to take time over money, because at a certain point, the secret Nordic people know is that time off buys you a better quality of life than more cash. Those four or five glorious weeks of paid summer vacations that people in the Nordic countries enjoy really just mean that the employer is spreading eleven months of pay over twelve.

From the point of view of employers, having employees who prefer free time to money can admittedly be problematic. It requires more effort to organize the work if you have to divide it between more people working irregular hours. And in some professions, workers become better at what they do the more they do it, so one person working longer hours is preferable to two people working part-time. This is especially true in fields that require extensive training or unusual talent. In the Nordic countries, where university education is free, it would certainly be a more efficient use of taxpayer dollars to educate just one doctor to work full-time, rather than two to work part-time. However, Nordic experience shows that in most fields, workers' skills aren't so specialized that finding adequate substitutes is difficult. And in some jobs, it might in fact be more efficient to have multiple workers work fewer hours, if the work requires concentration that inevitably ebbs after a certain number of hours per employee.

Having a flexible workplace can even benefit the company. In a 2012 interview, Jeanette Skilje, H&M's human resources chief, told the *Wall Street Journal* that H&M sees parental leave-taking as an opportunity for its employees to try out different positions within the company and develop new skills. All H&M employees have a person appointed to take on their job when they go on leave. She concluded that while people themselves might think they're irreplaceable, in reality nobody is. Summer vacations and parental leaves are a great opportunity for students or others looking to get a foot in the door to show what they can do. For employers these substitutions function as test-drives of new and old employees' talents, and of their ability to grow.

All this works best when every company has to do it. When more businesses are asked to adopt flexible practices, the cost to any one firm is lowered—something that has even been noted in the United States, in the 2013 *Economic Report of the President*, put out by the White House: "An individual employer may be less likely to offer flexible work schedules when other firms have not adopted the same practice out of the fear that it will attract less committed workers." That is precisely why the Nordic countries make these practices a matter of national policy, rather than leaving them up to individual companies—doing so is better overall for the companies. The Nordic approach protects the individual first, on the grounds that stronger individuals will build stronger companies, but it also protects the employers by instituting the same guidelines for all.

Studies have shown that a flexible, family-friendly workplace can motivate current staff, reduce staff turnover, help attract new staff, reduce workplace stress, and generally enhance worker satisfaction and productivity. An OECD report noted that companies that have introduced family-friendly measures often report significant reductions in staff turnover, absenteeism, and an increased likelihood that mothers return to the original employer after their maternity leave. Another study concluded that the United States could increase its productivity by offering all women fifteen weeks of paid maternity leave. The World Economic Forum has found that family-friendly policies can increase innovation by promoting a diverse workplace that includes more women. Overall, offering employees enough vacation and sick days to reduce stress, allow them to catch up on sleep, and improve their health have all been found to boost productivity as well as to save businesses money, in addition to adhering to common sense and contributing to the general quality of life. But none of this will happen automatically. As a Europe-wide study on gender equality in the workplace showed, in many cases companies can continue to get by and extract profits without offering their employees better work-life balance. This means that if a society wants its members—and its companies—to thrive with such benefits, laws are still required to help all businesses adopt these improvements together, at the same time.

The reason for setting up such requirements is simple, and Massachusetts senator Elizabeth Warren put it eloquently: "There is nobody in this country who got rich on his own. Nobody. You built a factory out there, good for you. But, I want to be clear: you moved your goods to market on the roads the rest of us paid for. You hired workers the rest of us paid to educate. You were safe in your factory because of police forces and fire forces that the rest of us paid for. You didn't have to worry that marauding bands would come and seize everything at your factory and hire someone to protect against this because of the work the rest of us did. Now look, you built a factory and it turned into something terrific or a great idea. God bless. Keep a big hunk of it. But part of the underlying social contract is you take a hunk of that and pay forward for the next kid who comes along."

Contrary to American assumptions, what Nordics refer to as their "well-being state" is not a system that kills innovation, competitiveness, or the American dream—that classic aspiration for upward social mobility and dynamic success. Americans toil away on an endless treadmill, virtually as servants of their employers, told that this is the only way to stay competitive. Yet their Nordic counterparts have the freedom to succeed professionally, contributing to the competitive advantage of their employers and their nation, while also enjoying life outside work.

Nordic businesses still remain innovative and globally competitive, benefiting from the standards set by the well-being state rather than being crippled by them.

Across the most important areas of life—family, work, education, health, love, money—people in Nordic societies enjoy forms of individualism, freedom, social mobility, and independence from societal obligations that are more quintessentially American than what Americans themselves today are generally able to experience. For the United States, in turn, to borrow ideas from the current successes of Nordic societies is not only workable and appropriate, but in fact could result in a restoration, and reinvigoration, of the most basic ideals that have defined the nation. Indeed, studying the Nordic model is an opportunity to pursue a deeper and more profound level of American-style individualism. All it requires is showing a little bit of faith in us, the human beings involved.

THE HUMAN SPIRIT

Americans believe, more than any other nation, in every individual's ability to craft his or her own fate. Getting rich is part of the American dream, of course, but Americans have also shown that they're motivated by loftier ideals. They have a special affection for selfless heroes and acts of charity—for those individuals who put the survival, well-being, and happiness of others ahead of their own. I have found myself deeply affected and inspired by the contagious, energetic, and self-motivated manner in which Americans from all walks of life kick off projects to improve the circumstances of people in their own community as well as on the other side of the world, without counting the hours or expecting financial rewards in return. But when it comes to social and economic policy, Americans suddenly seem to lose all faith in the human spirit.

The iconic American defender of libertarian ideals and self-interest, Ayn Rand, the author of *The Fountainhead* and *Atlas Shrugged*, experienced firsthand the most virulent and destructive form of socialism, in the Soviet Union. Under communism-inspired totalitarianism, people did lose their incentive to work, because all independence and individual agency were taken away from them. But the United States and the Nordic countries today are all free-market capitalist democracies. In this context concerns that providing citizens with generous services and workers with generous rights, and asking the successful to pay their share, will take away people's incentive to work represent a sad misjudgment of human nature.

We've seen how successful Nordic businesses are, and to be sure, in the Nordic private sector, the desire to make money is a powerful motivator. But Nordic societies are also leading innovators in the public and nonprofit arena, which has contributed to their dynamic competitiveness and prosperity as well. The creativity and ambition of Nordic government and nonprofit sectors are living proof that people in a capitalist democracy can be motivated by much more than simple greed.

Consider Denmark again, a country that is pursuing the world's most ambitious engineering solution to address climate change. Copenhagen has set a goal of becoming carbon-neutral by as early as 2025, and has been installing an ultra-high-tech wireless network of smart streetlamps and traffic lights that themselves save energy and also help traffic move more efficiently, reducing fuel consumption. All this is good for the environment, the nonprofit public sector, and the private sector. By aiming to wean itself as a nation off fossil fuels before 2050, for example, Denmark has become a world leader in the wind-power industry.

Sweden, meanwhile, has set itself the ambitious goal of completely eliminating deaths from traffic accidents, and in the process is reinventing city planning, road building, traffic rules, and the use of technology to make transport safer. The country established the goal in 1997, and since then has reduced road deaths by half. Today only three out of every one hundred thousand Swedes die on the roads each year, compared to almost eleven in the United States. Consequently transportation officials from around the world have started to seek Sweden's advice on traffic safety, and New York City mayor Bill de Blasio has based his street safety plan on Sweden's approach.

Of course one could also argue that the biggest Nordic innovation of all is the whole concept and execution of the well-being state.

Americans might be surprised, too, by the ways that some of the key building blocks of the global technology sector have been the result of nonprofit innovation. The core programming code of Linux, for example—the leading computer operating system running on the world's servers, mainframe computers, and supercomputers—was developed in Finland by a student at Helsinki University, Linus Torvalds, who released it free of charge as an open-source application. When Torvalds later received some valuable stock options, they were a gift of gratitude from some software developers. In addition Finns have made other significant contributions to the global open-source software movement, a community of coders who volunteer their time and skills to create free software for anyone to use. One of the world's most popular open-source databases, MySQL, was created by a Finn named Monty Widenius and his Swedish partners. Today just about all American corporate giants—including Google, Facebook, Twitter, and Walmart—rely on MySQL. Widenius and his team have, in the years since, nevertheless made good money, but they did so by providing support and other services, while the software itself remains free to the world.

Vying for global popularity with Nordic open-source software has been another, quite different product of the Nordic mind: the boom in so-called Nordic noir—crime novels and TV shows. With their psychologically dark themes, they can tell us something about the Nordic approach to creativity and innovation, too.

Stieg Larsson's Millennium trilogy of novels, starting with *The Girl with the Dragon Tattoo*, have been massive international best-sellers—made into both a Swedish movie and a Hollywood film starring Daniel Craig. Perhaps surprisingly, though, Larsson himself did not set out to be a best-selling author. For decades he was a journalist and nonprofit researcher; his specialty was working for antiracist causes. He sold the trilogy only shortly before his death. The books, which have been released posthumously, derive their strength from Larsson's deep sense that the injustices of the world need rectifying.

As with Larsson, other pieces of Nordic noir that have gained an international following have been made without the primary incentive of profits. The Danish TV show *The Killing*, an innovative crime drama that connects the mystery of a young girl's murder to local politics, weaves the tale into a touching portrait of the anguish experienced by the victim's family. In the United States *The Killing* gained a passionate following as a remake, while the British have fallen in love with the original Danish version. The show was produced by the Danish Broadcasting Corporation, the Danes' version of the BBC. In recent years this broadcasting company—DR, as it is called in Danish—has emerged as a powerhouse of high-quality TV drama watched all over the world. None of DR's success makes sense, at least if you look at it from a typical American standpoint. That's because DR, a public-service company, doesn't have to compete, and isn't required to turn a profit. It's funded by taxes—specifically, by an annual media license fee that every Danish household has to pay if they have a means of watching TV.

Since DR's worldwide success would seem to contradict some basic American assumptions about what incentivizes corporations to produce top-quality work, I wanted to find out what, exactly, has motivated the man who created *The Killing*. Søren Sveistrup, a tall man with a soldier's frame and a clean-shaven head, met me in Copenhagen wearing a black denim shirt and green cargo pants. He'd studied at Denmark's film school and tried his hand at writing movie scripts before being recruited by DR. He'd always been an ardent fan, he told me, of American movies and television shows—Clint Eastwood's work had been particularly close to his heart. And Sveistrup felt that the basic crime drama had been masterfully executed in the United States. His own ambition had been to innovate on the basic form, to elevate it by infusing it with a social critique—a long tradition in Nordic crime fiction.

Sveistrup was well aware that the budgets he works with in Denmark are only a small fraction of those enjoyed by similar British or American TV productions. But he thinks that Denmark, and DR, offer a different kind of advantage for someone looking to create an original TV show. "I think the Danish system is very good. We get spoiled. Compared to the Americans, of course we do. The whole welfare nation stuff is fantastic," Sveistrup said, referring to the general quality of life and sense of security that even he, working in a risky industry, can enjoy. "I think as a writer or just as an entrepreneur I have more possibilities in Denmark than I would have in other countries. I'm very grateful for that. I think public funding can help artists do something that they would not have done if they were by themselves."

When Sveistrup was working on *The Killing*, he received a monthly salary as he researched and wrote the script, and, typically for Nordics, he manages to mostly leave work early enough to pick up his children from day care and eat dinner with his family.

Again, from a certain American point of view, all this sounds like it could be a recipe for disaster: a bunch of artists spending taxpayer money for their pet projects without any accountability, not even to advertisers. Yet Sveistrup believes that while different environments can enable different kinds of work, the drive and ambition to create something extraordinary has, in the end, little to do with the specific structure of the monetary and material incentives involved, whether one is working in a Nordic-style well-being nation or in the trenches of the most brutal form of capitalism. The ambition, Sveistrup says, comes from inside.

"My experience is that every good, dramatic story comes from some kind of inner hunger or necessity to create it. If you talk to writers or directors, it has to do with some kind of misery. I don't know any plain happy person who could create something interesting," Sveistrup said. "What makes you have any kind of ambition, it's grounded in your past, in your childhood, in your youth. You took a bite of the apple, or maybe you didn't get the apple, or maybe you're trying to get attention, or re-create something that you lost. That aspect has nothing to do with the welfare state. That's the universal drive for a creative life. And if you're just happy, you have absolutely nothing to write about."

I smiled when Sveistrup said this, because it struck me as a very Nordic thing to say. Despite the fact that Nordic countries score top marks in practically every global ranking of quality of life and happiness, Nordic people can still be very somber folks. And it occurred to me that perhaps exactly what Sveistrup was saying was part of the secret of Nordic success. The creation of the Nordic well-being society has made life much more comfortable for all Nordic citizens, but they are still motivated by the drive to create, to achieve status and power, and to acquire money, just like all other humans. And yet at the same time, maybe the Nordic experience also reminds us that the human desire to excel isn't as fragile and weak as the American faith in the profit motive might suggest. Maybe there's more to life than money, even in America.

NINE

THE PURSUIT OF HAPPINESS

IT'S TIME TO RETHINK SUCCESS

ON NOT BEING SPECIAL

On June 1, 2012, David McCullough Jr. stepped up to the podium in front of the graduating class at Wellesley High School in Massachusetts to deliver a now-famous commencement speech. McCullough, one of the school's English teachers and the son of the Pulitzer Prize–winning historian David McCullough, looked the part: a kind and inspiring educator who makes a difference in the lives of his students. His temples showed a little gray, and his reading glasses sat low on his nose as he gazed over them at the sea of young people in the audience, arrayed in the sun in their caps and gowns, eager to hear his message.

McCullough warmed up the audience with a few amusing remarks. But only a few minutes into the speech, it seemed he was suddenly getting off message. "Normally, I avoid clichés like the plague, wouldn't touch them with a ten-foot pole, but here we are on a literal level playing field," McCullough said, referring to the school's football field, the venue for the event. "That matters. That says something. And your ceremonial costume—shapeless, uniform, one-size-fits-all. Whether male or female, tall or short, scholar or slacker, spray-tanned prom queen or intergalactic X-Box assassin, each of you is dressed, you'll notice, exactly the same. And your diploma—but for your name, exactly the same. All of this is as it should be, because none of you is special."

In America this sounded like heresy. The video of the speech went viral, sparking a media storm. McCullough's detractors complained that he was being overly negative on a day that should celebrate the promise of the graduates. He did have his supporters, and they tended to express relief; finally someone was telling the truth to a generation of narcissistic, spoiled, overprotected youth.

In a sense with his speech McCullough was taking aim at one of America's most cherished beliefs. The way that America allows, even expects, everyone to be special—to be different, to excel, and to pursue his or her own unique vision of happiness and success—is one of the great things about the country. Americans aren't the only ones who cherish this ideal; outsiders admire it as well. Many a Nordic citizen gazes at America with envy, wishing his or her uniqueness could be celebrated the way it would be in the United States. For in the Nordic countries, while autonomy is highly valued, no one is considered special, and no one is expected to be special. When I watched the video of McCullough's speech, I had only one cheerful thought: That dude's Finnish!

Having lived in the United States for a while now, I can see more clearly many of America's strengths, as well as some of the Nordic region's faults. The Nordic tendency to downplay the unique talents of each person as well as his or her unique pursuit of happiness and success can be petty and disheartening. Downplaying specialness is so deeply ingrained and pervasive that the Scandinavians—that is, the Swedes, Danes, and Norwegians— even have a literary phrase to describe this tendency.

The phrase is "the Law of Jante," and it is shorthand for a list of ten commandments created by the Danish-Norwegian writer Aksel Sandemose in his 1933 novel *A Fugitive Crosses His Tracks*. Sandemose's ten commandments referred to the mentality of a fictional town called Jante, but the rules were immediately understood to capture the larger disposition of Scandinavians in general. The commandments are:

1. You are not to think you are anything special.
2. You are not to think you are as good as we are.
3. You are not to think you are smarter than we are.
4. You are not to convince yourself that you are better than we are.
5. You are not to think you know more than we do.
6. You are not to think you are more important than we are.
7. You are not to think you are good at anything.
8. You are not to laugh at us.
9. You are not to think anyone cares about you.
10. You are not to think you can teach us anything.

The actual commandments are less known in Finland, but Finns certainly recognize the sentiment. It's not that Nordics are proud of their Law of Jante, mind you. More than anything, the commandments are meant as a critique of a rather sad aspect of the Nordic character that is often taken too far. Efforts to stand apart from the crowd, or even to display self-confidence, can strike people steeped in the Nordic tradition as egotism or narcissism. Successful Finns have been to known to feel that other Finns are jealous or disparaging of their achievements. Moreover, sometimes Finns betray a distasteful fondness for schadenfreude when a successful person falters.

The Nordic habit of conformity can be particularly hard on immigrants. Sweden is widely admired for its generous immigration policy, but on the whole many immigrants to the Nordic region find its citizens cold, hostile, and closed-minded. Often this impression is well-founded, although sometimes it is a misunderstanding. A Nordic person can seem reserved and distant to those from other cultures even when that person intends no malice or prejudice. That said, the Nordic impulse toward conformity can be so deeply ingrained, and Nordic norms can be so completely taken for granted, that Nordic people may not realize how alienating they can be to people from other cultures. (Of course Nordic norms can be restricting to Nordics themselves as well.)

The positive side of all this belittling of one's achievements or specialness is the worldview it conveys: one charmingly devoid of pomposity, and full of acknowledgment that we're all just humans here, regardless of our possibly successful actions. But if the pressure to conform and denigrate oneself is so oppressively present in Nordic societies, is it really possible for Nordic people to be happy? Can the Nordic countries truly claim to be lands of individualism, independence, freedom, and opportunity, if they force everyone to be a clone of everyone else? Surely the United States, even with its faults, is a place much more conducive to fostering human happiness, and to celebrating individual liberty and success?

In some ways I think that's true. While I find much room for improvement in America's social structures, I love Americans and their approach to life. They are the most helpful, energetic, and supportive people I've ever met. I admire the way Americans encourage one another in all endeavors and find ways to turn their ideas into action. American society is truly diverse, and while the United States struggles with its own issues of inequality and racism, for someone like me to live among a sea of people from all backgrounds has been an exhilarating and life-altering experience. That diversity and positive energy are what makes me want to be an American.

But here's the thing: What makes Nordic people uncomfortable is when "uniqueness" or "being special" includes the suggestion that certain people are more valuable than others. Americans and Nordics may start from a similar point, and acknowledge each individual's inherent value. But Americans tend to emphasize an individual's capacity for extraordinary achievement, and then focus on celebrating those who fulfill this promise. This makes Americans comfortable with hierarchies based on income, title, or other indicators of status, because these hierarchies are perceived as being based on merit. By contrast Nordics tend to continue emphasizing the equal value of each individual *regardless* of his or her achievements, and thus Nordic people dislike such hierarchies and celebrations of success.

What's behind this difference in attitudes? Today Americans still feel that by and large, every individual is responsible for constructing his or her own fate—the classic pursuit of happiness—and there is still much debate in the United States about the extent to which, if at all, an individual's success or failure is also shaped by accidents of birth. Nordic people have long ago moved beyond this debate. To most Nordics it's completely obvious that an accident of birth, like being born into poverty or a neighborhood without a good school, can severely disadvantage an individual and destroy any chances of success, no matter what he or she does. And vice versa: If you are born into wealth or a neighborhood with a much better school, obviously you are going to have a better chance at doing well. If you agree with this view, then every individual's success is also partly thanks to factors not of his or her own creation. As such, when one does succeed, one can certainly take pride in that, but there is less cause to feel overimpressed with one's own achievements, or be awed by the success of others. Other people helped make it possible, and more often than not, luck also played a part.

I'd be the first to agree that the Nordic attitudes described by the Law of Jante are outdated, and that people should have the freedom to be who they are, and to pursue their dreams, without pressure to be just like everyone else. Everyone should absolutely have the freedom to be openly proud of their achievements, especially when society has created truly equal opportunities for everyone. After all, it is exactly because of that equity that every individual can feel good about their success and the degree to which it is due to their own personal efforts, instead of, say, their parents' wealth or connections.

To take the idea of individual autonomy to its logical conclusion, Nordics would do well to be more supportive of different choices, and to allow their citizens to pursue happiness in different ways. While the structures of Nordic society do an excellent job at supporting people's autonomy and well-being, Nordic culture could do better at accepting variety and idiosyncrasy.

Meanwhile, though, McCullough's "You Are Not Special" speech had clearly hit a nerve in America, and many Americans themselves were wondering if all the cosseting, nudging, cajoling, wheedling, and fawning over every individual's potential to achieve exceptional success, and all the attendant striving, were actually resulting in anyone achieving happiness.

In fact, maybe what is needed in America is a complete re-thinking of the entire definition of success.

TO ACHIEVE OR TO BE?

American newspapers and magazines are full of stories of entrepreneurs, executives, athletes, and all kinds of whiz kids doing exceptional things. For me these stories are sources of both anxiety and excitement. On my best days I devour them hungrily, and they fill me with encouragement. Back in Finland I seldom encountered stories of such inspiring examples, which might help explain why Finns have the worst collective self-esteem of any nation I know. Go to Italy or Spain, and the locals can't stop telling you how great their own food, weather, scenery, or people are. Go to France, and you'll hear all about its cuisine, history, and literary heritage. Come to America, and it'll be made clear to you that the United States is the best country in the world. Go to Finland, and you'll be asked why you bothered to come.

So perhaps it was somewhat Finnish of me that when I sat at my kitchen table in New York, trying to feel inspired by the stories in newspapers and magazines about American super-achievers, sometimes I ended up feeling discouraged. Sure, I had always applied myself to my work tenaciously, and sometimes even creatively, but I love to sleep, watch TV, read, hang out with my family and friends, and lie around in my pajamas eating chocolate. I dislike competition, rushing to get things done, full schedules, and too much exercise. Just hearing about the incredibly busy, fast, athletic, confident, and successful people who accomplish astonishing numbers of things every single day in America drains the life out of me. Their mere existence, combined with the praise they receive, seems to re-proach my whole being.

In America being average is not good enough. Parents keep telling their children they are special, no doubt out of love and a sincere belief that their children are indeed special. But for the children trying to live up to all this, such expecta-tions can be a source of stress and pressure, especially if their achievements later in life fail to match the all-powerful self-image their parents instilled in them. As adults, what we're all supposed to do in America is overcome limits, get out of the comfort zone, push the envelope, and reach for more, more, always more. While this approach has accelerated progress and contributed to the lives of everyone on earth today, being satis-fied with what one has, by contrast, is often considered unam-bitious, even lazy.

As I absorbed the daily diet of American superachieving going on around me, I noticed a change in the way I thought about work. In Finland I had always wanted my job to be meaningful, and I had willingly put in long hours at the news-papers and magazines I worked for, even working weekends when necessary. At the same time I considered work just work, and life something that happened outside of work. Life was dinners with friends, long vacations, riding, swimming in lakes, spending time with family. I distinctly remember feeling sorry for Americans who didn't seem to know what to do with them-selves on vacation, or who didn't even take any vacations. In my eyes at the time, these Americans had become enslaved to work and forgotten what life is really about.

In the United States I listened to Americans talk about pas-sion for what you do, and even though the American rhetoric can sound hyperbolic to a Finn, slowly I began to understand it. Work can be something that you genuinely love, and not just something you do in order to have a life. Work itself can be a source of happiness, and not just a means to pay for the things that make you happy. When you see it that way, you don't have to be constantly waiting for the weekend or vacation, as many Finns do. But while I've come to appreciate the American way of seeing work as a source of energy and satisfaction, there are some enormous problems with the American approach to pursuing success today. These problems are undermining happiness in America and even ruining people's health and lives. What isn't so obvious are the ways that the Nordic theory of love sheds new light on these problems, too.

In a national survey Americans were asked to define the components of a successful life. They prioritized good health, a good marriage or relationship, knowing how to spend money wisely, a good balance between work and personal life, and having a job you love. Having a lot of money was rated very low—at twentieth place on a list of twenty-two contributors to a successful life. In another study the attributes parents most wanted to pass on to their children included honesty and truthfulness, reliability, closeness with family, and good education. They also hoped their children would work hard and become financially independent. But becoming powerful and influential was among the least-valued future scenarios.

And what about young people themselves? In another national survey Harvard researchers asked young Americans what was most important to them. Surprisingly, almost 80 percent of youth reported answers that seemed completely at odds with the selfless values that parents had reported wanting to teach their children. The young people picked high personal achievement or happiness as their top choice. They ranked the sort of less selfish goals that their parents reported trying to teach them lower, including fairness and caring for others. The vast majority of the youngsters also reported opinions about their parents that seemed to contradict completely what parents had said about themselves; children said they believed their parents' top priorities were also selfish goals like achievement and personal happiness. What explains this startling disconnect between the values American parents say they want to teach their kids, and the values their children are actually learning?

There are two possibilities: American adults might be lying when they talk about prioritizing compassion and love, since it looks as if in reality they value wealth and power. Or they might be telling the truth about their priorities, but something is forcing them to live against their own values in practice. Either way, how is it that the actions of American adults could have become so different from their words—so different, in fact, that even their own children get the wrong message? Why is the younger generation growing up to feel that what matters is the relentless and selfish quest to excel, to be special, to achieve?

Despite what parents say they want for their kids, the brutal reality in America today is that being a special superachiever is, more and more, the only way anyone can ensure a reasonably successful life for themselves—regardless of their core values. Consider this comment from the American journalist Alina Tugend: "Parents seem to be increasingly anxious that there just isn't going to be enough—enough room at good colleges or graduate schools or the top companies—for even the straight-A, piano-playing quarterback, and we end up convinced that being average will doom our children to a life that will fall far short of what we want for them." While individual Americans might be the most generous people in the world in their daily actions and deepest desires, they are stuck in a society that ensures none of the fundamental opportunities that people need to achieve even basic middle-class comforts. This condemns Americans to an anxiety-ridden battle where a person had better be special, because the alternative is not succeeding at all. The United States is remarkable among the advanced nations for the way it forces its people into lives so stressful they may have to turn against even their own values.

I once saw an ad in an American magazine for a financial institution of some kind. It featured a woman galloping into the distance on a beautiful horse, with her back to the viewer. The caption read: "Money means being able to tell the world to get lost." When I lived in Finland, I wasn't amassing significant wealth, and yet I'd always felt perfectly free to tell the world to get lost if I wanted to. I had five weeks of paid vacation every year, and Finns don't typically read their work e-mails on vacation. I'd never felt I needed to acquire wealth and power to ensure a successful and satisfying life. After I moved to America, I thought about the ad often. In the United States, to be able to do the things that are really important to you, like spending time with your family, offering your children a good education, and ensuring your family's health, you actually do need quite substantial amounts of money. But it's a catch-22. Americans who manage to build a career that earns them a lot of money usually can't take much time off. And if they have a job that doesn't demand so many hours, they don't usually make much money, which leads to constant anxiety, and often, the need to take on another job.

At least one very special, highly successful, and exceptionally wealthy American has given these problems some thought. The founder of the *Huffington Post*, Arianna Huffington, wrote in her recent book *Thrive* that Americans need a new definition of success. Rather than everyone working so hard, in Huffington's mind we should all strive for a healthier version of success that includes greater attention to our own personal well-being, the cultivation of wisdom, the ability to wonder, and giving back. When I heard this I cringed. Those are good goals for sure, and Huffington's heart seems to be in the right place. But the tools she is offering are not going to solve the problem. What Americans need, so that they can stop struggling so hard to be superachievers, is simple: affordable high-quality health care, day care, education, living wages, and paid vacations. Studies show that a majority of Americans would gladly work fewer hours than they do now, and only a minority would like to have a job with more responsibilities. It's not that Americans don't realize that they need to relax, as Arianna Huffington seems to think. It's that they can't afford to.

Still, we also have to admit that even when people get a basic level of financial security and the chance to catch their breath, happiness doesn't necessarily follow. In fact researchers and popular commentators often point to a strange paradox: People living in poverty or in other kinds of difficult circumstances often exhibit a brighter outlook on life than people who seem to have it all.

Indeed, just look at the difference between Americans and Finns—Americans ever the optimists, and Finns not so much. When global surveys rank the grumpy Nordics as some of the happiest people in the world, what does that even mean?

THE OPTIMISTS VS. THE PESSIMISTS

Sometimes when my American acquaintances hear me saying good things about the Nordic countries, they ask me to explain something. If Finland is such a great place, why does it have such a high suicide rate? Another way to ask that question is: What's the point of having great public services and well-functioning governments if people are unhappy? It's an intriguing paradox: Americans, of course, despite their insecurity and stressed-out lives, define themselves by their irrepressible optimism. Nordic people—especially Finns—feel secure and have a much higher quality of life than Americans, yet are more frequently pessimists.

In many ways I love the positive thinking one finds in America. At its best it's energizing and gratifying, and fills you with a can-do spirit. In Finland the way people grumble, and see impossibilities instead of opportunities, can deflate everyone's energy, and even become a hindrance when a project needs to move forward. My Finnish friends who've lived in the United States and then returned to Finland find that one of the most difficult things to bear back in Finland is the negativity. And yet, looking from my perch in the United States back at the Nordic region, I can't help but also wonder whether the abundance of positive thinking in America has a downside that's just as deep.

America's reign of optimism contributes to a culture in which negative feelings are often unwelcome. Everyone from a cancer patient to the unemployed and the downtrodden is always expected to see the silver lining, envision a better future, and express gratitude for whatever little they've got going for them. So what's wrong with that?

Negative feelings are often a necessary spark for progress. Too much optimism can actually hinder people in the pursuit of their goals. A professor of psychology at New York University and the University of Hamburg named Gabriele Oettingen and her colleagues have conducted studies that ask test subjects in a variety of situations to engage in mental scenarios related to a goal. Women trying to lose weight, injured people hoping to heal, and students aiming to get good grades, a date, or a job were asked to imagine different outcomes for their quest. Later researchers checked back to see what had happened. The more optimistic each person had been about his or her outcomes, the worse the results. As Oettingen explains, positive thinking can fool our minds into perceiving that we've already attained our goal, which slackens our readiness to pursue it. And it can have other problematic effects. The best-selling author Barbara Ehrenreich, for one, has argued that the American gospel of positive thinking contributed to the recent financial crisis, by encouraging the poor to take on mortgages they couldn't afford, and the rich to take risks that weren't reasonable.

A positive attitude in the face of adversity is an admirable quality, and makes a person much more pleasant to be around than constant negativity. But it can also distract people from pursuing changes necessary to improve their circumstances. Complaining can seem obnoxious and pointless, but it can also sometimes be perfectly justified and the necessary first step toward real change—not just change within oneself, but change in the world.

Still, I can understand why many Americans continue to choose even unwarranted optimism over warranted complaints. When you feel that your life might fall apart any minute, even a hint of negativity can seem like the last straw. At times in America, optimism was the only kind of thinking I could allow myself, even if it verged on delusion. And I learned that in the absence of the kind of true security that comes from things like being able to pay your bills, having affordable health care, knowing your children will get a good education no matter what, or being able to take time to rest, all you can do is either give in to depression or try to build your own personal well-being bubble—with yoga, meditation, diets, and keeping your thoughts in check. That—or eating fast food and burying your worries with the TV remote.

The harshness of American life helps explain the presence in the United States of a dubious, even predatory, wing of the self-help industry, which profits by selling unlikely promises to the unlucky. It's telling that self-help gurus hardly exist in the Nordic countries. They're not necessary. As in other areas of life in Nordic societies, this is an area where the basic goal of the Nordic theory of love—to provide every individual with independence—results in freedom. And the sort of freedom I'm talking about here is freedom from investing energy in false hope. Wishful thinking can take a nation only so far. Ultimately hope has to be generated by the actual presence of opportunity. And if it's really there, it doesn't require constant psychological energy and enthusiasm, or a constant stream of heroic tales of survival against all the odds, to sustain.

As I pondered the question Americans often posed to me—Why aren't Finns more optimistic, despite their supposedly great society?—I began to turn it around into a different question, a question that seemed to me the more relevant one: How have Finns managed to build such a great society, despite all their negativity? Perhaps the answer is that Finns have built a great society *because* of their pessimism, not in spite of it. The volume of outrage and complaints that pour out of Finns whenever they perceive an injustice in their society can be annoying—especially when that injustice might be considered minor in other countries. Nevertheless, perhaps this capacity for negative response is part of the secret of Finnish success. Finns are quick to demand real changes that improve their external circumstances. Where an American today might be inclined to turn inward, meditate, and nurture positive thinking, a Finn is going to go yell at the politicians until something gets fixed. No one would recommend that we all go around focusing only on our problems and challenges. But based on Gabriele Oettingen's research, the best way to achieve our goals is actually to combine positive thinking with realism. In other words, find the middle ground between Finns and Americans.

When I compare the lives of my Nordic acquaintances with those of my American friends, factoring in the curveballs that life throws people in any country, there is still no question: The Nordic people I know are by far more relaxed and stress-free. That might not be the final definition of happiness, but it's an awfully good start.

FREEDOM

About a year after I had first talked with Lars Trägårdh on Skype about the Swedish theory of love, I traveled to Stockholm and had lunch with him in a popular café in Stockholm's hip Södermalm neighborhood. I asked what it felt like for him to be back in Sweden after living in the United States for so many years. After all, he had practically fled Sweden as a teenager in the 1970s, never imagining he would return. At the time Swedish society had felt much too constricting for him, and he still has a soft spot for the American idea of freedom.

"I particularly like the West," Trägårdh had told me during our initial Skype conversation. "There's a libertarian in me who likes that kind of freedom. And as much as I rationally in my brain think that the Nordic social contract is extremely good for the vast majority of people, there's also a very strong American libertarian in me who would prefer not to have any constraints."

Now, over the café's daily special of meat sauce, mashed potatoes, and lingonberries, Trägårdh admitted that there were many things that he continued to miss about the United States. He loved the sociability of Americans and the way they constantly expand their social networks, while Swedes tend to stick with their old group of friends, holiday after holiday. But he has also found Sweden much changed, and for the better. It's a more open society, with more interesting urban life and more diversity than when he left as a youngster. And, he pointed out, the United States has changed too. When he first arrived in America, the country was just coming out of the 1960s and the "summer of love." Since then he has been troubled by changes in the American mind-set.

"One reason that I'm glad to be here in Sweden is that if I look at my friends in New York who have kids that are my children's age, there's just so much pressure early on with the testing. Here it is important to teach children to be independent, to play, to be children. That doesn't figure in New York. The idea of testing four-year-olds, there's something sick about that."

Trägårdh himself had found opportunities in the United States, including financial aid for his college studies, but his children would face a different America. And as Sweden has become more hospitable to him, the United States has become the opposite.

"Having a situation like we have in Sweden where you can be relaxed, things work well, it's not wrought with class issues, you're not paying lots of money and isolating yourself with your little group, and you don't have to insert your children into this highly competitive system so early—once you have children, those things do matter. And there is a financial side to it as well.

My friends who are academics in New York City are complaining about it. Even academics with fairly cushy salaries. They pay so much of their money for these things, and then they have to start saving for college too. So there is sort of a way in which you become really imprisoned."

As we ate and looked at various social research books and studies, he showed me a graph of results from the World Values Survey, a global research project measuring people's beliefs in different countries. Studying the data, Trägårdh has noticed two things. One is that Sweden lies at the highest end of the spectrum when it comes to valuing individual self-realization and personal autonomy, compared to other countries. Indeed, I could see that the dot representing Sweden on the graph was floating alone at the upper right-hand corner of the grid. The other Nordic countries hovered close by. This may come as a surprise to Americans, but the United States hung significantly lower on the graph, indicating that values were more old-fashioned and communitarian.

Seeing that Sweden was something of an outlier on this graph, one could reasonably ask whether Sweden was really a good example for any other country to follow—maybe Sweden was just unique, living in its own reality. Trägårdh had an answer to that. "These studies have been done since the 1980s, and if this was a movie instead of a photograph," he said, gesturing above the graph, "the whole world would be moving this way." He moved his hand toward the dot representing Sweden. The Nordic countries are not just strange and different. They're leading the way. All other advanced nations in the twenty-first century are moving in a similar direction when it comes to these core social values. And according to Trägårdh, that's because people everywhere in the world prefer more freedom rather than less. The American system of today, however, is one of

the laggards, and has yet to embrace the trend, or make significant progress in the direction the rest of the advanced world is
moving—toward more freedom.

"Social systems that do not promote or enable the pursuit of
individual liberty are always going to be at a disadvantage. This
used to be the great strength of the United States, social mobility
and the American dream," Trägårdh said. "But social mobility
without social investments is simply not possible. So if you start
to give up on public schools and a collective system for enabling
individual social mobility, you're going to end up with inequality, gated communities, collapse of trust, a dysfunctional political system. All these things you see now in the United States."

One summer Trevor and I traveled to Wyoming, and I knew
exactly what I wanted to do there. I wanted to go to a rodeo,
my first. We parked in a gravel lot and climbed to our seats
in the metal bleachers, the aroma of horses and earth wafting
around us in the late-afternoon sun. The event kicked off with
the rodeo princess galloping through the ring, muscling a huge
American flag around the arena from her horse. Then a girl
sang the national anthem, while the rugged rodeo riders stood
along the fences with their cowboy hats held over their hearts.
At the end of the anthem, the announcer reminded the audience
to be grateful for the freedoms that are afforded to everyone in
this great country.

After the rodeo, as Trevor drove us slowly back to our lodg-
ings along a pitch-black road populated with deer wandering
the woods and open plains, I thought back to what the rodeo
announcer had said after the national anthem: how grateful
Americans should be for their freedoms. It's an entirely worthy
sentiment that Americans love to express, and they do so often.
Many immigrants come to America from countries that don't

ensure basic freedoms the way the United States does, such as freedom of speech. At the same time it's almost as if Americans don't realize that there are many, many other nations in the world where citizens enjoy exactly the same freedoms that Americans do, and where not as much fuss is made about them. Moreover, Americans don't seem to realize that there are citizens in other parts of the world, like the Nordic region, who have acquired other kinds of freedoms that Americans lack. I gazed through the car window into the vast Wyoming night, the thrill of the rodeo and the wide-open Wild West landscape fresh in my mind, and asked myself: When are you *truly* free?

Are you free when you're a rugged cowboy, alone on the prairie, with no one asking anything of you, and no one giving anything to you? Or is it when you are a homesteader, off the grid, growing your own food, and relying on your family and neighbors when you need help? Or is it when you know that you can become whatever you want and make your own choices regardless of your parents' wealth or abilities, and when you can rest assured that should you or your family falter, your society will be there to keep you on your feet?

It is tempting to go with the first two scenarios, and why not? People in those situations are in many ways free. But then I thought back to a moment in the rodeo, when the action had stopped and the announcer had invited all the kids from the audience out into the ring, celebrated their attendance, and let them run around like little cowboys, chasing a trio of sheep. America loves its freedom, and it clearly loves its children. But it does precious little to provide for either in concrete ways. When those families left the rodeo, they were on their own.

Today nations that have progressed into the twenty-first century see freedom as something much richer. They see freedom as the assurance that all individuals get real opportunity, so they're free to pursue the good life for themselves, and real protection from the lottery of bad luck, so they're free from unnecessary fear and anxiety. And a lot of Americans today are desperate to have those freedoms.

On one visit to Finland I ended up in a bar with a group of old friends. One of them, a well-traveled man and father of two, demanded that I answer this question: "The Nordic model has done phenomenally well. That's a given," he started emphatically. "But what you have to tell *us* here in Finland is why the United States is so *overwhelmingly superior* to all other countries in the world. In business, in the military, in the arts. It is. But why? And why doesn't that show in ordinary Americans' lives?"

The first part of the question I could begin to answer. The United States is a big country with abundant natural resources. It has been able to build its society for more than a hundred years without having had any devastating wars fought on its soil and originally by benefiting from the extermination of the original native landholders and then from slave labor. It has been a magnet to people from all over the world, and it has excelled in encouraging people to work and create. Apart from the institution of slavery and ongoing problems with racism—which is a big caveat—the United States has been a world leader in democracy, opportunity, and freedom. When Alexis de Tocqueville arrived in America from France in the early 1800s, he was astonished by the progress and achievements he found in this young country. At the time Europe was still a continent of kings, czars, and landed gentry, and de Tocqueville saw the United States as an example of what the rest of the world would eventually become: a democracy, and a place where all people are free, equal, and earning their keep through their own work. For a long time the United States led the world in educating its people and spreading its wealth to a majority of them. For a long time America's superiority did manifest itself in ordinary people's lives: Americans were the freest and wealthiest of all.

My friend's second question was harder to answer. Why doesn't American superiority show in ordinary people's lives anymore? All advanced nations are dealing with the same twenty-first-century problems, brought on by globalization and technology, and yet the middle class in those nations has caught up with and in many ways surpassed the American middle class in quality of life.

What I could offer my friend was this: At some point Americans forgot that it's not enough to talk about equal opportunity, democracy, and freedom. These things need to be protected and supported by concrete actions—something that Americans of recent decades have neglected to do. The implications of this are profound. In more cases than not, the guilt and frustration that Americans feel about their difficulties in life, and their anxieties, almost certainly do not arise from any personal failings. The United States today puts people, even people who are doing well, into an intensely stressful logistical nightmare that is exhausting. Why do Americans have to put themselves through this, when there are other ways of life, proved and in place, already functioning well for the combined population of the twenty-six million people of the Nordic region?

When I look at my Nordic friends now, they seem so *free* to me. They work and have children, they engage in hobbies, they travel the world, and they never seem to worry about really going broke. They have health care, day care, and pensions. They can study whatever they want, and they don't have to risk their financial future to do so.

The Nordic countries have their own fiscal conservatives and libertarians who would like to see Nordic public services scaled down and handed over to the private sector instead. Some of them look to the United States as a shining example of the direction in which Nordic countries should proceed. When I hear such views, I worry. True, there is much Nordics could learn from the United States about innovation, entrepreneurship, personal responsibility, positive thinking, acceptance of diversity, and above all, the irrepressible drive to excel in whatever task is at hand. At the same time the Nordic countries have managed to create free societies that also provide security while at once supporting exceptional levels of autonomy and strengthening families. They are by no means perfect, and they have their own problems, but they have managed to give people the independence necessary to shape their own lives, and to love their family and friends without economic encumbrance and without debilitating anxiety. All these achievements should not be overlooked, and nor should they be dismissed as products of unique Nordic circumstance and culture. Make no mistake: These achievements may have been inspired by the Nordic theory of love, but they are not achievements of culture, they are achievements of policy. And any country can institute smart policies, especially America.

The longer I lived in the United States the more I began to love many aspects of my new life. There were the people—my American family and friends. There was the diversity—the multitude of ideas, religions, and cultures, the whole world inside one country's borders. There was the natural beauty I'd seen—the forests of Maine, the deserts and canyons of Utah and Arizona, the beaches of California, and the craggy mountains and sweet-smelling fields of Wyoming on a summer evening. There were the warm American values of loving your family, helping your neighbor, and showing kindness and generosity even to strangers. And there was the accumulation of talent drawn to this one country from all over the world, which has produced astonishing levels of excellence in every field of human endeavor imaginable. After coming to America I felt as if I was now truly part of the world, and I found the feeling exhilarating, as if I had been sitting in a small, quiet cabin and suddenly all the windows had been opened to reveal a carnival outside. I loved being inside the nice cabin, but I also wanted to become one more participant in the carnival outdoors.

When I pondered the good and bad of my life in the United States, on the bad side of the scale was the heavy burden of anxiety I felt on an almost daily basis about the prospect of starting a family, or simply surviving in the harsh conditions that America today imposes on its middle class. Much of my energy was spent worrying whether I would ever make enough money to achieve the kind of quality of life that I'd been able to attain in Finland, with a basic sense of security, fewer administrative hassles, and more time to spend with my loved ones. On the good side of the scale were all the things I loved about America. And the question that preoccupied me the most was this: Does it really have to be a choice between these two?

Individualism is one of the great foundations of Western culture. But unless society secures personal independence and basic security for the individual, it can lead to disaffection, anxiety, and chaos. For a long time now the United States has been turning toward its Wild West past, while the Nordic nations have been taking individualism in the logical direction of further progress, and into the future. While some of the praise heaped on the Nordic nations in the international media and various studies has surely been exaggerated and overpositive—no place is flawless, as Nordic people themselves will be the first to point out—the Nordic countries have undeniably created a model for what a high quality of life and a healthy society can look like in the twenty-first century. Bill Clinton's question to Finland's president Tarja Halonen about what advice she would give to other countries was a good one. The Nordic nations have set an example from which America could profitably borrow, and in the process, possibly return itself to its former glory as the best country in the world. If that were to happen, I, for one, might want to stay forever.

EPILOGUE

On Wednesday, November 6, 2013, I entered the U.S. District Court for the Eastern District of New York, in downtown Brooklyn, with my American husband, Trevor, and my Finnish friend Alli in tow. I made my way into a wood-paneled room lined with portraits of serious men, and sat down on a long wooden bench. On my left side sat an elderly Korean man, and on my right a young Chinese man. Other seats were taken by a group of women from the Caribbean, Asian men and women of all ages, and an elderly blonde woman speaking in Russian with a younger, bald man wearing earrings and a dark green tuxedo jacket. An old woman in a headscarf leaned on a walker and dozed off in the front row, and a mother in a hijab entertained her young child in a stroller with colored pens and paper.

Eventually we were called one by one to the table at the center of the room to proffer our paperwork and sign our certificates, and then we waited again. I read a book I had brought with me—*To Kill a Mockingbird*—and chatted with the man sitting to my left. He'd come to America from Korea in the 1970s, served four years in the American army, and ran his own business, not far from where I now lived, until he retired. The man on my right didn't seem to speak much English, and when the voter registration forms were passed around, he filled out the Chinese-language version.

Finally our family and friends were allowed into the room and the judge came in. Everyone stood up, and the judge led us in reciting the oath of allegiance for new citizens, and then the Pledge of Allegiance. She told us that she herself, as well as several of her colleagues in that very courthouse, had come to America as children without knowing English, and yet had risen to become federal judges. She also acknowledged the mistrust we might now feel toward the American government—a reference to the recent revelations of the government's electronic surveillance programs—but assured us that the United States is still a country of opportunity. After she finished, we were called one by one to receive our certificates. With that I became an American citizen.

As I walked out through the courthouse doors into the cool fall day with Trevor and Alli, I felt intoxicated. How did I get here? How did I, a girl from a small suburb in Finland, end up a citizen of the United States of America? I thought of all the millions of people around the world who needed this citizenship far more than I did, and of the hundreds of thousands of undocumented immigrants living in the United States, many of whom were brought to this country as children but still have trouble getting citizenship. But isn't this the essential American experience of today, I thought—squinting my eyes at the sun— this combination of pride in America's greatness and dismay at its brutal inequalities, all at the same time?

I also thought about how, as I'd prepared to become an American citizen, I'd read up on American history, and studied the Constitution and the Declaration of Independence. I realized what a privilege it was to become a member of this society. I could make an active choice to sign up for the basic ideals of the United States, for the fundamentals of freedom and justice, and that was all that was asked of me. No one asked me to change my religion, dress, diet, or customs. Nobody inquired whether I eat turkey at Thanksgiving or love American football. They did require me to speak English, but the test was rudimentary.

For all practical purposes I can be who I am, and as long as I accept the American idea of everyone's right to be who they are, I'm accepted. Not many countries in the world can say that for themselves.

As we stopped outside the courthouse doors to take a photo and get our bearings—where in the neighborhood could we get some apple pie?—a man with thick-rimmed glasses and a gray winter coat came out of the courthouse with his newly Americanized wife. He kept hugging her excitedly, while she smiled demurely, grasping her certificate in her hand just as I was grasping mine. Trevor offered to take a photo of them with their camera, and as they prepared to leave, the man glanced back at me.

"Enjoy America," he said, grinning. "I hope you like it."

ACKNOWLEDGMENTS

W hen I moved to the United States at the end of 2008, I knew only a handful of people in this vast nation. I had worked all my life in Finland, and I had never attempted to write a book, let alone one in English. While it's become a cliché to say that one has "depended on the kindness of strangers"—a strategy that didn't work too well for Blanche DuBois, who first uttered the famous line in Tennessee Williams's *A Streetcar Named Desire*—in my case, that's exactly what I've done. Numerous people in the United States have given me their friendship, support, and advice, and placed their faith in my abilities when they had little evidence that I actually possessed any. They all have my eternal gratitude.

My profound thanks go to my editor, Gail Winston, and everyone at HarperCollins, my agent, Kim Witherspoon, and everyone at Inkwell Management, Stephanie Mehta and everyone who worked at *Fortune* during my brief fellowship there, Sewell Chan of the *New York Times*, Jennie Rothenberg Gritz of the *Atlantic*, and Hugh Van Dusen and Wendy Wolf. They all took a chance on me and helped me start a writing career in the United States. Gail, in particular, never seemed discouraged when faced with the unwieldy first drafts of this book. Instead she proceeded to do what a great editor does: save the writer from herself.

I'm grateful to the KONE Foundation, the Alfred Kordelin Foundation, and the Finnish Association of Non-Fiction Writers for their support, and to the Helsingin Sanomat Foundation for funding the fellowship that allowed me to come to the United States in the first place.

I interviewed more than a hundred people for this book. Most of them are not named, but I thank them all. I am especially indebted to those who shared their personal experiences with me and introduced me to other people to interview. Special thanks to Jennifer Bensko Ha, Maria-Eugenia Dalton, Mads Egeskov Sørensen, Sigrid Egeskov Andersen, Brandur Ellingsgaard, Hannah Villadsen Ellingsgaard, Pamela Harrell-Savukoski, Kaarina Hazard, Ville Heiskanen, Nina Jähi, Tracy Høeg, Hanna and Olli Lehtonen, Mika Oksa, Kerstin Sjödén, and Fredrik Wass. Thank you, *kiitos, tack, tak*.

Several experts were exceptionally generous with their time and insights, including Lars Trägårdh, Pasi Sahlberg, Tine Rostgaard, Markus Jäntti, Laura Hartman, Leena Krokfors, Juhana Vartiainen, Sixten Korkman, Bengt Holmström, Heikki Hiilamo, Pauli Kettunen, Jaana Leipälä, Juha Hernesniemi, Sakari Orava, and Risto E. J. Penttilä. (They don't all agree with one another, and naturally the conclusions I've drawn and any mistakes are my own.) I'd also like to thank the employees of the multiple Finnish government agencies who answered my endless questions patiently and promptly. I must say, I love the Finnish bureaucrat!

Friends and colleagues encouraged me along the way, sent me articles and books to read, suggested people to interview, shared their own experiences with me, and generally kept me sane through the struggle and frustration of trying to think clearly and write well. I cannot thank enough Tulikukka de Fresnes, Anna-Liina Kauhanen, Taina and David Droeske, Mari Saarenpää, Veera Sylvius, Mari Teittinen, Noora Vainio, Alli Haapasalo, Chris Giordano, Laura and Saska Saarikoski, Spencer Boyer, Clare Stroud, Jessica DuLong, and Ben Rubin.

My family on both sides of the Atlantic never wavered in their love and support, even when it must have seemed to them that this book would never be done. Kirsti, Erkki, and Esa Partanen, Mikko and Veera Korvenkari, Sarah Corson, Dick Atlee, Ash Corson, Ann Corson, Jon Jaeger, Holly Lord, John Coyle, and everyone in the Lord family. Thank you for everything.

Finally there's Trevor Corson, who never tired of talking over ideas with me, or reading many, many—too many—drafts of this book before I ever dared show them to anyone else. To have your best friend and life partner be such a generous and encouraging person as well as such a fantastic colleague—all writers should be so lucky.

NOTES

All references below indicate items that are listed in the bibliography, unless otherwise noted. For bibliography items, the primary author's last name is given, plus page numbers for the longer documents; if the item has no author listed, or the same author has multiple entries in the bibliography, or several authors share the same last name, the first word or two of the item's title is given as well.

PROLOGUE

1   Description of panel discussion with President Clinton is based on an online video: Clinton Global Initiative.

3   Finnish high-school students: OECD, *Lessons*, 116; Ministry of Education and Culture, *Finland and PISA*.

3   *Newsweek*: Foroohar, 30–32.

4   *Monocle*: Morris, 18–22.

4   World Economic Forum: Schwab *Global Competitiveness Report 2011–2012; Global Competitiveness Report 2012–2013*.

4   Work-life balance: Ranking is based on the OECD's online tool, *Better Life Index*. Results for work-life balance in 2011–2012 were reported by Bradford; Thompson.

4   Innovation: European Commission, 7.

4   Happiness: Helliwell, 30.

5   *Financial Times*: Milne.

5   Failed states: Fund for Peace.

5   Ed Miliband comments: Miliband.

5   "Scandinavian" vs. "Nordic": In the Nordic nations "Scandinavia" is usually understood to include only Denmark, Norway, and Sweden due to their closely related North Germanic languages. Icelandic is a subset of the same language family. Finnish, by con-

trast, is a completely unrelated language of Uralic origin. These five nations use the term "Nordic" to refer to themselves as a culturally and politically unified region. To English-speakers, however, the term "Nordic" can evoke racist ideas popular in Nazi Germany, and thus in the United States "Scandinavia" is commonly used to refer to all five Nordic countries.

6   David Cameron and the Nordic nations: Bagehot.

6   *The Economist*'s special report: Wooldridge.

6   *Vanity Fair* on Scandinavia: Hotchner.

ONE: IN THE LAND OF THE FREE

12   Poisoned cookies: Greenhouse.

13   Helen Mirren: Hattenstone.

17   Sick days and parental leaves in Finland: Citizens have a universal right to about one year of paid sick leave and ten months of paid parental leave. Pay during a leave is subsidized by the government and covers part of the leave taker's salary (for parental leave, about 70 percent). Some employers offer better benefits, usually due to collective agreements. Employers can fire a sick employee only if an illness has prevented the employee from performing his or her tasks for an extended period of time, usually a year. See Kela, *Health*, 8–10; Kela, *Maternity*, 2–8; Virta.

20   Credit cards: Credit card interest rates and fees are notoriously difficult to compare, but one survey in 2011 put the average American annual percentage rate at 15 percent, with rates ranging from about 11 to 25 percent, while another survey put the Finnish range from about 7.5 to 14.5 percent. I myself had never received one single credit card offer in the mail in Finland. See Tomasino; Ranta.

20   Cell phones: Since my arrival in the United States, American cell phone carriers have started to sell phones and plans separately, and Finnish carriers have started to offer package deals. However, a 2014 report found that mobile data in Finland were still among the cheapest in the world, while American data were among the most expensive. Finns paid $5.18 for 500 MB of mobile data while Amer-

icans paid $76.21. See International Telecommunication Union, 132.

22   Anxiety-inducing articles about superachievers and the unfortunate: Baker; Holmes; Lublin; Seligson; Abelson; Jubera; Mascia.

22   Food-borne illness: Moss.

22   Toxic plastic bottles: Grady.

22   Toxic toys: Lipton.

22   Antibiotics and cattle: Kristof, "The Spread."

23   Countries by GDP per capita: OECD, *National*, 25.

24   Anxiety disorders and sales of prescription drugs: National Institute of Mental Health; IMS Health; Smith.

24   Women's financial insecurity: When the study was repeated in 2013, the results were very similar, with 27 percent of women with household income of more than two hundred thousand dollars fearing "becoming a bag lady." See Coombes; Allianz.

25   Uninsured in the United States: According to the U.S. Census Bureau, 16.7 percent of Americans, or 50.7 million people, lacked health insurance in 2009. See DeNavas-Walt, 22.

26   *Newsweek* on the best country in the world: Foroohar, 30–32.

27   David Beckham's operation: Beckham was operated on in Turku, Finland, by a Finnish sports-injury specialist named Sakari Orava. See Young.

30   Parents doing children's homework: The prestigious Sidwell Friends School in Washington, DC, went so far as to write a letter to parents urging them to let students do their own English homework without editing by parents or tutors. See Sidwell.

31   Parents texting with college-age offspring, influencing their college opportunities, and being their best friends: Volk Miller; DeParle, "For Poor"; Williams.

32   "Helicopter parenting": Gottlieb, "How"; Gunn; Kolbert.

33   Sales of antianxiety and antidepression drugs: McDevitt.

34   Finnish children named Ridge and Brooke: Population Register Centre.

37   Career women on finding a spouse: Bolick; Gottlieb, "Marry"; Rosin.

37   Marriage among high-school educated whites: Murray.

37   Debate over marriage: Chait; Cherlin; DeParle, "For Women"; Frum; Samarrai; Schuessler.

38   Twenty-thousand dollars for giving birth: Wildman.

39   Law on American parental leaves: U.S. Department of Labor.

TWO: THE NORDIC THEORY OF LOVE

47   *Pippi Longstocking* in translation: Astridlindgren.se.

49   *Är svensken människa?*: Berggren, *Är*; Neander-Nilsson.

51   Trägårdh and Berggren's discussion on *Pippi Longstocking*: Berggren, "Pippi," 12.

54   Finland's war losses 1939–1944: Some 700,000 Finns, from a population of 3.7 million, fought in the wars, and 93,000 died. See Leskinen, 1152–55.

55   "The number of Finns who sacrificed their lives": American deaths in the Korean and Vietnam Wars amount to 95,000, almost the same as Finland's losses (93,000) in the two wars against the Soviet Union. The Finnish population was 5.5 million in July 2015, while America's was 320 million. Leskinen, 1152–53; Leland, 3.

57   Child well-being in different countries: UNICEF.

57   World's best countries for mothers: Save, 10.

58   Trägårdh and Berggren on family as a social institution: Berggren, "Social," 15.

60   "We're living in the middle of an amazing era": Brooks.

THREE: FAMILY VALUES FOR REAL

64   Average annual cost of child care for an infant in the state of New York was $10,400, and in New York City $16,250 in 2009. See Office of Senator Kirsten Gillibrand, *Child Care*.

65   Costs of giving birth: Truven; Rosenthal, "American Way."

65   Law on American parental leaves: U.S. Department of Labor.

65   Workers covered by the law granting right to parental leave: Klerman.

66   Pregnant women losing their jobs and lack of job security in the United States: Bakst; Graff; Liptak; Redden; Suddath; Swarns; New York State Office of the Attorney General.

66   Parental leaves around the world: Addati, 16.

66   Sick leave in different countries: Heymann; World Policy Forum.

66   Cities and states offering paid sick leave in the United States: White House Office, "White House Unveils."

66   California's paid family leave program: Employment Development.

66   Examples of corporate family leave policies: Grant.

67   Americans' access to paid leave: Bureau of Labor Statistics, "Table 32" and "Table 38."

67   Length of maternity leave taken in the United States: U.S. Department of Health, 40.

70   Cost of Hanna's hospital stay: In 2015 the maximum charge for a day in a basic room at a public hospital in Finland was €38.10. The hospital Hanna stayed in charged double for a private family room. She paid for four days at a rate of €76.20 and for one day at a rate of €38.10, bringing her total bill to €342.90, which in July 2015 equaled about $375. The price included room and board, doctors' fees, all operations, and drugs provided in-house. Ministry of Social Affairs and Health, *Terveydenhuollon*; HUS.

71   Average length of stay for normal delivery in different countries: OECD, *Health at a Glance 2015*, 109.

72   Nordic maternity benefits as a percentage of salary: Nordic Social, 42.

72   Parental leave in Norway: Norwegian Labour.

72   Administration of parental leave benefits in Nordic countries: Aula, 33–34, 42–44.

73   Breast-feeding in Finland: Uusitalo.

73   The length of parental leaves and other information on Finnish family benefits can be found on the Web site of Kela, the Social Security Institution of Finland. In order to qualify for paternity leave, a father must reside in the home with the mother and the child. See Kela, *Benefits for Families*.

74   Access to day care for Nordic parents: After the birth of a child, the right to public day care in Nordic countries typically starts later

than many American parents would expect it to, not until a child is between six months and one year old, depending on the country. From an American perspective, one could argue that the lack of public day care options for younger infants limits parents' ability to return to work sooner, should they want to. However, in Nordic countries most parents are happy to take full advantage of the long parental leaves that are guaranteed to everyone, thus this has not become an issue. Nordic Social, 57–63.

74   Finnish children in day care by age and type of institution: Säkkinen.

75   Public day-care fees in Finland: Ministry of Education *Varhaiskasvatuksen*.

75   Swedish parental leave: Försäkringskassan.

76   Swedish day-care fees: Nordic Social, 73.

76   Nordic children enrolled in day care by age: Nordic Social, 62.

76   Part-time parental leave in Nordic countries: Duvander, 43.

76   Caring at home for a sick child: Nordic Social, 52–53.

76   Vacation time in Finland: Ministry of Employment and Economy.

76   Paid vacation in other Nordic countries: European Foundation, 17–19; Fjölmenningarsetur.

78   Finland's baby box: Tierney; Kela, *Maternity*.

81   "Why, in the world's most affluent": Newman, Kindle loc. 207.

81   "Citizens of Norway, Denmark, Finland": Newman, 39–40.

82   Nordic unemployment benefits and policies: Nordic Social, 79–102; Kela, *Unemployment*.

84   Marco Rubio's speech: Quotes are from a transcript published on Senator Rubio's Web site. See Rubio.

84   Job training for the unemployed in Finland: Kela, *Unemployment*.

85   Married, cohabiting, and single parents in different countries: OECD, *Doing Better for Families*, 28.

86   Studies on problems experienced by children in single-parent families: Amato; Berger, 160–161; U.S. Department of Health, 12; DeParle, "For Women"; Murray.

86   Claim that government programs destroy families: for example, see Edsall; Levin; Rubio.

86   Cross-national comparison of single parenthood: Casey.

86 Family structure in different countries: Livingston; OECD, *Doing Better*, 25–28; OECD, *Family Database*; Statistics Finland.

87 "The patterns of family formation": Newman, 159.

88 Parental leave benefits for someone without work history, in Finland and other Nordic countries: Nordic Social, 40–42; Kela, *Allowance* and *Amount*.

89 Single parents in employment: OECD, *Doing Better*, 216, 225, 238.

90 Jennifer M. Silva on young working-class Americans and marriage: Silva.

91 Share of female parliamentarians and cabinet members in different countries: OECD, *Women*, 28–29.

92 Time spent on child care and housework by gender: Bureau of Labor Statistics, "Table 1" and "Table 9"; Miranda, 11–12; Parker, *Modern*.

92 Finnish children in day care: Säkkinen.

92 Breast-feeding guidelines and reality in Finland: To be exact, WHO recommends breast-feeding, with complementary foods, up to the age of two or beyond, and Finland recommends it up to the age of one or beyond. Aula, 49; World Health Organization; National Institute of Health, *Tietopaketit*; Uusitalo.

94 Daddy quotas in Nordic countries: Denmark introduced a father's quota in 1997 but abolished it in 2002. Other Nordic countries continue to have them. The information on Nordic parental leaves is current as of July 2015. See Duvander, 38–39; Nordic Social, 41–49; Rostgaard, 8–9; OECD, *Closing*, 208; Poulsen; Försäkringskassan; Kela, *Paternity*; Norwegian.

94 Daddy quotas' impact on housework, child care, and paid work: Addati, 52; Nordic Social 49; OECD, *Closing*, 208–9; Patnaik; National Institute of Health, *Tilastotietoa*.

95 American men's attitudes and challenges related to paternity leave: Berdahl; Cain Miller, "Paternity Leave"; Harrington; Ludden; Mundy.

96 Marissa Mayer's pregnancy: Sellers; Swisher.

97 Sheryl Sandberg's *Lean In*: Sandberg, chaps. 7 and 9.

97 Nordic and American women as managers: Blau; OECD, *Closing* 156, 177.

98 American stay-at-home moms: Cohn.

98 Nordic and American women in the labor force: In 1990 the United States had the sixth-highest female labor participation rate among twenty-two OECD countries. By 2010 its rank had fallen to seventeenth. See Blau; OECD *Closing*, 156, 177, 235.

99 American families with two working parents: Parker.

99 Cost of day care in the U.S.: Child Care Aware.

100 Nordic children in day care: Nordic Social, 62.

100 Ideal length of maternity leave for women's careers: Addati, 8–9; OECD, *Closing*, 209; World Economic Forum, *Global Gender* (2015), 43; OECD, *Babies*, 21; Cain Miller, "Can."

101 Gender gap in different countries: World Economic Forum, *Global Gender* (2013) 20; World Economic Forum, *Global Gender* (2015), 4, 8.

102 White House Report on family policies and economic growth: Executive Office of the President, 43.

102 Family and medical leave laws in American states: National Conference, *State Family*.

103 Consequences of California's paid parental leave: Appelbaum; *Economic Report of the President*, 130.

103 The Family Act: Office of Senator Kirsten Gillibrand, *American*.

104 President Obama's leave proposals: *Economic Report of the President*, 130; White House Office, "White House Unveils."

104 ILO's recommendations and development of parental leaves: Addati, 9, 11, 16, 20, 22, 25–27.

105 International organizations' support for paid leaves and affordable child care: European Commission; OECD, *Closing*, 18–19; World Economic Forum, *Global Gender* (2015), 36–43.

FOUR: HOW CHILDREN ACHIEVE

110 Charter school performance: Center for Research on Education Outcomes.

111 Children of the rich outperform other children: Reardon.

112 Finland and the United States in PISA: Kupari; Ministry of Education, *Finland and PISA*; Ministry of Education, PISA12; OECD,

Country; OECD, *Lessons*; OECD, *PISA 2009 Results*; OECD, *PISA 2012 Results: What Students Know*; Sahlberg, "Why."

114 History of Finland's education system: OECD, *Lessons*, 118–123; Sahlberg, *Finnish*, chap. 1.

116 "Some predicted a gloomy future": Sahlberg, *Finnish*, 19.

117 Sahlberg's visit at the Dwight School: In-person observations by the author; some of the material here has been published previously in the *Atlantic*. See Partanen.

118 Independent schools and private universities in Finland: The one exception is the International School of Helsinki, which has permission from the Ministry of Education to charge annual tuition of almost ten thousand dollars because it follows an international curriculum and serves mainly children of foreign families living in the country temporarily. E-mail interview with Anne-Marie Brisson of the Ministry of Education and Culture (Aug. 4, 2015); e-mail interview with Laura Hansén of the Ministry of Education and Culture (Aug. 10, 2015); Ministry of Education and Culture, *Basic*, *Funding*, and *Valtioneuvosto*; Basic Education Act 628/1998, chap. 3 and chap. 7, section 31; Yle.

118 Right to free education in Finland: Ministry of Justice, section 17.

120 Poor economics and supply vs. demand approach to education: Banerjee, chap. 4.

121 American students in private schools, expansion of for-profit schools, and private testing services: Chingos, 10; Miron; Kena, 74.

121 Private schools in Sweden: OECD, *Equity*, 71; OECD, *Improving*, 93–96.

121 Standardized testing in various countries: Morris.

121 India's school vouchers: Muralidharan; Shah.

121 Obama's and Romney's views on education: Gabriel; Romney; White House Office, "Remarks by the President on Education Reform."

122 "A civilized society cannot allow": Banerjee, 78.

123 Parents' wealth and education and American students' school success: OECD, *Country*; OECD, *Lessons*, 34; OECD, *Economic Policy*, 188; OECD, *PISA 2012 Results: Excellence Through Equity*, 39; Reardon.

124 Child poverty in different countries: UNICEF Innocenti; UNICEF Office, 7.

125 Debate on poverty and school reform: See, for example, Klein; Rhee; Thomas.

125 Risks related to child poverty: UNICEF Innocenti, 4.

125 Countries with more inequality but less variety in educational outcomes than the United States: OECD, *Lessons*, 34.

125 Income inequality in Finland: OECD, *Society*, 66–67.

128 Examples of influential studies on the benefits of early-childhood education: Campbell; Schweinhart.

128 Expanding early-childhood education in the United States: National Center for Education Statistics, "Table 5.1"; White House Office, *President Obama's Plan*; Harris.

128 Nordic children in day care: Ministry of Education and Culture, *Every Child*; Nordic Social, 57–62; Säkkinen.

129 Finnish day-care activities and goals: Skype interview with Eeva Hujala of Tampere University (Jan. 31, 2013); author interviews with parents; daily schedules posted online by Finnish day-care centers.

131 Finnish day-care regulations and quality: At the time of writing in 2015, the Finnish government was planning to allow a staff-to-child ratio of one adult for eight children over the age of three. Ministry of Education and Culture, *Early Childhood*; Taguma; UNICEF Office, 21.

131 Sam Kass on day care: Kass spoke at *Parenting* magazine's 2012 Mom Congress in Washington, DC.

134 Teacher education in Finland: OECD, *Lessons* 125; Sahlberg, *Finnish*, chap. 3; interview with Leena Krokfors of Helsinki University (Oct. 12, 2012).

134 Teacher education in the United States: Foderaro; Greenberg; Levine; National Council on Teacher Quality; NYC Department; Putnam; Smith.

135 Criticism of Teach for America: Naison; Ehrenfreund; Rich, "Fewer"; Winerip.

135 Teachers' salaries: OECD, *Education*, 454.

135 High performers in PISA invest in teachers: OECD, *Does Money*.

136 Standardized tests in the United States: The 2001 "No Child Left Behind" law signed by President George W. Bush made the tests a requirement for receiving federal funds. In recent years a movement opposing excessive testing has gained ground. In 2015 the Obama administration acknowledged that its policies had helped push testing and teacher evaluations too far. Efforts to reform "No Child Left Behind" were ongoing at the time of writing. For reform efforts, see Rich, "'No Child'"; Steinhauer; Strauss; Zernike, "Obama."

137 Rating schools and teachers based on students' test scores: Aviv; Banchero; Harris; OECD, *Country*, 5; Otterman; Rizga; Santos, "City Teacher Data" and "Teacher Quality."

137 Autonomy of Finnish schools: Interviews with Pasi Sahlberg (Dec. 8, 2011, May 11, 2012, and Oct. 25, 2014); Sahlberg, "Quality," 28; OECD, *Lessons*, 123–27; interview with principal Mika Oksa (Mar. 7, 2012).

139 Finnish teachers unions: According to the Trade Union of Education in Finland, 95 percent of teachers in Finland are members, even though unionization in Finland is completely voluntary. See http://www.oaj.fi/cs/oaj/public_en.

139 Cost of standardized tests in the United States: Chingos.

139 Schools cheating on tests: The most infamous cheating scandal in the United States so far happened in Atlanta, where eighty-two educators in thirty schools confessed to inflating students' test scores in one school year. Eleven public school teachers were convicted of crimes, and some were sentenced to several years in prison, for repeatedly erasing and replacing students' answers on tests. Widespread cheating has been reported in dozens of cities. See Aviv; Fausset; Rich, "Scandal"; U.S. Government Accountability Office.

141 Subjects taught in Finnish schools: The Finnish National Core Curriculum and minimum instruction hours for all subjects can be found online at the Finnish National Board of Education Web site.

141 Arts education in American schools: Dillon; McMurrer; U.S. Department of Education, "Prepared Remarks of U.S. Secretary of Education"; Parsad.

141 Finland adding more lessons in arts and crafts: Ministry of Education and Culture, *Työryhmä*.

142 Dan Rather interviewing Linda Darling-Hammond: Stanford-Scope.

143 Tiistilä School: I attended the upper school from the fall of 1987 to the spring of 1990. My reporting there for this book took place on Sept. 10–11, 2013. I rely on my own observations as well as interviews with school staff and students, particularly the school principal, Mirja Pirinen, and the assistant principal, Marikka Korhonen.

143 Size of Finnish schools and classes: Ministry of Education and Culture, *Opetusryhmien tila*, 22, 25–26; OECD, *Lessons*, 124.

144 Finnish law stating that children need time for hobbies and rest: Basic Education Act 628/1998, chap. 6, section 24.

144 Impact of private tutoring and other family spending on the American educational gap: Associated Press, "School Spending"; Duncan, 3–4; Greenstone, *Dozen*, 12, and *Thirteen*, chap. 2; Phillips.

145 Afternoon care for Finnish school children: In 2011, 98 percent of Finnish municipalities offered afternoon care for students in first or second grade. Ministry of Education and Culture, *Perusopetuksen*.

145 Time spent in school in different countries: OECD, *Education*, 428.

146 Ranking schools in Finland: The Finnish National Matriculation Examination Board published results for individual academic high schools on its Web site for the first time in 2015, but the schools were listed in alphabetical order and the results were hard to understand without further analysis. That job was left to the media. Overall, Finnish education administrators and researchers have shown profound dislike for such rankings. See Kortelainen; Laitinen; Mäkinen; Takala; Ylioppilastutkintolautakunta.

146 Collaboration in Finnish schools: Author interviews with Finnish teachers; Toivanen; Peltomäki; Schleicher, 19.

146 Problems related to team sports in American schools: Lavigne; Ripley, "The Case"; Wolverton.

147 Exchange students' observations in different countries: Ripley, "The Smartest," 71–72, 99–101, 196.

150 Parental involvement and student achievement: Robinson.

150 Fredrick M. Hess on "Finlandophilia": Jenny Anderson.

151 Diversity in Finland and the United States: Grieco; Statistics Finland, *Foreigners*.

152 Norwegian approach to education: Abrams; OECD, *Education Policy Outlook Norway*.

152 Swedish approach to education: Hartman; OECD, *Improving Schools in Sweden*.

154 School funding in Finland: Eurydice; STT.

155 "Local property wealth per capita in a given state's richest school district": Carey, "School Funding's," 6.

155 School funding in the United States: Carey, "School Funding's"; Baker; Ushomirsky; U.S. Department of Education, "For Each and Every Child," 17–20.

155 "Imagine two towns": U.S. Department of Education, "For Each and Every Child," 17.

156 Education spending in different countries: In 2011, Luxembourg, Switzerland, Norway, Austria, and the United States spent the most out of all OECD countries on primary and secondary education (usually ages six to fifteen) when measured as dollars per student, including public and private spending. As a percentage of GDP, the U.S. came in eighth in total education spending for all levels of education (including universities), while Finland came in eleventh. OECD, *Country*, 4; OECD, *Education at a Glance 2014*, 222; OECD, *Education Spending*; OECD, *Lessons*, 28, 130.

156 Dan Rather on education administration in Finland and Los Angeles: Dan.

157 Finns borrowing ideas from other countries: Interview with Leena Krokfors of Helsinki University (Oct. 12, 2012); interviews with Pasi Sahlberg (Dec. 8 , 2011, May 11, 2012, and Oct. 25, 2014); Sahlberg, *Finnish*, 34–35.

158 University rankings: Times.

158 "When President Obama has said": Carey, "Americans Think."

159 Adult literacy, numeracy, and technological skills in different countries: OECD, *OECD Skills Outlook*.

160 Higher education spending and costs for families in the United

States: In 2015 the College Board estimated that undergraduate tuition, fees, room, and board at American public institutions costs on average $19,548 for one academic year, and at private nonprofit institutions $43,921 for one academic year—bringing the total average published price for a private four-year college education for one student to $175,000. See College Board; *Economic Report of the President*, 132–34, 137–38; Kirshstein; OECD, Education spending (indicator).

160 University fees and stipends in Finland: Public financial support for a student in higher education consists of a study grant, housing supplement, and government guarantee for student loans. In the spring of 2016 the monthly study grant was €336.75 for all students over the age of eighteen not living with their parents. The maximum monthly rent subsidy came to €201.60 for all students not living with their parents nor renting accommodation owned by their parents. Thus the maximum financial aid for living expenses came to slightly less than six hundred dollars per month, at March 2016 exchange rates. In addition, rents in student housing and terms for student loans are reasonable, and other subsidies for meals and transportation may apply. See Student Union; Kela, *Government Guarantee*; Kela, *Housing Supplement*, Kela, *Study Grant*.

161 American college admissions for those who can pay or are children of alumni: Mandery; Zernike, "Paying."

163 Finnish goal of meaningful education or employment for all youths under the age of twenty-five: Ministry of Education and Culture, *Koulutustakuu*.

FIVE: HEALTHY BODY, HEALTHY MIND

168 Life of uninsured Americans: Buckley; Kristof, "A Possibly Fatal."

169 Americans dying for lack of health insurance: Doyle; FactCheck. Org; IOM, *Care* and *America's;* Krugman, "Death"; Sommers; Weiner.

170 Hospitals charging the uninsured: Arnold, "When Nonprofit"; Brill; Silver-Greenberg; Rosenthal, "As Hospital."

170 Medical bankruptcy in the United States: Brill; Himmelstein; La Montagne; Sack; Underwood.

171 Health-care systems in different countries: Reid.

173 Health insurance coverage in the United States in 2014: The percentages add up to more than 100 percent because people may be covered by more than one type of health insurance during the year. Smith.

174 Medicaid eligibility: Artiga.

178 Americans losing and gaining health insurance: Hayes; Rosenbaum: Sanger-Katz.

178 Americans postponing retirement because of health insurance: Fronstin.

178 Employment rates in different countries: OECD, *OECD Factbook 2014*, 133.

182 Cost of employer-sponsored health insurance in the United States: Claxton; Rosenthal, "The $2.7 Trillion."

184 Out-of-pocket maximums and other health-care fees in Finland: More information can be found on the Web sites of the Finnish Ministry of Social Affairs and Health; and Kela, the Social Insurance Institution of Finland. Health-care services for children under the age of eighteen count toward their guardian's out-of-pocket maximum. After the out-of-pocket maximum for prescription drugs is reached, the patient has to pay less than three dollars per prescription. For coverage of drugs, see Finnish Medicines Agency.

184 Government subsidies for private health care in Finland: Blomgren; Kela, *Statistical Yearbook*, 166–67, 169.

185 Access to specialists and elective surgery in different countries: Davis 20; Gubb 8, 16–18; OECD, *Health at a Glance 2015*, 128–29.

187 Health outcomes, survival rates, access to care and comparisons of health-care systems in different countries: Commonwealth Fund, "Why Not the Best," 24–25; Davis; OECD, *Health at a Glance 2015*, 46–45, 58–59, 81, 151, 153, 155.

188 "American medicine is the best in the world when it comes to": NPR.

189 Harvard study on medical bankruptcy: Himmelstein.

190 Costs for patients after ObamaCare: Goodnough, "Unable"; Health Care.gov; Rosenthal, "After Surgery," "As Insurers," and "Costs."

190 Health-care spending in different countries: OECD *Health at a Glance 2015,* 164–65.

191 Prices of procedures in different countries: International Federation.

191 "Americans pay, on average, about four times as much for a hip replacement": Rosenthal, "The 2.7 Trillion."

192 Why American health care is so expensive: Bach; Brill; Fujisawa; Gawande; International Federation; OECD, *Health at a Glance 2015,* 114–15, and *Why*; Rampell; Rosenthal, "In Need," "The Soaring Cost," and "Medicine's"; Squires.

196 Sarah Palin on death panels: Drobnic Holan.

197 The price of a hip replacement in American hospitals: Rosenthal, "Availability."

198 American doctors spending time getting drugs and treatments covered: Davis, 23; Ofri.

200 Drug and treatment coverage in Finland: Finnish Medicines Agency; e-mail interview with Lauri Pelkonen of the Ministry of Social Affairs and Health (Aug. 21, 2015); interview with Jaana Leipälä of the National Institute of Health and Welfare (Oct. 17, 2013).

201 How drug and treatment coverage works in the United States: Bach; Brill; Jacobs; Lim; Rosenthal, "Insured," Siddiqui.

202 Trust in doctors in different countries: Blendon.

202 Births relying on midwives vs. obstetricians: OECD, *Health at a Glance 2013,* 68.

203 American doctors overusing MRI tests and antibiotics: OECD, *Health at a Glance 2013,* 86–87, 110–11; *Health at a Glance 2015,* 102–3, 136–37.

205 Guy Thompto on freedom: The online commentator going by the name Thompto left his comment (July 11, 2012) on a *New York Times* opinion piece written by the Czech film director Milos Forman titled "Obama the Socialist? Not Even Close" (July 10, 2012).

207 A patient's right to choose in Nordic countries: Anell, 44, 61–62;

Ministry of Social Affairs and Health, *Hoitopaikan valinta*; Olejaz, 46–47, 73, 113–14; Ringard, 22, 42.

208 "Universal Laws of Health Care Systems": Reid, 27.

209 Finns believe in national health-care system: Taloudellinen tiedotustoimisto.

209 Maximum wait times for access to care and patient fees in Finland: Ministry of Social Affairs and Health, *Hoitoon pääsy* and *Terveydenhuollon maksut*.

213 Price of multiple sclerosis drugs in the United States: Hartung.

214 Medicare and Medicaid nursing home and home health-care coverage: Bernstein; Medicare.gov, *Your Medicare* and *How Can I*; Taha; Thomas.

214 Median financial net worth of Americans aged 55–64: Sommer.

214 Median annual cost of a private nursing home in the United States: Genworth.

214 Americans worried about financing retirement: Bank of America; Morin.

215 Women quitting work to care for elderly family members: Searcey.

217 Elder care in Nordic countries: Help Age International; Nordic Social, 155–162; Osborn *International*; interview with Tine Rostgaard from Aalborg University (Sept. 10, 2013).

219 Affordable Care Act's impact by 2015: Blumenthal David; Krugman, "Rube"; Pear, "Number."

220 Taxes and funding of American health care: Gruber; Horpedahl; Rae.

222 Rising health-care costs for American workers: Commonwealth, *Why Are*; IOM, *America's*; Osborn, *The Commonwealth*; Schoen; Swift.

226 Americans supporting government role in health care: Balz; Gallup; Connelly; Pew Research Center, "Millennials," 35–36; Pew Research Center, "Political," 68–69.

227 Efforts to create public health-care options in the United States: Associated Press, "Governor"; McDonough; Office of Senator Jamie Eldridge; Perkins; Varney; Wheaton.

228 Drug companies' profits, advertising, and R&D: Richard Anderson; Brill; Rosenthal, "The Soaring Cost."

228 Obama seeking to negotiate Medicare drug prices: Morgan; Pear, "Obama."

228 Legislation requiring drug companies to justify prices: Editorial Board; Silverman.

228 Employers interested in not offering health insurance to employees: Goldstein; Pear, "I.R.S."

229 Ron Paul and debate audience members on whether an uninsured man should die: RonPaul2008dotcom.

230 Story about self-employed man who could have paid for insurance but didn't, then got cancer: Kristof, "A Possibly."

230 Unpaid medical bills fall on the taxpayer: Brill; Goodnough, "Hospitals."

231 Insurance companies raising prices: Pear, "Health Insurance"; Schoen.

231 Americans' vengeful attitude toward insurance companies: Andrews.

231 Millennials' attitudes about health care: Pew Research Center, "Millennials."

SIX: OF US, BY US, AND FOR US

233 Mitt Romney on 47 percent of Americans: Romney was speaking at a private fund-raiser in Florida on May 17, 2012, when he said: "There are 47 percent of the people who will vote for the president no matter what. All right, there are 47 percent who are with him, who are dependent upon government, who believe that they are victims, who believe that government has a responsibility to care for them, who believe that they are entitled to health care, to food, to housing, to you name it. That that's an entitlement. And the government should give it to them. . . . These are people who pay no income tax." See MoJo News Team.

234 Newt Gingrich on food stamps: Byers.

234 "That will kill the ability of America": "Republican Candidates."

235 Finns and Americans receiving welfare: I'll be the first to admit that this comparison is not a fair measurement of the overall social assistance Finland and the United States offer their residents. Finland, for example, sends automatic monthly child benefits to all families with children. Rather, I am making a point here about negative views of the "welfare" state. The comparison is based on the 381,851 Finns receiving *toimeentulotuki* and the 47.7 million Americans receiving food stamps in 2013. See Congressional Budget Office, *Supplemental*; Virtanen.

237 Finns and Americans employed: Employment rates are calculated as the ratio of the employed to the working-age population (aged fifteen to sixty-four). Employed people are defined as those who report that they have worked in gainful employment for at least one hour in the previous week or who had a job but were absent from work during the reference week. In 2010–2012, 69 percent of Finns were thus employed, as opposed to 67 percent of Americans. Other Nordic countries did even better: Iceland 79 percent, Norway 76 percent, Sweden and Denmark both 73 percent. See OECD, *OECD Factbook*, 132–133.

237 *New York Times* article on Chisago County: Appelbaum.

238 Distribution of American household income and benefits: Congressional Budget Office, *Trends* 3, 21.

238 Submerged state: While Social Security benefits are delivered as government checks, Suzanne Mettler notes even that program was deliberately fashioned by the Roosevelt Administration to resemble private insurance, which makes its status as a government social program less than obvious to some beneficiaries. In Mettler's study, 44 percent of recipients of Social Security payments said that they had not used a government program, as did 52 percent of the respondents who had claimed the child care tax credit, 47 percent of those who had taken Earned Income Tax Credit, and 64 percent of those who had employer-sponsored and thus tax-exempted health insurance. The same applied to 43 percent of recipients of unemployment benefits, and 40 percent of people on Medicare. Mettler.

241 Iceland's banking crisis: Icelandic Parliament.

242 Competitiveness, freedom and state of Nordic economies: Miller; OECD *Economic Surveys* for Denmark, Finland, Iceland, Norway, and Sweden; Schwab, *Global Competitiveness Report 2015–2016.*

243 Finland's economy during and after the euro crisis: Arnold, *Finland*; Irwin; Krugman, "Annoying"; Milne; Moody's; Moulds; O'Brien, *The Euro* and *Why;* Standard and Poor's, "Finland."

243 Government debt, GDP, and deficits in different countries: OECD, *Government,* 58–59, 62–63; OECD, *National,* 25.

246 Congress vs. cockroaches: Public Policy Polling.

246 Hobbes and human wars: Hobbes, 56, 81.

246 Rousseau and human laws: Rousseau.

247 Mill on freedom: Mill.

248 Alexis de Tocqueville and American democracy: Tocqueville.

248 "How could you judge" and "Wasn't a state": Micklethwait, 48, 56.

248 Smith and the invisible hand: Smith.

250 "Put simply": Micklethwait, 87.

251 A third of Americans believe armed rebellion is necessary: Farleigh.

252 The author's personal taxes in Finland and the United States in 2011: Technically, the parental leaves and sick days of Finnish entrepreneurs are not paid for by taxes. Rather, all self-employed workers are required by law to buy entrepreneur's pension insurance, which covers these benefits, as well as social security payments. However, these payments are approximately equivalent to American self-employment tax, and thus they are included in these calculations.

252 The tax rates of the Romneys and the Obamas: Confessore; Leonhardt; Mullins; White House Office, *President Obama.*

254 Taxation in different countries: Lindbeck, 1297–98, 1301; OECD, *Consumption* chap. 5, 34–35, 120–30, 134, 140; OECD, *OECD Factbook,* 230–231; OECD, "Table 1.7"; OECD, *Taxing,* 19–24, 45, 129, 546; Tax Policy Center, "Historical."

256 Top marginal tax rates in different countries: OECD, "Table 1.7."

256 Income distribution in the United States: Tax Policy Center, "Distribution."

256 Americans support higher taxes on the wealthy: Newport; Ohlemacher; Parker, "Yes"; Steinhauser.

256 "The effective tax rate for the wealthiest": Senate.

257 Buffett, King, and Obama on their tax rates: Buffett, "A Minimum" and "Stop"; King; Lander.

258 Danish "flexicurity": Andersen.

258 The Swedish economy and budget rules: In 2015 the Swedish government announced that it would like to see the budget surplus rule dropped since the country's finances were stable and it would free money for investments. The discussion was ongoing at the time of writing. Duxbury; Regeringskansliet; OECD. *OECD Economic Surveys: Sweden*.

259 Government spending per GDP and efficiency in arranging services: Adema; OECD, *Government*, 70–71.

261 Proposals and efforts for smarter government in the United States: Paul Blumenthal; Chappell; Dorment; *Education Week*; Kaiser; National Conference, *Redistricting*, *State Family*, and *State Minimum*; National Employment Law Project, "City"; Teles; United for the People; White House Office, "White House Unveils"; Employment Development.

261 Proposals for tax reform: Brundage; Buffett, "A Minimum"; Krugman, "Taxes"; Nixon; Norris; White House, *Reforming*.

SEVEN: THE LANDS OF OPPORTUNITY

265 Hedge fund managers made almost one billion: According to *Forbes* the twenty-five highest-earning hedge fund managers made $24.3 billion in 2013, while *Institutional Investor's Alpha* put that number at $21.15 billion. One billion each is the average—some made more, some less. To get into the top twenty-five, you had to make about $300 million. See Taub; Vardi.

265 American median income: DeNavas-Walt and Proctor, 5.

265 The homeless in New York: Feuer; Stewart.

266 Income inequality in the United States: Congressional Budget Office, *Trends*; Krugman, "The Undeserving"; National Employment Law Project, "Occupational"; Saez; Yellen.

266 Explanations for rising inequality: Frank; OECD, *Divided*, 28–41.

267 Americans prefer Swedish income distribution: Norton.

269 Income inequality, equality of opportunity and social mobility: Chetty; Corak, "Do Poor" and "Income Inequality"; Hertz; Jäntti; OECD, *Growing Unequal*; Pickett; interview with Markus Jäntti (Sept. 29, 2013.)

270 Ed Miliband on the American dream: Miliband.

270 Finnish school reform and social mobility: One study found that dispensing with separate tracks and creating a unified public school in Finland diminished the correlation between sons' and fathers' incomes by a quarter. See Pekkarinen.

274 Middle-class incomes in the United States and other countries: DeNavas-Walt and Proctor, 23; Leonhardt and Quealy.

275 OECD recommendations for countering inequality: OECD, *Divided*, 18–19.

275 Americans view inequality as the greatest threat: Pew Research Center, "Middle Easterners."

275 American states and cities raising the minimum wage: National Conference, *State Minimum*; National Employment Law Project, "City."

275 Krugman on the rich paying taxes: Krugman, "Now That's."

275 Stiglitz on Nordic countries: Stiglitz.

276 Wealth and happiness: Lewis.

EIGHT: BUSINESS AS UNUSUAL

281 Supercell: Interview with Ilkka Paananen (Oct. 23, 2013); Junkkari; Kelly; Reuters; Saarinen, "Hurjaa" and "Supercell-miljonäärit"; Scott, "SoftBank" and "Supercell Revenue"; Wingfield.

284 *Wall Street Journal* on Acne Studios: Yager.

285 KONE and elevator innovation: Full disclosure: The author of this book received a nonfiction writing grant from the KONE Foundation. The foundation is independent from the company and gives out more than 20 million euros annually to promote Finnish research, arts, and culture.

286 KONE and skyscrapers: Davidson; *Economist*.

287 Ease of doing business in different countries: World Bank.

288 Ease of laying off employees in different countries: OECD, *Employment*, 78.

289 Minimum wages and fast-food chains: In August 2015 a Big Mac in Finland cost €4.10 while in the United States the average price was $4.80. The exchange rate at the time put the Finnish Big Mac at the equivalent of $4.60. See Alderman; Allegretto.

292 Executive pay in Nordic countries: Pollard.

294 GDP per hours worked, total hours worked per worker and employment rates in different countries: OECD, *OECD Compendium*, 23, *Hours*, and OECD *Factbook*, 132–133.

295 H&M's parental leave policy: Hansegard.

296 "An individual employer may be": *Economic Report of the President* 129, 132.

296 Family-friendly policies benefit employers: Bassanini 11; Huffington, *Beyond*; OECD, *Babies*, 24; World Economic Forum, *Global Gender* (2013), 31.

297 Employers' reluctance to offer better work-life balance: University of Cambridge.

297 "There is nobody in this country who got rich": Real Clear Politics.

300 Road deaths in different countries: International Transport, 22.

300 Linus Torvalds: Rivlin.

NINE: THE PURSUIT OF HAPPINESS

305 "Normally, I avoid clichés like the plague": Wellesley.

306 American views about a successful life: Bowman, 17; Futures; Weissbourd.

314 "Parents seem to be increasingly anxious": Tugend.

316 Americans would like to work less: Delaney; Rampell.

318 Downsides of optimism: Ehrenreich; Oettingen.

321 Testing four-year-olds: Many kindergartens in New York City admit students based on their performance on a standardized test. See Senior.

BIBLIOGRAPHY

Abelson, Reed. "Insured, but Bankrupted by Health Crises." *New York Times*, June 30, 2009. Web.

Abrams, Samuel E. "The Children Must Play." *New Republic*, Jan. 28, 2011. Web.

Addati, Laura, et al. *Maternity and Paternity at Work: Law and Practice Across the World.* International Labour Office. Geneva: ILO, 2014. Web.

Adema, Willem, et al. "Is the European Welfare State Really More Expensive? Indicators on Social Spending, 1980–2012; and a Manual to the OECD Social Expenditure Data Base (SOCX)." *OECD Social, Employment and Migration Working Papers* 124. Paris: OECD Publishing, 2011. Web.

Aho, Erkki. "52 Finnish Comprehensive Schools." In *100 Social Innovations from Finland.* Edited by Ilkka Taipale. Helsinki: Peace Books from Finland, 2009.

Alderman, Liz, and Steven Greenhouse. "Living Wages, Rarity for U.S. Fast-Food Workers, Served up in Denmark." *New York Times*, Oct. 27, 2014. Web.

Allegretto, Sylvia, et al. *Fast Food, Poverty Wages: The Public Cost of Low-Wage Jobs in the Fast-Food Industry.* UC Berkeley Labor Center, 2013. Web.

Allianz. *The 2013 Allianz Women, Money, and Power Study.* Web.

Amato, Paul. R. "The Impact of Family Formation Change on the Cognitive, Social and Emotional Well-Being of the Next Generation." *Marriage and Child Wellbeing* 15:2 (2005): 75–96. Web.

Andersen, Torben M., et al. *The Danish Flexicurity Model in the Great Recession.* VoxEU.org, Apr. 8, 2011. Web.

Anderson, Jenny. "From Finland, an Intriguing School-Reform Model." *New York Times*, Dec. 12, 2011. Web.

Anderson, Richard. "Pharmaceutical Industry Gets High on Fat Profits." *BBC News*, Nov. 6, 2014. Web.

Andrews, Michelle. "Patients Balk at Considering Cost in Medical Decision-Making, Study Says." *Washington Post*, Mar. 11, 2013. Web.

Anell, Anders, et al. "Sweden: Health System Review." *Health Systems in Transition* 14:5 (2012): 1–159. Web.

Appelbaum, Binyamin, and Robert Gebeloff. "Even Critics of Safety Net Increasingly Depend on It." *New York Times*, Feb. 11, 2012. Web.

Appelbaum, Eileen, and Ruth Milkman. "Paid Family Leave Pays Off in California." *Harvard Business Review*, Jan. 19, 2011. Web.

Arnold, Chris. "When Nonprofit Hospitals Sue Their Poorest Patients." *NPR*, Dec. 19, 2014. Web.

Arnold, Nathaniel, et al. *Finland: Selected Issues*. Washington, DC: International Monetary Fund, 2015. Web.

Artiga, Samantha, and Elizabeth Cornachione. *Trends in Medicaid and CHIP Eligibility Over Time*. Kaiser Family Foundation, 2015. Web.

Associated Press. "Governor Abandons Single-Payer Health Care Plan." *New York Times*, Dec. 17, 2014. Web.

Associated Press. "School Spending by Affluent Is Widening Wealth Gap." *New York Times*, Sept. 30, 2014. Web.

Astridlindgren.se. *Astrid Lindgren and the World*. N.d. Web. Accessed July 23, 2015.

Aubrey, Allison. "Burger Joint Pays $15 an Hour. And, Yes, It's Making Money." *NPR*, Dec. 4, 2014. Web.

Aula, Maria Kaisa, et al. "Vanhempainvapaatyöryhmän muistio." ["Memorandum of Working Group on Family Leaves."] *Sosiaali- ja terveysministeriön selvityksiä* 12. Helsinki: Ministry of Social Affairs and Health, 2011. Web.

Aviv, Rachel. "Wrong Answer." *The New Yorker*, July 21, 2014. Web.

Bach, Peter S. "Why Drugs Cost So Much." *New York Times*, Jan. 14, 2015. Web.

Bagehot. "Nice Up North." *The Economist*, Jan. 27, 2011. Web.

Baker, Bruce D., et al. *Is School Funding Fair? A National Report Card*. Education Law Center, 2015. Web.

Baker, Peter. "The Limits of Rahmism." *New York Times Magazine*, Mar. 8, 2010. Web.

Bakst, Dina. "Pregnant, and Pushed Out of a Job." *New York Times*, Jan. 30, 2012. Web.

Balz, Dan, and Jon Cohen. "Most Support Public Option for Health Insurance, Poll Finds." *Washington Post*, Oct. 20, 2009. Web.

Banchero, Stephanie. "Teachers Lose Jobs Over Test Scores." *Wall Street Journal*, July 24, 2010. Web.

Banerjee, Abhijit V., and Esther Duflo. *Poor Economics—A Radical Rethinking of the Way to Fight Global Poverty*. New York: PublicAffairs 2011. Kindle file.

Bank of America. "Going Broke in Retirement Is Top Fear for Americans." *Merrill Edge Report*, May 27, 2014. Web.

Basic Education Act 628/1998. Amendments up to 1136/2010. Finlex. Web. Accessed Aug. 2, 2015.

Bassanini, Andrea, and Danielle Venn. "The Impact of Labour Market Policies on Productivity in OECD countries." *International Productivity Monitor* 17 (2008): 3–15. Web.

Berdahl, Jennifer L., and Sue H. Moon. "Workplace Mistreatment of Middle Class Workers Based on Sex, Parenthood, and Caregiving." *Journal of Social Issues* 69:2 (2013): 341–66. Web.

Berger, Lawrence M., and Sarah A. Font. "The Role of the Family and Family-Centered Programs and Policies." *Policies to Promote Child Health* 25:1 (2015): 155–76. Web.

Berggren, Henrik, and Lars Trägårdh. *Är svensken människa?* Stockholm: Norstedts Förlag, 2006.

———. "Pippi Longstocking: The Autonomous Child and the Moral Logic of the Swedish Welfare State." In *Swedish Modernism: Architecture, Consumption and the Welfare State*. Edited by Helena Mattsson and Sven-Olov Wallenstein, 10–23. London: Black Dog Publishing, 2010.

———. "Social Trust and Radical Individualism: The Paradox at the Heart of Nordic Capitalism." In *Shared Norms for the New Reality: The Nordic Way*, 13–27. Stockholm: Global Utmaning, 2010. Web.

Bernstein, Nina. "Pitfalls Seen in a Turn to Privately Run Long-Term Care." *New York Times*, Mar. 6, 2014. Web.

Blau, Francine D., and Lawrence M. Kahn. "Female Labor Supply: Why Is the US Falling Behind?" *American Economic Review* 103:3 (2013): 251–56. Web.

Blendon, Robert J., et al. "Public Trust in Physicians—U.S. Medicine in International Perspective." *New England Journal of Medicine* 371 (2014): 1570–72. Web.

Blomgren, Jenni, et al. "Kelan sairaanhoitokorvaukset tuloryhmittäin. Kenelle korvauksia maksetaan ja kuinka paljon?" ["The Social Insurance Institution of Finland's Health Care Reimbursements by Income Quintile. To Whom Are Reimbursements Paid and What Are the Amounts?"] *Sosiaali- ja terveysturvan selosteita* 93. Helsinki: Kela, 2015. Web.

Blumenthal, David, et al. "The Affordable Care Act at Five." *New England Journal of Medicine Online First*, May 6, 2015. Web.

Blumenthal, Paul. "States Push Post-Citizens United Reforms as Washington Stands Still." *Huffington Post*, July 11, 2013. Web.

Bolick, Kate. "All the Single Ladies." *Atlantic*, Nov. 2011. Web.

Bowman, Carl, et al. *Culture of American Families*. Institute for Advanced Studies in Culture, 2012. Web.

Bradford, Harry. "The 10 Countries with the Best Work-Life Balance: OECD." *Huffington Post*, Jan. 6, 2011. Web.

Brill, Steven. "Bitter Bill: Why Medical Bills Are Killing Us." *Time*, Feb. 20, 2013. Web.

Brooks, David. "The Talent Society." *New York Times*, Feb. 20, 2012. Web.

Brundage, Amy. *White House Report—The Buffett Rule: A Basic Principle of Tax Fairness*. White House, Apr. 10, 2012. Web.

Buckley, Cara. "For Uninsured Young Adults, Do-It-Yourself Health Care." *New York Times*, Feb. 17, 2009. Web.

Buffett, Warren E. "A Minimum Tax for the Wealthy." *New York Times* Nov. 25, 2012. Web.

———. "Stop Coddling the Super-Rich." *New York Times*, Aug. 14, 2011. Web.

Bureau of Labor Statistics. "Table 1. Time spent in primary activities and percent of the civilian population engaging in each activity, averages per day by sex, 2014 annual averages." *American Time Use Survey*. N.d. Web. Accessed July 29, 2015.

———. "Table 32. Leave Benefits: Access, private industry workers." *National Compensation Survey, March 2015*. Web.

———. "Table 38. Paid Vacations: Number of Annual Days by Service Requirement, private industry workers." *National Compensation Survey, March 2015*. Web.

———. "Table 9. Time adults spent caring for household children as a primary activity by sex, age, and day of week, average for the combined years 2010–2014." *American Time Use Survey*. N.d. Web. Accessed July 29, 2015.

Byers, Dylan. "What Newt Said About Food Stamps." *Politico*, Jan. 6, 2012. Web.

Cain Miller, Claire. "Can Family Leave Policies Be Too Generous? It Seems So." *New York Times*, Aug. 9, 2014. Web.

———. "Paternity Leave: The Rewards and the Remaining Stigma." *New York Times*, Nov. 7, 2014. Web.

Campbell, Frances A., et al. "Early Childhood Education: Young Adult Outcomes from the Abecedarian Project." *Applied Developmental Science* 6:1 (2002): 42–57. Web.

Carey, Kevin, and Marguerite Roza. *School Funding's Tragic Flaw*. Education Sector and the Center on Reinventing Public Education, University of Washington, 2008. Web.

———. "Americans Think We Have the World's Best Colleges. We Don't." *New York Times*, June 28, 2014. Web.

Casey, Timothy, and Laurie Maldonado. *Worst Off—Single-Parent Families in the United States*. Legal Momentum, 2012. Web.

Cecere, David. "New Study Finds 45,000 Deaths Annually Linked to Lack of Health Coverage." *Harvard Gazette*, Sept. 17, 2009. Web.

Center for Research on Education Outcomes (CREDO). *National Charter School Study 2013*. Stanford, CA: CREDO at Stanford University, 2013. Web.

Chait, Jonathan. "Inequality and the Charles Murray Dodge." *New York*, Jan. 31, 2012. Web.

Chappell, Bill. "Supreme Court Backs Arizona's Redistricting Commission Targeting Gridlock." *NPR*, June 29, 2015. Web.

Cherlin, Andrew J. "The Real Reason Richer People Marry." *New York Times*, Dec. 6, 2014. Web.

Chetty, Raj, et al. "Where Is the Land of Opportunity? The Geography of Intergenerational Mobility in the United States." *Quarterly Journal of Economics* 129:4 (2014): 1553–1623. Web.

Child Care Aware. *Parents and the High Cost of Child Care: 2015 Report.* Web.

Chingos, Matthew M. *Strength in Numbers: State Spending on K–12 Assessment Systems.* Brown Center on Education Policy at Brookings, 2012. Web.

Claxton, Gary, et al. *Employer Health Benefits 2015.* Kaiser Family Foundation and Health Research & Educational Trust, 2015. Web.

Clinton Global Initiative. "Opening Plenary Session CGI 2010 pt. 1." Online video clip. Original.livestream.com. N.d. Web. Accessed July 20, 2015.

Cohn, D'Vera, et al. "After Decades of Decline, a Rise in Stay-At-Home Mothers." Pew Research Center, Apr. 8, 2014. Web.

College Board. "Trends in College Pricing 2015." *Trends in Higher Education Series.* College Board, 2015. Web.

Commonwealth Fund. "Why Are Millions of Insured Americans Still Struggling to Pay for Health Care?" *Medium*, June 16, 2015. Web.

———. "Why Not the Best? Results from the National Scorecard on U.S. Health System Performance, 2011." Commonwealth Fund, 2011. Web.

Confessore, Nicholas, and David Kocieniewski. "For Romneys, Friendly Code Reduces Taxes." *New York Times*, Jan. 24, 2012. Web.

Congressional Budget Office. *Supplemental Nutrition Assistance Program.* May 2013. Web.

———. *Trends in the Distribution of Household Income Between 1979 and 2007.* October 2011. Web.

Connelly, Marjorie. "Polls and the Public Option." *New York Times*, Oct. 28, 2009. Web.

Coombes, Andrea. "'Bag Lady' Fears Haunt About Half of Women." *Marketwatch*, Aug. 22, 2006. Web.

Corak, Miles. "Income Inequality, Equality of Opportunity, and Intergenerational Mobility." *Journal of Economic Perspectives* 27:3 (2013): 79–102. Web.

———. "Do Poor Children Become Poor Adults? Lessons from a Cross Country Comparison of Generational Earnings Mobility." Institute for the Study of Labor (IZA), 2006. Web.

Davidson, Justin. "The Rise of the Mile-High Building." *New York*, Mar. 24, 2015. Web.

Davis, Karen, et al. *Mirror, Mirror on the Wall: How the Performance of the U.S. Health Care System Compares Internationally*. Commonwealth Fund, 2014. Web.

Delaney, Arthur, and Ariel Edwards-Levy. "More Americans Would Take a Pay Cut for a Day Off." *Huffington Post*, Aug. 1, 2015. Web.

DeNavas-Walt, Carmen, and Bernadette D. Proctor. *Income and Poverty in the United States: 2013*. Washington, DC: U.S. Government Printing Office, 2014. Web.

DeNavas-Walt, Carmen, et al. *Income, Poverty, and Health Insurance Coverage in the United States: 2009*. Washington, DC: U.S. Government Printing Office, 2010. Web.

DeParle, Jason. "For Poor, Leap to College Often Ends in Hard Fall." *New York Times*, Dec. 22, 2012. Web.

DeParle, Jason, and Sabrina Tavernise. "For Women Under 30, Most Births Occur Outside Marriage." *New York Times*, Feb. 17, 2012. Web.

Dillon, Sam. "Schools Cut Back Subjects to Push Reading and Math." *New York Times*, Mar. 26, 2006. Web.

Dorment, Richard. "22 Simple Reforms That Could #FixCongress Now." *Esquire*, Oct. 15, 2014. Web.

Doyle, Joseph J., Jr. "Health Insurance, Treatment and Outcomes: Using Auto Accidents as Health Shocks." *Review of Economics and Statistics* 87:2 (2005): 256–70. Web.

Drobnic Holan, Angie. "PolitiFact's Lie of the Year: 'Death Panels'." *Tampa Bay Times PolitiFact.com*, Dec. 18, 2009. Web.

Duncan, Greg, and Richard J. Murnane. *Whither Opportunity? Rising Inequality, Schools, and Children's Life Chances.* Executive Summary. New York: Russell Sage and Spencer Foundation, 2011. Web.

Duvander, Ann-Zofie, and Johanna Lammi-Taskula. "1. Parental Leave." In *Parental Leave, Childcare and Gender Equality in the Nordic Countries. TemaNord 2011:562,* edited by Ingólfur V. Gíslason and Guðný Björk Eydal, 31–64. Copenhagen: Nordic Council of Ministers, 2011. Web.

Duxbury, Charles. "Sweden Seeks to Drop Budget Surplus Target." *Wall Street Journal,* Mar. 3, 2015. Web.

Economic Report of the President. Washington, DC: U.S. Government Printing Office, 2013. Web.

The Economist. "The Other Mile-High Club." *The Economist,* June 15, 2013. Web.

Editorial Board. "Runaway Drug Prices." *New York Times,* May 5, 2015. Web.

Edsall, Thomas B. "What the Right Gets Right." *New York Times,* Jan. 15, 2012. Web.

Education Week. "Quality Counts Introduces New State Report Card; U.S. Earns C, and Massachusetts Ranks First in Nation." *Education Week,* Jan. 8, 2015. Web.

Ehrenfreund, Max. "Teachers in Teach for America Aren't Any Better Than Other Teachers When It Comes to Kids' Test Scores." *Washington Post,* Mar. 6, 2015. Web.

Ehrenreich, Barbara. "Overrated Optimism: The Peril of Positive Thinking." *Time,* Oct. 10, 2009. Web.

Eklund, Klas. "Nordic Capitalism: Lessons Learned." In *Shared Norms for the New Reality: The Nordic Way,* 5–11. Stockholm: Global Utmaning, 2010. Web.

Employment Development Department State of California. *Disability Insurance (DI) and Paid Family Leave (PFL) Weekly Benefit Amounts.* N.d. Web. Accessed July 25, 2015.

———. *Fact Sheet. Paid Family Leave (PFL).* N.d. Web. Accessed July 25, 2015.

European Commission. "Investing in Children: Breaking the Cycle of Disadvantage." *Commission Recommendation*, Feb. 20, 2013. Web.

———. *Innovation Union Scoreboard 2011*. Brussels: European Union, 2012. Web.

European Foundation for the Improvement of Living and Working Conditions. *Developments in Collectively Agreed Working Time 2012*. 2013. Web.

Eurydice. *Finland—Early Childhood and School Education Funding*. European Commission, 2015. Web.

Executive Office of the President of the United States. *The Labor Force Participation Rate Since 2007: Causes and Policy Implications*. July 2014. Web.

FactCheck.Org. *Dying from Lack of Insurance*. Sept. 24, 2009. Web.

Fairleigh Dickinson University's Public Mind Poll. "Beliefs About Sandy Hook Cover-Up, Coming Revolution Underlie Divide on Gun Control." May 1, 2013. Web.

Fausset, Richard. "Judge Reduces Sentences in Atlanta School Testing Scandal." *New York Times*, Apr. 30, 2015. Web.

Feuer, Alan. "Homeless Families, Cloaked in Normalcy." *New York Times*, Feb. 3, 2012. Web.

Finnish Medicines Agency Fimea and Social Insurance Institution of Finland (Kela). *Finnish Statistics on Medicines 2013*. Helsinki: Fimea and Kela, 2014. Web.

Fjölmenningarsetur. *Vacation Pay / Holiday Allowance*. N.d. Web. Accessed July 25, 2015.

Foderaro, Lisa W. "Alternate Path for Teachers Gains Ground." *New York Times*, Apr. 18, 2010. Web.

Foroohar, Rana. "The Best Countries in the World." *Newsweek*, Aug. 23 & 30, 2010, 30–32. Web.

Försäkringskassan. *About Parental Benefits*. N.d. Web. Accessed July 25, 2015.

Frank, Robert H. "A Remedy Worse Than Disease." *Pathways*, Summer 2010. Web.

Fronstin, Paul. "Views on Health Coverage and Retirement: Findings from the 2012 Health Confidence Survey." *EBRI Employee Benefit Research Institute Notes* 34.1 (2013): 2–9. Web.

Frum, David. "Is the White Working Class Coming Apart?" *Daily Beast*, Feb. 6, 2012. Web.

Fujisawa, Rie, and Gaetan Lafortune. "The Remuneration of General Practitioners and Specialists in 14 OECD Countries: What Are the Factors Influencing Variations Across Countries?" *OECD Health Working Papers* 41, 2008. Web.

Fund for Peace. *Failed States Index 2012.* N.d. Web. Accessed July 21, 2015.

Futures Company. *The Life Twist Study.* American Express, 2013. Web.

Gabriel, Trip. "Vouchers Unspoken, Romney Hails School Choice." *New York Times*, June 11, 2012. Web.

Gallup. *Healthcare System: Historical Trends.* N.d. Web. Accessed Aug. 15, 2015.

Gawande, Atul. "Big Med." *The New Yorker*, Aug. 12, 2012. Web.

Genworth. *2013 Cost of Care Survey.* N.d. Web. Accessed Aug. 14, 2015.

Gittleson, Kim. "Shake Shack Is Shaking up Wages for US Fast-Food Workers." *BBC*, Jan. 30, 2015. Web.

Goldstein, Amy. "Few Employers Dropping Health Benefits, Surveys Find." *Washington Post*, Nov. 19, 2014. Web.

Goodnough, Abby, and Robert Pear. "Unable to Meet the Deductible or the Doctor." *New York Times*, Oct. 17, 2014. Web.

———. "Hospitals Look to Health Law, Cutting Charity." *New York Times*, May 25, 2014. Web.

Gottlieb, Lori. "How to Land Your Kid in Therapy." *Atlantic*, July/August 2011. Web.

———. "Marry Him!" *Atlantic*, Mar. 2008. Web.

Grady, Denise. "In Feast of Data on BPA Plastic, No Final Answer." *New York Times*, Sept. 6, 2010. Web.

Graff, E.J. "Our Customers Don't Want a Pregnant Waitress." *American Prospect* 31 (Jan. 2013). Web.

Grant, Rebecca. "Silicon Valley's Best and Worst Jobs for New Moms (and Dads)." *Atlantic*, Mar. 2, 2015. Web.

Greenberg, Julie, et al. *2014 Teacher Prep Review*. National Council on Teacher Quality, rev. Feb. 2015. Web.

Greenhouse, Linda. "Justice Recalls Treats Laced with Poison." *New York Times*, Nov. 17, 2006. Web.

Greenstone, Michael, et al. *Dozen Economic Facts About K-12 Education*. Hamilton Project, 2012. Web.

———. *Thirteen Economic Facts About Social Mobility and the Role of Education*. Hamilton Project, 2013. Web.

Grieco, Elizabeth M., et al. "The Foreign-Born Population in the United States: 2010." *American Community Survey Reports*. United States Census Bureau, 2012. Web.

Gruber, Jonathan. "The Tax Exclusion for Employer-Sponsored Health Insurance." *National Tax Journal* 64.2 (2011): 511–530. Web.

Gubb, James. *The NHS and the NHS Plan: Is the Extra Money Working?* Civitas, Institute for the Study of Civil Society, 2006. Web.

Gunn, Dwyer. "Sit. Stay. Good Mom!" *New York*, July 6, 2012. Web.

Hansegard, Jens. "For Paternity Leave, Sweden Asks If Two Months Is Enough." *Wall Street Journal*, July 31, 2012. Web.

Harrington, Brad, et al. *The New Dad: Take Your Leave*. Boston: Boston College Center for Work & Family, 2014. Web.

Harris, Elizabeth A. "Cuomo Gets Deals on Tenure and Evaluations of Teachers." *New York Times*, Mar. 31, 2015. Web.

———. "Most Parents Got Top Choices for Pre-K, Blasio says." *New York Times*, June 8, 2015. Web.

Hartman, Laura, ed. "Konkurrensens konsekvenser. Vad händer med svensk välfärd?" ["The Consequences of Competition: What Is Happening to Swedish Welfare?"] Stockholm: SNS Förlag, 2011.

Hartung, Daniel M., et al. "The Cost of Multiple Sclerosis Drugs in the US and the Pharmaceutical Industry: Too Big to Fail?" *Neurology*, Apr. 24, 2015. Web.

Hattenstone, Simon. "Nothing Like a Dame." *Guardian*, Sept. 2, 2006. Web.

Hayes, Susan L., and Cathy Schoen. "Stop the Churn: Preventing Gaps in Health Insurance Coverage." *Commonwealth Fund Blog*, July 10, 2013. Web.

HealthCare.gov. *Out-of-Pocket Maximum/limit*. N.d. Web. Accessed Nov. 25, 2015.

Helliwell, John, et al. *World Happiness Report*. Sustainable Development Solutions Network, 2012. Web.

Help Age International. *Global Agewatch Index 2014*. Web.

Hertz, Tom. "Understanding Mobility in America." Center for American Progress, 2006. Web.

Heymann, Jody, et al. *Contagion Nation: A Comparison of Paid Sick Leave Policies in 22 Countries*. Center for Economic and Policy Research, May 2009. Web.

Himmelstein, David U., et al. "Medical Bankruptcy in the United States 2007: Results of a National Study." *American Journal of Medicine*, 122:8 (2009): 741–746. Web.

Hobbes, Thomas. *Leviathan*. 1651. Kindle file.

Holmes, Elizabeth. "Don't Hate Her for Being Fit." *Wall Street Journal*, July 20, 2012. Web.

Horpedahl, Jeremy, and Harrison Searles. *The Tax Exemption of Employer-Provided Health Insurance*. Mercatus Center at George Mason University, 2013. Web.

Hotchner, A. E. "Nordic Exposure." *Vanity Fair*, Aug. 2012. Web.

Huffington, Arianna. "Beyond Money and Power (and Stress and Burnout): In Search of New Definition of Success." *Huffington Post*, May 29, 2013. Web.

———. *Thrive: The Third Metric to Redefining Success and Creating a Life of Well-Being, Wisdom, and Wonder*. New York: Harmony Books, 2014. Kindle file.

HUS. *Synnytyksen jälkeen. Hoitoajat ja potilasmaksut*. N.d. Web. Accessed July 25, 2015.

Icelandic Parliament. *Report of the Special Investigation Commission*. 2010. Web.

IMS Health. "Top 25 Medicines by Dispensed Prescriptions (U.S.)" N.d. Web. Accessed July 22, 2015.

International Federation of Health Plans. *2013 Comparative Price Report*. N.d. Web. Accessed Aug. 13, 2015.

International Telecommunication Union. *Measuring the Information Society Report 2014.* Geneva: ITU, 2014. Web.

International Transport Forum. *Road Safety Annual Report 2014.* Paris: OECD Publishing, 2014. Web.

IOM (Institute of Medicine). *America's Uninsured Crisis: Consequences for Health and Health Care.* Washington, DC: National Academies Press, 2009. Web.

———. *Care Without Coverage: Too Little, Too Late.* Washington, DC: National Academies Press, 2002. Web.

Irwin, Neil. "Finland Shows Why Many Europeans Think Americans Are Wrong About the Euro." *New York Times*, July 20, 2015. Web.

Jacobs, Douglas B., and Benjamin D. Sommers. "Using Drugs to Discriminate—Adverse Selection in the Insurance Marketplace." *New England Journal of Medicine* 372 (2015): 399–402. Web.

Jäntti, Markus, et al. "American Exceptionalism in a New Light: A Comparison of Intergenerational Earnings Mobility in the Nordic Countries, the United Kingdom and the United States." Institute for the Study of Labor (IZA), 2006. Web.

Jubera, Drew. "A Georgia County Shares a Tale of One Man's Life and Death." *New York Times*, Aug. 22, 2009. Web.

Junkkari, Marko. "Supercellin perustajat ovat kaikkien aikojen veronmaksajia." ["The Founders of Supercell Are Among the Biggest Taxpayers of All Time."] *Helsingin Sanomat*, Nov. 3, 2014. Web.

Kaiser Family Foundation. "Massachusetts Health Care Reform: Six Years Later," May 2012. Web.

Kela. *Allowance for the Unemployed, Students and Rehabilitees.* Social Insurance Institution of Finland (Kela), N.d. Web. Accessed July 26, 2015.

———. *Amount of Child Home Care Allowance.* N.d. Web. Accessed July 26, 2015.

———. *Benefits for Families with Children.* N.d. Web. Accessed July 25, 2015.

———. *Government Guarantee for Student Loans.* N.d. Web. Accessed Aug. 9, 2015.

————. *Health and Rehabilitation Brochure.* N.d. Web. Accessed July 21, 2015.

————. *Home and Family Brochure.* N.d. Web. Accessed July 21, 2015.

————. *Housing Supplement.* N.d. Web. Accessed Aug. 9, 2015.

————. *Maternity Grant and Maternity Package.* N.d. Web. Accessed July 25, 2015.

————. *Paternity Allowance During Paternity Leave.* N.d. Web. Accessed July 29, 2015.

————. *Statistical Yearbook of the Social Insurance Institution 2013*, 2014. Web.

————. *Study Grant.* N.d. Web. Accessed Aug. 9, 2015.

————. *Unemployment: Benefits for the Unemployed Brochure.* N.d. Web. Accessed July 26, 2015.

Kelly, Gordon. "Supercell's CEO Reveals the Culture He Built to Produce a £2.5 Billion Company in Two Years." Wired.co.uk, Nov. 13, 2013. Web.

Kena, Grace, et al. *The Condition of Education 2015.* U.S. Department of Education, National Center for Education Statistics, 2015. Web.

King, Stephen. "Stephen King: Tax Me, for F@%&'s Sake!" *Daily Beast*, Apr. 30, 2012. Web.

Kirshstein, Rita J. *Not Your Mother's College Affordability Crisis.* Delta Cost Project at American Institutes for Research, 2012. Web.

Klein, Joel I. "Urban Schools Need Better Teachers, Not Excuses, to Close the Education Gap." *U.S. News & World Report*, May 9, 2009. Web.

Klerman, Jacob, et al. *Family and Medical Leave in 2012: Executive Summary.* Cambridge, MA: Abt Associates, 2012. Web.

Kolbert, Elizabeth. "Spoiled Rotten." *The New Yorker*, July 2, 2011. Web.

Kortelainen, Mika, et al. "Lukioiden väliset erot ja paremmuusjärjestys." ["Differences Between Academic High Schools, and Their Rankings"] *VATT tutkimukset* 179. Helsinki: Government Institute for Economic Research 2014. Web.

Kristof, Nicholas. "A Possibly Fatal Mistake." *New York Times*, Oct. 12, 2012. Web.

————. "The Spread of Superbugs." *New York Times*, Mar. 6, 2010. Web.

Krugman, Paul. "Annoying Euro Apologetics." *New York Times* July 22, 2015. Web.

———. "Death by Ideology." *New York Times*, Oct. 14, 2012. Web.

———. "Now That's Rich." *New York Times*, May 8, 2014. Web.

———. "Rube Goldberg Survives." *New York Times*, Apr. 3, 2014. Web.

———. "Taxes at the Top." *New York Times,* Jan. 19, 2012. Web.

———. "The Undeserving Rich." *New York Times*, Jan. 19, 2014. Web.

Kupari, Pekka, et al. "PISA12—Ensituloksia." [PISA12—First Results.] *Opetus—ja kulttuuriministeriön julkaisuja* 20. Ministry of Education and Culture, 2013. Web.

Laitinen, Joonas, and Johanna Mannila. "Ressun keskiarvoraja jälleen korkein pääkaupunkiseudun kuntien omissa lukioissa." ["Ressu High School Once Again Requires the Highest Grade Point Average for Entry Among Municipal High Schools in the Helsinki Metropolitan Area."] *Helsingin Sanomat*, June 11, 2015. Web.

LaMontagne, Christina. "Medical Bankruptcy Accounts for Majority of Personal Bankruptcies." *Nerdwallet*, Mar. 26, 2014. Web.

Lander, Mark. "Obama, Like Buffett, Had Lower Tax Rate Than His Secretary." *New York Times*, Apr. 13, 2012. Web.

Lavigne, Paula. "Bad Grades? Some Schools OK with It." *ESPN*, Oct. 18, 2012. Web.

Leland, Anne, and Mari-Jana Oboroceanu. *American War and Military Operations Casualties: Lists and Statistics*. Congressional Research Service, Feb. 26, 2010. Web.

Leonhardt, David. "Putting Candidates' Tax Returns in Perspective." *New York Times*, Jan. 24, 2012. Web.

Leonhardt, David, and Kevin Quealy. "The American Middle Class Is No Longer the World's Richest." *New York Times,* Apr. 22, 2014. Web.

Leskinen, Jari, and Antti Juutilainen, eds. *Jatkosodan pikkujättiläinen.* [The Continuation War's Small Giant.] Helsinki: WSOY, 2005.

Levin, Yuval. "Beyond the Welfare State." *National Affairs* 7 (Spring 2011). Web.

Levine, Arthur. *Educating School Teachers*. Education Schools Project, 2006. Web.

Lewis, Michael. "Extreme Wealth Is Bad for Everyone—Especially the Wealthy." *New Republic*, Nov. 12, 2014. Web.

Lim, Carol S., et al. "International Comparison of the Factors Influencing Reimbursement of Targeted Anti-Cancer Drugs." *BMC Health Services Research* 14 (2014): 595. Web.

Lindbeck, Assar. "The Swedish Experiment." *Journal of Economic Literature* 35 (1997): 1273–1319. Web.

Liptak, Adam. "Case Seeking Job Protections for Pregnant Women Heads to Supreme Court." *New York Times*, Nov. 30, 2014. Web.

Lipton, Eric S., and David Barboza. "As More Toys Are Recalled, Trail Ends in China." *New York Times*, June 19, 2007. Web.

Livingston, Gretchen, and Anna Brown. "Birth Rate for Unmarried Women Declining for First Time in Decades." Pew Research Center, Aug. 13, 2014. Web.

Lublin, Joann S., and Leslie Kwoh. "For Yahoo CEO, Two New Roles." *Wall Street Journal*, July 17, 2012. Web.

Ludden, Jennifer. "More Dads Want Paternity Leave. Getting It Is a Different Matter." *NPR*, Aug. 13, 2014. Web.

Mäkinen, Esa, et al. "Kaikki Suomen lukiot paremmuusjärjestyksessä: Etelä-Tapiola kiilasi Ressun ohi." ["All of Finland's High Schools Ranked: South Tapiola Cut Ahead of Ressu."] *Helsingin Sanomat*, May 25, 2015. Web.

Mandery, Evan J. "End College Legacy Preference." *New York Times*, Apr. 24, 2014. Web.

Mascia, Jennifer. "An Accident, and a Life Is Upended." *New York Times,* Dec. 21, 2009. Web.

McDevitt, Kaitlin. "The Big Money: Depression and the Recession." *Washington Post*, Aug. 30, 2009. Web.

McDonough, John. "The Demise of Vermont's Single-Payer Plan." *New England Journal of Medicine* 372 (2015): 1584–1585. Web.

McMurrer, Jennifer, et al. *Instructional Time in Elementary Schools.* Center on Education Policy, 2008. Web.

Medicare.gov. *How Can I Pay for Nursing Home Care?* N.d. Web. Accessed Aug. 14, 2015.

————. *Your Medicare Coverage. Home Health Services.* N.d. Web. Accessed Aug. 14, 2015.

Mettler, Suzanne, and Julianna Koch. "Who Says They Have Ever Used a Government Social Program? The Role of Policy Visibility." Feb. 28, 2012. Web.

Micklethwait, John, and Adrian Wooldridge. *The Fourth Revolution: The Global Race to Reinvent the State.* New York: Penguin Press, 2014. Kindle file.

Miliband, Ed. Speech at the Sutton Trust's Social Mobility Summit in London, the United Kingdom, May 21, 2012. Web.

Mill, John Stuart. *On Liberty.* 1859. Kindle file.

Miller, Terry, and Anthony B. Kim. *2015 Index of Economic Freedom.* Heritage Foundation, 2015. Web.

Milne, Richard, and Michael Stothard. "Rich, Happy and Good at Austerity." *Financial Times* Special Report, May 30, 2012. Web.

Ministry of Education and Culture. *Finland and PISA.* N.d. Web. Accessed July 20, 2015.

————. *Basic Education in Finland.* N.d. Web. Accessed Aug. 2, 2015.

————. *Early Childhood Education and Care in Finland.* N.d. Web. Accessed Aug. 3, 2013.

————. *Every Child in Finland Has the Same Educational Starting Point.* N.d. Web. Accessed Jan. 12, 2015.

————. *Financing of Education.* N.d. Web. Accessed Aug. 3, 2015.

————. *Koulutustakuu osana yhteiskuntatakuuta.* [Education Guarantee as Part of the Social Guarantee.] N.d. Web. Accessed Aug. 10, 2015.

————. "Opetusryhmien tila Suomessa" ["The State of Class Sizes in Finland."] *Opetus- ja kulttuuriministeriön työryhmämuistioita ja selvityksiä* 4, 2014. Web.

————. "Perusopetuksen aamu- ja iltapäivätoiminnan sekä koulun kerhotoiminnan laatukortteja valmistelevan työryhmän muistio." [Report by the Preparatory Committee for Assessing the Quality of Morning, Afternoon and Other Clubs Offered to Students in Basic Education.] *Opetus- ja kulttuuriministeriön työryhmämuistioita ja selvityksiä* 8, 2012. Web.

————. *PISA12—Still Among the Best in the OECD—Performance Declining.* N.d. Web. Accessed Aug. 2, 2015.

————. *Työryhmä: Perusopetusta uudistetaan—taide- ja taitoaineisiin, äidinkieleen ja yhteiskuntaoppiin lisää tunteja.* [Committee: Basic Education to Be Reformed—More Instruction Hours for Arts, Crafts, Language Arts and Social Studies.] Feb. 24, 2012. Web.

————. *Valtioneuvosto myönsi kahdeksan perusopetuksen järjestämislupaa.* [Finnish Government Granted Eight Basic Education Licenses.] June 12, 2014. Web.

————. *Varhaiskasvatuksen asiakasmaksut.* [Early-Childhood Education Fees.] N.d. Web. Accessed Jan. 9, 2016.

Ministry of Employment and Economy. *Annual Holidays Act Brochure.* June 2014. Web.

Ministry of Justice. Constitution of Finland. June 11, 1999 (731/1999, amendments up to 1112 / 2011 included). Web. Accessed Aug. 2, 2015.

Ministry of Social Affairs and Health. *Hoitoon pääsy (Hoitotakuu).* [Access to Care (Health Care Guarantee).] N.d. Web. Accessed Aug. 14, 2015.

————. *Hoitopaikan valinta.* [Choosing the Facility for Care.] N.d. Web. Accessed Aug. 14, 2015.

————. *Terveydenhuollon maksut.* [Health-Care Copays.] N.d. Web. Accessed Aug. 14, 2015.

Miranda, Veerle. "Cooking, Caring and Volunteering: Unpaid Work Around the World." *OECD Social, Employment and Migration Working Papers* 116. Paris: OECD Publishing, 2011. Web.

Miron, Gary, and Charisse Gulosino. *Profiles of For-Profit and Nonprofit Education Management Organizations: Fourteenth Edition—2011–2012.* Boulder, CO: National Education Policy Center, 2013. Web.

MoJo News Team. "Full Transcript of the Mitt Romney Secret Video." *Mother Jones*, Sept. 19, 2012. Web.

Moody's Investors Service. "Announcement: Moody's Changes the Outlook to Negative on Germany, Netherlands, Luxembourg and Affirms Finland's AAA Stable Rating." July 23, 2012. Web.

Morgan, David. "Obama Administration Seeks to Negotiate Medicare Drug Prices." *Reuters*, Feb. 2, 2015. Web.

Morin, Rich. "More Americans Worry About Financing Retirement." Pew Research Center, Oct. 22, 2012. Web.

Morris, Allison. "Student Standardised Testing: Current Practices in OECD Countries and a Literature Review." *OECD Education Working Papers* 65. Paris: OECD Publishing, 2011. Web.

Morris, Tom, and Dan Hill. "The Liveable Cities Index—2011." *Monocle*, July/August 2011, 18–22.

Moss, Michael. "Food Companies Are Placing the Onus for Safety on Consumers." *New York Times*, May 15, 2009. Web.

———. "Peanut Case Shows Holes in Safety Net." *New York Times*, Feb. 8, 2009. Web.

Moulds, Josephine. "How Finland Keeps Its Head Above Eurozone Crisis." *Guardian*, July 24, 2012. Web.

Mullins, Brody, et al. "Romney's Taxes: $3 Million." *Wall Street Journal*, Jan. 24, 2012. Web.

Mundy, Liza. "Daddy Track: The Case for Paternity Leave." *Atlantic*, January/February 2014. Web.

Muralidharan, Karthik, and Venkatesh Sundararaman. "The Aggregate Effect of School Choice: Evidence from a Two-stage Experiment in India." *NBER Working Paper* 19441. Sept. 2013, rev. Oct. 2014. Web.

Murray, Charles. "The New American Divide." *Wall Street Journal*, Jan. 21, 2012. Web.

Naison, Mark. "Professor: Why Teach for America Can't Recruit in My Classroom." *Washington Post*, Feb. 18, 2013. Web.

National Center for Education Statistics. "Table 5.1. Compulsory school attendance laws, minimum and maximum age limits for required free education, by state: 2013." *State Education Reforms*. Web.

National Conference of State Legislatures. *Redistricting Commissions and Alternatives to Legislature Conducting Redistricting*. N.d. Web. Accessed Aug. 18, 2015.

National Conference of State Legislatures. *State Family and Medical Leave Laws*. Dec. 31, 2013. Web.

———. *2015 Minimum Wage by State*. June 30, 2015. Web.

National Council on Teacher Quality. *2013 State Teacher Policy Yearbook: National Summary*. Jan. 2014. Web.

National Employment Law Project. "City Minimum Wage Laws: Recent Trends and Economic Evidence." May 2015. Web.

———. "Occupational Wage Declines Since the Great Recession." Sept. 2015. Web.

National Institute of Health and Welfare. "Tietopaketit: Imetys." [Information Packages: Breast-Feeding.] *Lastenneuvolakäsikirja*. N.d. Web. Accessed July 29, 2015.

———. *Tilastotietoa perhevapaiden käytöstä*. [Statistics on Use of Family Leaves.] N.d. Web. Accessed July 29, 2015.

National Institute of Mental Health. *Any Anxiety Disorder Among Adults*. N.d. Web. Accessed July 22, 2015.

Neander-Nilsson, Sanfrid. *Är svensken människa?* Stockholm: Fahlcrantz & Gumaelius, 1946.

New York State Office of the Attorney General. *Can You Be Fired?* N.d. Web. Accessed July 24, 2015.

Newman, Katherine S. *The Accordion Family. Boomerang Kids, Anxious Parents, and the Private Toll of Global Competition*. Boston: Beacon Press, 2012. Kindle file.

Newport, Frank. "Americans Continue to Say Wealth Distribution Is Unfair." *Gallup*, May 4, 2015. Web.

Nixon, Ron, and Eric Lichtblau. "In Debt Talks, Divide on What Tax Breaks Are Worth Keeping." *New York Times*, Oct. 2, 2011. Web.

Nordic Social Statistical Committee. *Social Protection in the Nordic Countries 2012/2013*. Copenhagen: Nordic Statistical Committee, 2014. Web.

Norris, Floyd. "Tax Reform Might Start with a Look Back to '86." *New York Times*, Nov. 22, 2012. Web.

Norton, Michael I., and Dan Ariely. "Building a Better America—One Wealth Quintile at a Time." *Perspectives on Psychological Science* 6:1 (2011): 9–12. Web.

Norwegian Labour and Welfare Organization (NAV). *Parental Benefit*. July 13, 2015. Web.

NPR. "Cardiologist Speaks from the Heart about America's Medical System." *NPR*, Aug. 19, 2014. Web.

NYC Department of Education. *Teacher and Pupil-Personnel Certification*. Web. Nd. Accessed Aug. 3, 2015.

O'Brien, Matt. "The Euro Is a Disaster Even for the Countries That Do Everything Right." *Washington Post*, July 17, 2015. Web.

———. *Why Bad Things Happen to Good Economies*. World Economic Forum, July 30, 2015. Web.

OECD. "Does Money Buy Better Performance in PISA?" *PISA in Focus*, Feb. 2012. Web.

———. *Babies and Bosses: Reconciling Work and Family Life*. Paris: OECD Publishing, 2007. Web.

———. *Closing the Gender Gap: Act Now*. Paris: OECD Publishing, 2012. Web.

———. *Consumption Tax Trends 2014*. Paris: OECD Publishing, 2014. Web.

———. "Country Note: United States." *Results from PISA 2012*. Web.

———. *Divided We Stand: Why Inequality Keeps Rising*. Paris: OECD Publishing, 2011. Web.

———. *Doing Better for Families*. Paris: OECD Publishing, 2011. Web.

———. *Economic Policy Reforms: Going for Growth*. Paris: OECD Publishing, 2010. Web.

———. *Education at a Glance 2014: OECD Indicators*. Paris: OECD Publishing, 2014. Web.

———. *Education Policy Outlook Norway*. Paris: OECD Publishing, 2013. Web.

———. Education spending (indicator). doi: 10.1787/ca274bac-en. Web. Accessed Aug. 9, 2015.

———. *Equity and Quality in Education: Supporting Disadvantaged Students and Schools*. Paris: OECD Publishing, 2012. Web.

———. *Government at a Glance 2015*. Paris: OECD Publishing, 2015. Web.

———. *Growing Unequal? Income Distribution and Poverty in OECD Countries*. Paris: OECD Publishing, 2008. Web.

———. *Health at a Glance 2013: OECD Indicators*. Paris: OECD Publishing, 2013. Web.

———. *Health at a Glance 2015: OECD Indicators*. Paris: OECD Publishing, 2015. Web.

———. *Hours worked* (indicator), 2015. Web.

———. *Improving Schools in Sweden: OECD Perspective*. Paris: OECD Publishing, 2015. Web.

———. *Lessons from PISA for the United States: Strong Performers and Successful Reformers in Education*. Paris: OECD Publishing, 2011. Web.

———. *National Accounts at a Glance 2014*. Paris: OECD Publishing, 2014. Web.

———. *OECD Compendium of Productivity Indicators 2015*. Paris: OECD Publishing, 2015. Web.

———. *OECD Economic Surveys: Denmark 2013*. Paris: OECD Publishing, 2014. Web.

———. *OECD Economic Surveys: Finland 2014*. Paris: OECD Publishing, 2014. Web.

———. *OECD Economic Surveys: Iceland 2015*. Paris: OECD Publishing, 2015. Web.

———. *OECD Economic Surveys: Norway 2014*. Paris: OECD Publishing, 2014. Web.

———. *OECD Economic Surveys: Sweden 2015*. Paris: OECD Publishing, 2015. Web.

———. *OECD Employment Outlook 2013*. Paris: OECD Publishing, 2013. Web.

———. *OECD Factbook 2014: Economic, Environmental and Social Statistics*. Paris: OECD Publishing, 2014. Web.

———. *OECD Skills Outlook 2013: First Results from the Survey of Adult Skills*. Paris: OECD Publishing, 2013. Web.

———. *PISA 2009 Results: What Students Know and Can Do—Student Performance in Reading, Mathematics and Science* (vol. 1). Paris: OECD Publishing, 2010. Web.

———. *PISA 2012 Results: Excellence Through Equity: Giving Every Student the Chance to Succeed* (vol. 2). OECD Publishing, 2013. Web.

———. *PISA 2012 Results: What Students Know and Can Do—Student*

Performance in Mathematics, Reading and Science (vol. 2, rev. ed. February 2014). Paris: OECD Publishing, 2014. Web.

———. *Society at a Glance 2011: OECD Social Indicators*. Paris: OECD Publishing, 2011. Web.

———. "Table 1.7. Top Statutory Personal Income Tax Rate and Top Marginal Tax Rates for Employees 2014." N.d. Web. Accessed Aug. 17, 2015.

———. *Taxing Energy Use 2015: OECD and Selected Partner Economies*. Paris: OECD Publishing, 2015. Web.

———. *Taxing Wages 2015*. Paris: OECD Publishing, 2015. Web.

———. "Why Is Health Spending in the United States So High?" N.d. Web. Accessed Aug. 13, 2015.

———. *Women, Government and Policy Making in OECD Countries: Fostering Diversity for Inclusive Growth*. Paris: OECD Publishing, 2014. Web.

OECD Family Database. *SF1.3 Living arrangements of children*. N.d. Web. Accessed July 26, 2015.

Oettingen, Gabriele. "The Problem with Positive Thinking." *New York Times*, Oct. 24, 2014. Web.

Office of Senator Jamie Eldridge. *A Public Option for Massachusetts*. May 16, 2011. Web.

Office of Senator Kirsten Gillibrand. *American Opportunity Agenda: Expand Paid Family and Medical Leave*. N.d. Web. Accessed July 30, 2015.

———. *Child Care Costs Rising $730 Each Year in New York*. N.d. Web. Accessed July 24, 2015.

Ofri, Danielle. "Adventures in 'Prior Authorization.'" *New York Times*, Aug. 3, 2014. Web.

Ohlemacher, Stephen, and Emily Swanson. "AP-GfK Poll: Most Americans Back Obama Plan to Raise Investment Taxes." *Associated Press*, Feb. 22, 2015.

Olejaz, Maria, et al. "Denmark: Health System Review." *Health Systems in Transition* 14:2 (2012): 1–192. Web.

Osborn, Robin, and Cathy Schoen. "Commonwealth Fund 2013 International Health Policy Survey in Eleven Countries." Commonwealth Fund, 2013. Web.

Osborn, Robin, et al. "International Survey of Older Adults Finds Short-comings in Access, Coordination, and Patient-Centered Care." *Health Affairs Web First*, Nov. 19, 2014. Web.

Otterman, Sharon. "Once Nearly 100%, Teacher Tenure Rate Drops to 58% as Rules Tighten." *New York Times*, July 27, 2011. Web.

Parker, Kim. "Yes, The Rich Are Different." Pew Research Center, Aug. 27, 2012. Web.

Parker, Kim, and Wendy Wang. "Modern Parenthood: Roles of Moms and Dads Converge as They Balance Work and Family." Pew Research Center, Mar. 14, 2013. Web.

Parsad, Basmat, and Maura Spiegelman. *Arts Education in Public Elementary and Secondary Schools 1999–2000 and 2009–2010*. Washington, DC: National Center for Education Statistics, 2012. Web.

Partanen, Anu. "What Americans Keep Ignoring About Finland's School Success." *Atlantic*, Dec. 29, 2011. Web.

Patnaik, Ankita. "Reserving Time for Daddy: The Short and Long-Run Consequences of Father's Quotas." Jan. 15, 2015. Web.

Pear, Robert. "Health Insurance Companies Seek Big Rate Increases for 2016." *New York Times*, July 3, 2015. Web.

———. "I.R.S. Bars Employers from Dumping Workers into Health Exchanges." *New York Times*, May 25, 2014. Web.

———. "Number of Uninsured Has Declined by 15 Million Since 2013, Administration says." *New York Times*, Aug. 12, 2015. Web.

———. "Obama Proposes That Medicare Be Given the Right to Negotiate the Cost of Drugs." *New York Times*, Apr. 27, 2015. Web.

Pekkarinen, Tuomas, et al. "School Tracking and Intergenerational Income Mobility: Evidence from the Finnish Comprehensive School Reform." *Journal of Public Economics* 93.7–8 (2009): 965–75. Web.

Peltomäki, Tuomas, and Jorma Palovaara. "Opetukseen halutaan avoimuutta." [Requests Made for Openness in Teaching.] *Helsingin Sanomat*, Jan. 16, 2013. Web.

Perkins, Olivera. "Obamacare Not Enough, So Some in Labor Want Single-Payer System." *Plain Dealer*, Sept. 12, 2014. Web.

Pew Research Center. "Middle Easterners See Religious and Ethnic Hatred as Top Global Threat." Oct. 16, 2014. Web.

———. "Millennials in Adulthood: Detached from Institutions, Networked with Friends." Mar. 7, 2014. Web.

———. "Political Polarization in the American Public." June 12, 2014. Web.

Phillips, Anna M. "Tutoring Surges with Fight for Middle School Spots." *New York Times*, Apr. 15, 2012. Web.

Pickett, Kate, and Richard Wilkinson. *The Spirit Level: Why Greater Equality Makes Societies Stronger.* New York: Bloomsbury Press, 2010. Kindle File.

Pollard, Niklas, and Balazs Koranyi. "For Nordic Bosses, Joys of Home Trump Top Dollar Pay." *Reuters*, Mar. 10, 2013. Web.

Population Register Centre. *Name Service.* N.d. Web. Accessed July 23, 2015.

Poulsen, Jørgen. "The Daddy Quota—the Most Effective Policy Instrument." Nordic Information on Gender. Jan. 15, 2015. Web.

Public Policy Polling. "Congress Less Popular Than Cockroaches, Traffic Jams." Jan. 8, 2013. Web.

Putnam, Hannah, et al. *Training Our Future Teachers.* National Council on Teacher Quality, 2014. Web.

Rae, Matthew, et al. *Tax Subsidies for Private Health Insurance.* Henry J. Kaiser Family Foundation, 2014. Web.

Rampell, Catherine. "Coveting Not a Corner Office, but Time at Home." *New York Times*, July 7, 2013. Web.

———. "How Much Do Doctors in Other Countries Make?" *New York Times*, July 15, 2009. Web.

Ranta, Elina. "Älä maksa liikaa—katso mikä kortti on paras." ["Don't Pay Too Much—See Which Card Is Best."] *Taloussanomat*, Apr. 9, 2011. Web.

Rather, Dan. "Finnish First," *Dan Rather Reports*, Episode 702, Jan. 17, 2012. iTunes.

Real Clear Politics. "Elizabeth Warren: 'There Is Nobody in This Country Who Got Rich on Their Own.'" Online video clip. *Real Clear Politics Video*, Sept. 21, 2011. Web.

Reardon, Sean F. "No Rich Child Left Behind." *New York Times*, Apr. 27, 2013. Web.

Redden, Molly, and Dana Liebelson. "A Montana School Just Fired a Teacher for Getting Pregnant. That Actually Happens All the Time." *Mother Jones*, Feb. 10, 2014. Web.

Regeringskansliet. (Government Offices of Sweden.) *The Swedish Fiscal Policy Framework*. 2011. Web.

Reid, T. R. *The Healing of America: A Global Quest for Better, Cheaper, and Fairer Health Care*. New York: Penguin Books, 2010. Kindle file.

"Republican Candidates Debate in Manchester, New Hampshire, January 7, 2012." Transcript. American Presidency Project. Web.

Reuters. "Clash of Clans Maker Supercell Doubles Profit." *New York Times*, Mar. 24, 2015. Web.

Rhee, Michelle. "Poverty Must Be Tackled But Never Used as an Excuse." *Huffington Post*, Sept. 5, 2012. Web.

Rich, Motoko. "'No Child' Law Whittled Down by the White House." *New York Times*, July 6, 2012. Web.

———. "Fewer Top Graduates Want to Join Teach for America." *New York Times*, Feb. 5, 2015. Web.

———. "Scandal in Atlanta Reignites Debate Over Tests Role." *New York Times*, Apr. 2, 2013. Web.

Ringard, Ånen, et al. "Norway: Health System Review." *Health Systems in Transition* 15: 8 (2013): 1–162. Web.

Ripley, Amanda. "The Case Against High-School Sports." *Atlantic*, Oct. 2013. Web.

———. *The Smartest Kids in the World*. New York: Simon & Schuster, 2013.

Rivlin, Gary. "Leader of the Free World." *Wired*, Nov. 2003. Web.

Rizga, Kristina. "Everything You've Heard About Failing Schools Is Wrong." *Mother Jones*, Aug. 22, 2012. Web.

Robinson, Keith, and Angel L. Harris. "Parental Involvement Is Overrated." *New York Times*, Apr. 12, 2014. Web.

Romney, Mitt. "A Chance for Every Child." Remarks on Education at Latino Coalition's Annual Economic Summit in Washington, DC, May 23, 2012. Transcript. American Presidency Project. Web.

Ronpaul2008dotcom. "Full CNN Tea Party Express Republican Debate." Online video clip. YouTube, Sept. 13, 2011. Web.

Rosenbaum, Sara, et al. "Mitigating the Effects of Churning Under the Affordable Care Act: Lessons from Medicaid." Commonwealth Fund, 2014. Web.

Rosenthal, Elisabeth. "After Surgery, Surprise $117,000 Medical Bill from Doctor He Didn't Know." *New York Times*, Sept. 20, 2014. Web.

———. "American Way of Birth, Costliest in the World." *New York Times*, June 30, 2013. Web.

———. "As Hospital Prices Soar, a Stitch Tops $500." *New York Times*, Dec. 2, 2013. Web.

———. "As Insurers Try to Limit Costs, Providers Hit Patients with More Separate Fees." *New York Times*, Oct. 25, 2014. Web.

———. "Costs Can Go Up Fast When E.R. Is in Network but the Doctors Are Not." *New York Times*, Sept. 28, 2014. Web.

———. "In Need of a New Hip, But Priced Out of the U.S." *New York Times*, Aug. 3, 2013. Web.

———. "Insured, but Not Covered." *New York Times*, Feb. 7, 2015. Web.

———. "Medicine's Top Earners Are Not the M.D.s." *New York Times*, May 17, 2014. Web.

———. "The $2.7 Trillion Medical Bill." *New York Times*, June 1, 2013. Web.

———. "The Soaring Cost of Simple Breath." *New York Times*, Oct. 12, 2013. Web.

Rosenthal, Jaime A., et al. "Availability of Consumer Prices from US Hospitals for a Common Surgical Procedure." *JAMA Internal Medicine* 173:6 (2013): 427–32. Web.

Rosin, Hanna. "The End of Men." *Atlantic* July/August 2010. Web.

Rostgaard, Tine. *Family Policies in Scandinavia*. Denmark: Aalborg University, 2015. Web.

Rousseau, Jean-Jacques. *The Social Contract*. 1762. Kindle file.

Rubio, Marco. "Reclaiming the Land of Opportunity: Conservative Reforms for Combating Poverty." Remarks at the U.S. Capitol, Jan. 8, 2014. Web.

Saarinen, Juhani. "Hurjaa voittoa tekevän Supercellin toimitusjohtaja ylistää Helsinkiä." [Supercell Makes Astonishing Profits and Its CEO Praises Helsinki.] *Helsingin Sanomat*, Apr. 18, 2013. Web.

———. "Supercell-miljonäärit valloittivat tulolistojen kärjen—katso lista sadasta eniten ansainneesta." [Supercell Millionaires Rose to the Top of Income Rankings—See the Top 100.] *Helsingin Sanomat*, Nov. 3, 2014. Web.

Sack, Kevin. "From the Hospital to Bankruptcy Court." *New York Times*, Nov. 25, 2009. Web.

Saez, Emmanuel. "Striking It Richer: The Evolution of Top Incomes in the United States." Jan. 25, 2015. Web.

Sahlberg, Pasi. "Quality and Equity in Finnish Schools." *School Administrator*, Sept. 2012: 27–30. Web.

———. "Why Finland's Schools Are Top-Notch." *CNN*, Oct. 6, 2014. Web.

———. *Finnish Lessons—What Can the World Learn from Educational Change in Finland?* New York: Teachers College Press, 2011.

Säkkinen, Salla, et al. "Lasten päivähoito 2013." [Children's Day Care 2013.] *Tilastoraportti 33, 2013.* National Institute for Health and Welfare, 2014.

Samarrai, Fariss. "Love and Work Don't Always Work for Working Class in America, Study Shows." *UVAToday*, Aug. 13, 2013. Web.

Sandberg, Sheryl. *Lean In—Women, Work, and the Will to Lead.* New York: Alfred A. Knopf, 2013. Kindle file.

Sanger-Katz, Margot. "$1,000 Hepatitis Pill Shows Why Fixing Health Costs Is So Hard." *New York Times*, Aug. 2, 2014. Web.

Santos, Fernanda. "City Teacher Data Reports Are Released." *WNYC Schoolbook*, Feb. 24, 2012. Web.

Santos, Fernanda, and Robert Gebeloff. "Teacher Quality Widely Diffused, Ratings Indicate." *New York Times*, Feb. 24, 2012. Web.

Save the Children. *The Urban Disadvantage: State of the World's Mothers 2015.* Web.

Schleicher, Andreas, ed. *Preparing Teachers and Developing School Leaders for the 21st Century: Lessons from around the World.* Paris: OECD Publishing, 2012. Web.

Schoen, Cathy, et al. "State Trends in the Cost of Employer Health Insurance Coverage, 2003–2013." Commonwealth Fund, 2015. Web.

Schuessler, Jennifer. "A Lightning Rod over America's Class Divide." *New York Times*, Feb. 5, 2012. Web.

Schwab, Klaus. *Global Competitiveness Report 2011–2012.* Geneva: World Economic Forum, 2011. Web.

———. *Global Competitiveness Report 2012–2013.* Geneva: World Economic Forum, 2012. Web.

———. *Global Competitiveness Report 2015–2016.* Geneva: World Economic Forum, 2015. Web.

Schweinhart, Lawrence J., et al. *The High/Scope Perry Preschool Study Through Age 40. Summary, Conclusions and Frequently Asked Questions.* High/Scope Educational Research Foundation, 2005. Web.

Scott, Mark. "SoftBank Buys 51% of Finnish Mobile Game Maker for $1.5 Billion." *New York Times*, Oct. 15, 2013. Web.

———. "Supercell Revenue and Profit Soared in 2013." *New York Times*, Feb. 12, 2014. Web.

Searcey, Dionne. "For Women in Midlife, Career Gains Slip Away." *New York Times*, June 23, 2014. Web.

Seligson, Hannah. "Nurturing a Baby and a Start-Up Business." *New York Times*, June 9, 2012. Web.

Sellers, Patricia. "New Yahoo CEO Mayer Is Pregnant." *Fortune*, July 17, 2012. Web.

Senate Budget Committee. "Conrad Remarks at Hearing on Assessing Inequality, Mobility and Opportunity." Feb. 9, 2012. Web.

Senior, Jennifer. "The Junior Meritocracy." *New York*, Jan. 31, 2010. Web.

Shah, Parth J. "Opening School Doors for India's Poor." *Wall Street Journal*, Mar. 31, 2010. Web.

Siddiqui, Mustageem, and S. Vincent Rajkumar. "The High Cost of Cancer Drugs and What We Can Do About It." *Mayo Clinic Proceedings* 87:10 (2012): 935–43. Web.

Sidwell Friends School. *Letter to Parents.* N.d. Web. Accessed July 23, 2015.

Silva, Jennifer M. "Young and Isolated." *New York Times*, June 22, 2013. Web.

Silver-Greenberg, Jessica. "Debt Collector Is Faulted for Tough Tactics in Hospitals." *New York Times*, Apr. 24, 2012. Web.

Silverman, Ed. "Angry over Drug Prices, More States Push Bills for Pharma to Disclose Costs." *Wall Street Journal*, Apr. 24, 2015. Web.

Smith, Adam. *An Inquiry into the Nature and Causes of the Wealth of Nations*. 1776. Kindle file.

Smith, Daniel. "It's still the 'Age of Anxiety.' Or Is It?" *New York Times*, Jan. 14, 2012. Web.

Smith, Jessica C., and Carla Medalia. *Health Insurance Coverage in the United States: 2014*. U.S. Census Bureau, Current Population Reports. Washington, D.C.: U.S. Government Printing Office, 2015. Web.

Smith, Morgan. "Efforts to Raise Teacher Certification Standards Falter." *Texas Tribune*, Aug. 22, 2014. Web.

Sommer, Jeff. "Suddenly, Retiree Nest Eggs Look More Fragile." *New York Times*, June 15, 2013. Web.

Sommers, Benjamin D., et al. "Mortality and Access to Care Among Adults After State Medicaid Expansions." *New England Medical Journal*, July 25, 2012. Web.

Squires, David A. "Explaining High Health Care Spending in the United States: An International Comparison of Supply, Utilization, Prices, and Quality." Commonwealth Fund, 2012. Web.

———. "Finland Long-Term Ratings Lowered to 'AA+' on Weak Economic Growth; Outlook Stable." Oct. 10, 2014. Web.

———. "Standard & Poor's Takes Various Rating Actions on 16 Eurozone Sovereign Governments." Jan. 13, 2012. Web.

StanfordScope. "Dan Rather's Interview with Linda Darling-Hammond on Finland." Online video clip. YouTube, Jan. 30, 2012. Web.

Statistics Finland. "5. Majority of Children Live in Families with Two Parents." Nov. 21, 2014. Web.

———. *Foreigners and Migration*, 2013. Web.

———. "Number of Educational Institutions Fell Further." Feb. 12, 2015. Web.

Steinhauer, Jennifer. "Senate Approves a Bill to Revamp 'No Child Left Behind.'" *New York Times*, July 16, 2015. Web.

Steinhauser, Paul. "Trio of Polls: Support for Raising Taxes on the Wealthy." *CNN*, Dec. 6, 2012. Web.

Stewart, Nikita. "As Homeless Shelter Population Rises, Advocates Push Mayor on Policies." *New York Times*, Mar. 11, 2014. Web.

Stiglitz, Joseph. "Inequality Is Not Inevitable." *New York Times*, June 27, 2014. Web.

Strauss, Valerie. "What Was Missing—Unfortunately—in the No Child Left Behind Debate." *Washington Post*, July 17, 2015. Web.

STT. "Vanhempien koulutustaustasta voi tulla koulujen rahoitus-mittari." [Parents' Education May Become the Measuring Stick for School Funding.] *Helsingin Sanomat*, May 28, 2012. Web.

Student Union of the University of Helsinki. *Membership Fee Academic Year 2015–2016*. Web.

Suddath, Claire. "Can the U.S. Ever Fix Its Messed-Up Maternity Leave System?" *Bloomberg Businessweek*, Jan. 27, 2015. Web.

Swarns, Rachel L. "Pregnant Officer Denied Chance to Take Sergeant's Exam Fights Back." *New York Times*, Aug. 9, 2015. Web.

Swift, Art. "Americans See Health Care, Low Wages as Top Financial Problems." Gallup, Jan. 21, 2015. Web.

Swisher, Kara. "Survey Says: Despite Yahoo Ban, Most Tech Companies Support Work-from-Home for Employees." *All Things D*, Feb. 25, 2013. Web.

Taguma, Miho, et al. *Quality Matters in Early Childhood Education and Care: Finland 2012*. Paris: OECD Publishing, 2012. Web.

Taha, Nadia. "Medicaid Help Without Falling into Poverty." *New York Times*, Nov. 19, 2013. Web.

Takala, Hanna. "Kommentti: Lukiovertailut—aina väärin sammu-tettu?" [Comment: High School Rankings—Always Done Wrong?] *MTV*, May 25, 2015. Web.

Taloudellinen tiedotustoimisto. *Kansan Arvot 2013*. [Public Values 2013.] N.d. Web. Accessed Aug. 14, 2015.

Taub, Stephen. "The Rich List: The Highest-Earning Hedge Fund Man-agers of the Past Year." *Institutional Investor's Alpha*, May 6, 2014. Web.

Tax Policy Center. "Distribution tables by percentile by year of impact: T11-0089—Income breaks 2011." May 12, 2011. Web.

———. "Historical Top Marginal Personal Income Tax Rates in OECD Countries, 1975–2013." Apr. 16, 2014. Web.

Teles, Steven M. "Kludgeocracy in America." *National Affairs* 17, 2013. Web.

Thomas, Katie. "In Race for Medicare Dollars, Nursing Home Care May Lag." *New York Times*, Apr. 14, 2015. Web.

Thomas, Paul. "Is Poverty Destiny? Ideology vs. Evidence in School Reform." *Washington Post*, Sept. 19, 2012. Web.

Thompson, Derek. "The 23 Best Countries for Work-Life Balance (We Are Number 23)." *Atlantic*, Jan. 4, 2012. Web.

Tierney, Dominic. "Finland's 'Baby Box': Gift from Santa Claus or Socialist Hell?" *Atlantic*, Apr. 13, 2011. Web.

Times Higher Education. *World University Rankings 2015–2016.* Web.

Tocqueville, Alexis de. *Democracy in America: And Two Essays on America*. London: Penguin Classics, 2003.

Toivanen, Tero. "Mitä asioita olisi hyvä sisällyttää lukion opettajien väliseen verkostoyhteistyöhön uudessa oppimisympäristössä?" [What Should Be Included in High School Teachers' Network Cooperation in New Learning Environment?] *Sosiaalinen media oppimisen tukena* 26. Sept. 2012. Web.

Tomasino, Kate. "Rate Survey: Credit Card Interest Rates Hold Steady." *Creditcards.com*, Oct. 26, 2011. Web.

Truven Health Analytics. "The Cost of Having a Baby in the United States." Jan. 2013. Web.

Tugend, Alina. "Redefining Success and Celebrating the Ordinary." *New York Times*, June 29, 2012. Web.

U.S. Department of Education. "For Each and Every Child—A Strategy for Education Equity and Excellence." Washington, DC: U.S. Government Printing Office, 2013. Web.

———. "Prepared Remarks of U.S. Secretary of Education Arne Duncan on the Report: 'Arts Education in Public Elementary and Secondary Schools: 2009–2010.'" Apr. 2, 2012. Web.

U.S. Department of Health and Human Services, Health Resources and Services Administration, Maternal and Child Health Bureau. *Child Health USA 2013*. Rockville, MD: U.S. Department of Health and Human Services, 2013. Web.

U.S. Government Accountability Office. "K-12 Education: States' Test Security Policies and Procedures Varied." May 16, 2013. Web.

Underwood, Anne. "Insured, but Bankrupted Anyway." *New York Times*, Sept. 7, 2009. Web.

UNICEF Innocenti Research Centre. "Measuring Child Poverty: New League Tables of Child Poverty in the World's Rich Countries." *Innocenti Report Card* 10. Florence: UNICEF Innocenti Research Centre, 2012. Web.

UNICEF Office of Research. "Child Well-being in Rich Countries: A Comparative Overview." *Innocenti Report Card* 11. Florence: UNICEF Office of Research, 2013. Web.

United for the People. *State and Local Support.* N.d. Web. Accessed Aug. 18, 2015.

U.S. Department of Labor. "Health Benefits, Retirement Standards, and Workers Compensation: Family and Medical Leave." *Employment Law Guide.* N.d. Web. Accessed July 24, 2015.

University of Cambridge. *Charting Gender's "Incomplete Revolution."* June 27, 2012. Web.

Ushomirsky, Natasha, and David Williams. *Funding Gaps 2015.* Education Trust, 2015. Web.

Uusitalo, Liisa, et al. *Infant Feeding in Finland 2010.* Helsinki: National Institute for Health and Welfare, 2012. Web.

Vardi, Nathan. "The 25 Highest-Earning Hedge Fund Managers and Traders." *Forbes*, Feb. 26, 2014. Web.

Varney, Sarah. "The Public Option Did Not Die." *NPR* and *Kaiser Health News*, Jan. 12, 2012. Web.

Virta, Lauri, and Koskinen Seppo. "Työntekijän sairaus ja työsopimussuhteen jatkuvuus." [Employee's Illness and Continuation of Employment.] *Työterveyslääkäri*; 25:2 (2007) 90–93. Web.

Virtanen, Ari, and Sirkka Kiuru. *Social Assistance 2013.* Helsinki: National Institute for Health and Welfare, 2014. Web.

Volk Miller, Kathleen. "Parenting Secrets of a College Professor." *Salon*, Feb. 27, 2012. Web.

Waiting for "Superman." Director: Davis Guggenheim. Distribution: Paramount Vantage, 2010. Film.

Weiner, Rachel. "Romney: Uninsured Have Emergency Rooms." *Washington Post*, Sept. 24, 2012. Web.

Weissbourd, Rick, et al. *The Children We Mean to Raise: The Real Messages Adults Are Sending About Values.* Harvard Graduate School of Education, 2014. Web.

Wellesley Public Media. "You Are Not Special Commencement Speech from Wellesley High School." Online video clip. YouTube, June 7, 2012. Web.

Wheaton, Sarah. "Why Single Payer Died in Vermont." *Politico*, Dec. 20, 2014. Web.

White House Office of the Press Secretary. *President Obama's Plan for Early Education for All Americans*. Feb. 13, 2013. Web.

———. "President Obama's and Vice President Biden's Tax Returns and Tax Receipts." Apr. 18, 2011. Web.

———. "Remarks by the President on Education Reform at the National Urban League Centennial Conference." July 29, 2010. Web.

———. "White House Unveils New Steps to Strengthen Working Families Across America." Jan. 14, 2015. Web.

White House. *Reforming the Tax Code*. N.d. Web. Accessed Aug. 18, 2015.

Wildman, Sarah. "Health Insurance Woes: My $22,000 Bill for Having a Baby." *Double X*, Aug. 3, 2009. Web.

Williams, Paige. "My Mom Is My BFF." *New York*, Apr. 22, 2012. Web.

Winerip, Michael. "A Chosen Few Are Teaching for America." *New York Times*, July 11, 2010. Web.

Wingfield, Nick. "From the Land of Angry Birds, a Mobile Game Maker Lifts Off." *New York Times*, Oct. 8, 2012. Web.

Wolverton, Brad. "The Education of Dasmine Cathey." *Chronicle of Higher Education*, June 2, 2012. Web.

Wooldridge, Adrian. "The Next Supermodel." *The Economist*, Feb. 2, 2013: Special Report.

World Bank. *Doing Business 2016: Measuring Regulatory Quality and Efficiency*. Washington, DC: World Bank, 2016. Web.

World Economic Forum. *Global Gender Gap Report 2013*. Geneva: World Economic Forum, 2013. Web.

———. *Global Gender Gap Report 2015*. Geneva: World Economic Forum, 2015. Web.

World Health Organization. *Health Topics: Breastfeeding*. N.d. Web. Accessed July 29, 2015.

World Policy Forum. "Are Workers Entitled to Sick Leave from the First Day of Illness?" N.d. Web. Accessed July 25, 2015.

Yager, Lynn. "How to Succeed in Fashion Without Trying Too Hard." *Wall Street Journal*, Mar. 15, 2013. Web.

Yellen, Janet L. "Perspectives on Inequality and Opportunity from the Survey of Consumer Finances." Speech given at the Conference on Economic Opportunity and Inequality, Federal Reserve Bank of Boston. Oct. 17, 2014. Web.

Yle. "More Finns Ready to Pay for University Education." *Yle*, Aug. 8, 2013. Web.

Ylioppilastutkintolautakunta. *Koulukohtaisia tunnuslukuja*. *N.d.* Web. Accessed Aug. 8, 2015.

Young, Brett. "Calmness No Achilles Heel for Beckham's Surgeon." *Reuters*, 19, Mar. 2010. Web.

Zernike, Kate. "Obama Administration Calls for Limits on Testing in Schools." *New York Times*, Oct. 24, 2015. Web.

———. "Paying in Full as the Ticket into Colleges." *New York Times*, Mar. 30, 2009. Web.

INDEX

ABOUT THE AUTHOR

Anu Partanen's work has appeared in the *New York Times* and the *Atlantic*. A journalist in Helsinki for many years, she has also worked at *Fortune* magazine as a visiting reporter through the Innovation Journalism Fellowship at Stanford University. She lives in New York City.